VALERIE TAYLOR

VALERIE TAYLOR

with BEN MCKELVEY

An Adventurous Life

hachette
AUSTRALIA

All photos are copyright © Valerie Taylor with the exception of the full-page portrait of Valerie Taylor on p. 16 of the photo sections, which is courtesy © Kara Rosenlund www.kararosenlund.com

Line illustrations by Valerie Taylor

hachette
AUSTRALIA

Published in Australia and New Zealand in 2019
by Hachette Australia
(an imprint of Hachette Australia Pty Limited)
Level 17, 207 Kent Street, Sydney NSW 2000
www.hachette.com.au

10 9 8 7 6 5 4 3 2 1

 A catalogue record for this
book is available from the
National Library of Australia

ISBN: 978 0 7336 4172 5 (paperback)

Cover design by Christabella Designs
Cover photographs courtesy of Valerie Taylor
Typeset in ITC Baskerville Std by Kirby Jones
Printed and bound in Australia by McPherson's Printing Group

The paper this book is printed on is certified against the Forest Stewardship Council® Standards. McPherson's Printing Group holds FSC® chain of custody certification SA-COC-005379. FSC® promotes environmentally responsible, socially beneficial and economically viable management of the world's forests.

To the ocean and her inhabitants and all those who have
her wellbeing at heart

CONTENTS

A life in the ocean

I pull down my mask, fit my regulator, step off the side of the boat and slide from the Fijian coastline into a dream. I'm in the Pacific Ocean, I'm in the Coral Sea, I'm in the Persian Gulf, Bass Strait. I descend into water that changes from turquoise to azure to navy. I'm in a lake, in a lagoon, in a river, an estuary.

I'm wearing pale-blue rubber flippers and a pink wetsuit. Always blue flippers, always pink wetsuit. I have a matching ribbon in my hair, pink silk tying back a mane of sometimes faded platinum, sometimes yellow gold.

The water is warm. The water is frigid. I don't notice the temperature of the water at all.

My darling Ron is below me. He is above me, putting film into a camera. Ron is no longer alive.

There are other people underwater too: Fijian warriors, American millionaires, Saudi adventurers, filmmakers, environmentalists and thrill-seekers. They're friends and companions, strangers, competitors, adversaries. They're all bit players.

They all take cues from Ron, and sometimes it seems the animals do too. He holds a camera in a homemade underwater housing. Home is a fibro shack in Mortdale, a mansion in Roseville. Home is a retirement apartment in Fairlight overlooking Sydney Harbour where Ron and I chose to never retire.

I look out for underwater signals that only he and I know.

Ron is strong in the water and a warrior swims close to him with an iron bar in his hands, ready to protect him. Those beautiful men; this beautiful man. This will be Ron's last ever dive.

I see sharks scarred, mottled, silver, grey, white; hulking behemoths and svelte dancers. The animals hunt and feed and migrate and mate. They are off in the distant blue existing only as shadows. They are dangerously close, baring their teeth and gnawing at our cages.

I'm a teen, and a grey nurse shark has startled and terrified me. The ocean is a mystery to all of us.

I'm a nymph diving behind a spearfishing champion I wish would marry me.

I'm a professional woman, and a great white shark, soon to be the star of the film *Jaws*, has punched through the canopy of the Southern Ocean like a great geyser of muscle and teeth.

It's a glorious scene. They all are. It's all there, my whole underwater life on the big screen and small and in boxes that won't let in moisture at *National Geographic*, and Paramount and Channel Nine and as a trillion ones and zeros on hard drives and in the Cloud.

The life of the ocean is in those ones and zeros too. Not all of it, but almost all of the change. The water is crystal clear, the coral vibrant. There's slicked oil and bleached reefs. There's abundant fish and mammals. They are scarce. Some are gone forever.

I have spent my life documenting the Anthropocene. I didn't know it when I started but I know now.

I feel arthritic pain in my arm and there's no doubt I am nearly eighty-four years old. A pregnant bull shark sees a fish next to me and charges. The shark feeds and banks away. The pain in my arm recedes and I am somewhat younger. I'm on the same Fijian reef as before and I try to will in a tiger shark towards Ron's camera. His sickness is obvious even underwater; it's in his movement and posture.

One more wonderful shot, my darling, just one more.

I'm younger again, in San Diego surrounded by blue sharks. Each with their long nose, long body and faint but electric tint, they put me in mind of a luxurious French sports sedan. They're very beautiful but quite agitated.

I feel something; not pain, but something else: pressure, cold. I look down and see a cloud forming around me, dark purple and green in the deep shimmering blue.

I reach down and feel through my wetsuit, through my skin and flesh all the way to the bone. This is not the first time I've been bitten by a shark, nor the last. It is, however, the worst bite I will suffer.

I'm calm. If we are to be bitten, then we are to be bitten. If one of us is attacked, the other films. This is something Ron has long said.

One must choose a life of adventure, and of mystery and discovery, but with that choice one must also choose the attendant risks. One must choose the ocean too, all of it. These are my words, not Ron's.

No one has noticed the attack except Ron. I see him suspended and still in the water, flippers down, shoulders level, staring at me over his camera. He films; he is an honest man, true to his word, even now.

The cloud of blood grows and billows, and it occurs to me that there is mystery below the water and there is mystery above it, too.

I come back to Fiji and to 2019, where another large bull shark approaches. Now I notice it is I who has a Fijian warrior shadowing me.

It's all too wonderful. It's all been too wonderful.

Let's start at the beginning.

CHAPTER ONE

The beginning

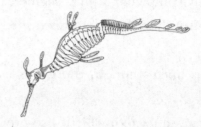

One never forgets pain. Real pain, that is, not the discomfort that is so often misattributed these days. Discomfort can be forgotten, like last week's dinner choice, but pain embeds and perseveres; it informs and guides. It can bring an atheist to faith or a churchgoer to despair. It can change the trajectory of lives, sometimes for worse, sometimes for better.

I will never forget the pain of having polio, nor would I want to. Those nine weeks I spent partly paralysed and in pain did more to make me who I am than any other factor in my life. Any other factor except for Ron Taylor, of course, but he comes in much later.

My story starts in November 1935, at the Women's Hospital on Crown Street in Sydney. I was born to a mother who was a descendant of colonial-era settlers, and a father who was the son of ten-pound poms, in a time of tempered hope.

The Australian pound had started to recover after taking a battering during the Great Depression, a surge led by a manufacturing sector that offered employment to any who wanted it. Huge public building projects such as Sydney Airport, the Sydney Harbour Bridge and Town Hall Station had been recently completed, and it seemed there was more reason for optimism than there had been since the end of the Great War.

The day I was born, though, there was a change in the spring air.

In the days leading up to my birth two events of note took place. The German Reich, led by an angry nationalist named Herr Hitler, had unfurled a new flag: a black geometric pattern set against a white circle on a red background. And, Australia's favourite adventurer, Charles Kingsford Smith, lost radio contact in the Andaman Sea in his plane the *Lady Southern Cross*.

The Sun, Daily Telegraph and the *Sydney Morning Herald* were all gloomily speculating as to whether this new German flag would soon fly over invading armies across Europe, and whether Kingsford Smith would be found alive. Both fears proved to be well founded.

I spent the first three years of my life in Sydney, but I remember almost nothing in that period bar a bout of diphtheria, another deadly disease now all but extinct thanks to the wonders of immunisation and the power of science.

What I remember of diphtheria is the fear of my mother's

fingers approaching as she reached into my throat, preparing to pull out the mucus that had been generated by the disease. I remember it, I assume, because the experience is fixed to the memory of the pain that came next, like a side-car affixed to a motorcycle. As I said, one never forgets pain.

All of my significant childhood memories after that incident were forged in New Zealand.

My father was born an East Londoner, my mother the daughter of a fruit-picking family from Mildura. How they met I do not know, but when I was born and for the duration of my childhood my father worked as an engineer for the battery company Exide and my mother was a housewife. When I was three an opportunity was presented to my father: the company needed someone to establish a small battery factory in some pastoral land at the southern end of New Zealand's North Island. It was an opportunity too good to pass up, so we moved to Lower Hutt, located near the edge of Wellington harbour, early in 1939. My father established his factory within walking distance of the State Commission house my parents rented and where my mother cared for me and my baby brother, Greg.

By August 1939 the factory was established and producing car batteries. My father was ready to return to Australia, but on the first day of September, German tanks, planes and troops thundered across the Polish border. Two days later New Zealand and Australia declared war on Nazi Germany. All inessential passage between Australia and New Zealand was halted, and my father's factory quickly became a supplier of combat matériel.

My family was now in New Zealand for the duration of the conflict. I have strong memories of World War II, and those memories have sometimes made me quite patriotic, splitting my allegiances between England, Australia and New Zealand.

From a modern perspective, it's hard to fathom how all-encompassing an event like a world war is for civilians, even in the most remote part of it. We would all hang on every morsel of news, every evening radio broadcast, every news reel at the cinema. An Allied defeat was a dagger in the heart; a glorious victory by our soldiers sparked such pride that we felt as though we held the bayonets ourselves.

My family was especially keen to hear about the heroics of the Maori Battalion in Greece, Crete, North Africa and Italy. We lived close to a nearly wholly Maori neighbourhood in Lower Hutt, and my schoolfriend Mary was Maori.

One of the most vivid memories of the war for me was of my school class being taken into Wellington to cheer the Maori Battalion as it marched through the streets before shipping overseas, stopping to perform their ferocious Haka and then marching on, chanting their battle song as they disappeared.

I remember that song to this day: it was a rousing call for the battalion to march to victory and glory, to remain staunch and true, and to carry the people's honour as they marched. I was so proud when I heard that the Nazi Field Marshal Erwin Rommel had said that with the Maori Battalion he could have conquered the world. I wished I could have fought with those proud men; rifle in hand, enemy ahead. I think all the kids in the street wished the same thing. We played goodies and baddies where the enemy soldiers marched up and down giving the German salute while our side used guns made from wooden pegs to shoot them down. We all had to take our turn at playing the enemy.

I realised not everyone's role in the war was to do or die. For instance, my father's duty would never bring him face to face with the enemy, but I understood that what he did was just as essential as the gunfighters. Batteries were needed to power the Allied war machine, from planes to tanks.

One of the essential elements of battery-making was lead, and with no natural lead available in New Zealand it often fell to my father to ride his bike around the streets of suburban Lower Hutt asking for contributions of household lead. I would often go along as he went from door to door, asking for any lead that might be available.

'For the war effort,' my father would say. I remember people being desperately keen to contribute if they could.

Most commonly we collected toy lead soldiers, which, after being melted into a liquid, were purified and drained off to then be coated over wooden separators, essential for battery manufacture. Those hundreds of toy soldiers would transfer from the battlefields of a child's mind to those of Europe and the Pacific.

I felt proud helping my father hunt for lead.

Like many women in that war, my mother accepted that her role was to keep her husband and children fed and clothed, and to maintain a home worth protecting – no small feat as more and more household items became first rationed, then scarce and finally a pre-war memory.

As a daughter, I was expected to share my mother's role. I would help her in the kitchen and look after my little brother, and also in this time of war I would help provide the household with kitchen essentials. Mushrooms when it rained, apples from an abandoned orchard, blackberries in late summer. All free for the taking.

Sometimes this meant lining the basket on my bike with newspaper and cycling to the rail tracks where the train has to slow down at a roundabout. I would call to the drivers in the engine for coal to put in my basket. We had coal, but like everything else it was rationed and a few extra lumps made a warmer room.

I also used to ride my bike to the nearby Griffin's biscuit factory and beg for the dough offcuts from the workers I could see through the factory window. I soon discovered both exploits were more successful when I took along my little brother. I would pinch him to make him cry just at the right moment, creating a pathetic scene more likely to see me return home with a full basket of coal or a big lump of dough.

I remember the air-raid shelters and the blackouts and the memorials. I know now it was a difficult time, but it is not one I remember as difficult because I was too young to know any different.

In many ways the war was exciting for the very young. There was a giant game being played, far away in another country. Every night we would crowd around the radio listening to the war news. The war was part of my early life; the radio news was all I knew. It wasn't until many years later that I fully realised the devastating impact this conflict had on so many millions of people.

Then one day, the war ended. I remember my father's joy, and riding our bikes to his factory so he could paint, in bold red letters 'EXIDE' on the roof, my father yelling at me to get out of the way as the paint dribbled down the ridges of the corrugated iron onto the grass. The factory had been disguised as a farm barn for the duration of the war in case the enemy invaded, meaning the company name – Exide Batteries – was never on display.

The bombers never came, and now they never would.

In the afternoon of that day we all went into Wellington, where the biggest celebration I had ever seen was underway. Beneath cold, grey skies hundreds of people were dancing and hugging and singing and the word 'peace' was being shouted over and over again. Rain came and I was amazed my mother didn't force me into a coat.

The gleeful chaos of that day crystallised in my mind when a Scottish band marched into town. Their drums and pipes reached deep inside me, and it seems inside my mother as well. When we heard that music we both cried. I still weep a little when a bagpipe plays alongside a Celtic drum. The music catches my heart in a way no other sound ever has.

Our family stayed in New Zealand for a while after the war, although my father always maintained that we would go back to Australia one day. I'm not sure why we stayed so long; it wasn't a time when children asked questions of their parents.

I remember those few years after the end of the war being marked by a series of firsts: my first balloon, first pineapple, first banana, first firecracker – all the things that had been unavailable during the war. I remember the first proper chocolate bar coming to our house. When I bit into it I tasted a wonderful kaleidoscope of flavour, but it made my brother Greg ball up his face and wince.

'Hot, hot, hot,' he complained, being so unaccustomed to using the sweet sensors in his tongue.

My tenth birthday came shortly after the end of the war, and I think that by eleven or twelve I had started to understand what my life was supposed to be. I was to be a woman like my mother. I would feed and keep, and tend and nurture. I would find a man with a job he could keep for his whole life, marry him and take care of him, and have children. I would expect no more or less than that. It was what was expected of a girl of my generation.

Then one morning I woke with a terrible aching pain.

I told my mother I didn't feel well, but she was a woman who didn't believe in pain that didn't come with a bleeding wound. She told me I must dress and be at school by the time the bell rang.

I managed to drag myself into my uniform, but that was no small feat. It was agony to move my limbs. I just wanted to go back to bed. I tried to mount my bicycle, but that proved impossible, so I gritted my teeth and lumbered to the bus stop.

When I limped into class I slumped over my desk and was unable to move even when the teacher threatened me with the ruler. After school I managed to catch the bus home. I went straight to bed thinking that rest would bring improvement.

There was no rest and there was no improvement, only more pain.

In the morning I was physically unable to lift my arms over my head and that's when my mother became alarmed. She took me to the hospital, and there I was held down while a doctor inserted a long and painful needle into my spine. A lumbar puncture can be given easily today, but seventy years ago it was a lengthy and unpleasant experience.

That confirmed the diagnosis they had started to fear: I had polio.

A virus with a very high transmission rate, polio came and went in epidemic waves. Most who contracted the disease had few or no symptoms, and that fact combined with a long incubation and infection period meant that a polio outbreak could often only be identified when those unlucky enough to have the disease enter their central nervous system started complaining of muscle and joint pain.

A polio epidemic was spreading around the world. I was one of many thousands who would succumb to the virus.

I was immediately taken away from my mother, isolated and transported to a huge ward in Wellington Hospital, filled exclusively with patients infected with polio. This was 1949 and the polio vaccine was coming, but it would come too late for us. In the polio ward we were observed; apart from being fed soup, custard and sometimes milk, all that could be done was to wait to see if we would become some of the last casualties of one of the great diseases. While there I had no capacity to think of anything but loneliness and pain; no capacity for compassion, not even time for self-pity. Just aching limbs.

I wanted my agony to end. I wanted my mother. I wanted to go home.

Babies came into the ward, crying bundles of blankets, becoming silent as they succumbed to the disease. The doctors would stand around my bed having hushed conversations about my chances of recovery. I didn't care what they had to say. I knew I was going to survive.

Sometimes I would ask for my mother; I wanted her so much.

'You would only infect her, dear. You don't want that, do you?' nurses would reply. Of course I didn't want that.

I spent three weeks in that ward, each day exactly like the last, each hour like the last. Pain in the morning, pain in the evening. The only way I understood that there had been a passage of time was through the only window I could see from my bed.

There was a solitary tree visible through the glass. When I arrived at hospital it was barren except for a few specks of green. As I lay in my hospital bed, spring started to take hold and the tree took on colour and small leaves. On the last day in the ward I saw white flowers appear. It was an apple tree.

Three weeks later when I was no longer contagious, I was moved into another huge ward, full of patients recovering from polio.

Death was no longer a possibility, but partial paralysis was still a risk.

In that second ward I started to escape my suffering, travelling on imaginary journeys that, to this day, are some of the most exhilarating and memorable of my life. I went down the Mississippi River to Kentucky and Arkansas from Missouri with a bold boy named Huckleberry Finn and I was friends with his itinerant, rambunctious and wholly intriguing friend Tom Sawyer. I visited with a young woman named Lorna Doone in seventeenth-century pastoral England, where a suitor was trying to destroy her family's name and fortune. I went on an adventure with an innkeeper's son named Jim Hawkins who, at the behest of the pirate Long John Silver, went off to the high seas in search of a place called Treasure Island. I think that was my favourite story of all. I am still looking for that island.

These wonderful flights of fancy were all made possible thanks to a Christian group called The Church of the Brethren – sanguine missionaries with long hair who visited the ward and delivered just the right books at just the right time.

Those books changed my life. They were my introduction into a world larger than Lower Hutt, larger than all of New Zealand. A world that wasn't all kitchens and grocery stores and vegetable gardening. It was only much later that I would conceive that I might get to those other worlds, but I never forgot that they existed. They were also my introduction to what would become something of a silent, one-word mantra in my life: *adventure*.

I couldn't quite put my finger on exactly what adventure was then, but I knew that with every page I read I came a little closer to understanding. While in hospital, those books became my raison d'être and almost every daylight hour was spent with a book resting on a wooden holder where I could read it without moving. I would beg the passing nurses to turn the page for me.

A week later I was given a proper book rest. It took several days' practice, but with constant trying I managed to teach my left hand to climb up the legs on the rest to the edge of the book so I could turn the page without help.

My sense of achievement did not last long.

The next day a nurse placed a lead bracelet on my wrist, leaving me once again helpless. The bracelet was part of a therapy to help strengthen my weak arms and hands by moving against a restriction. The nurses were kind but knew I would never stop until I could read at my preferred pace. I worked to lift my other hand to the book to turn the pages, and as soon as I could, another bracelet joined the first.

I hated those bracelets, but I now know that sometimes kindness often seems like cruelty. The enforced resistance and agonising boundary-pushing was the beginning of the treatments pioneered by Sister Elizabeth Kenny, an Australian nurse to whom I believe I owe much of my present-day mobility.

Sister Kenny was a Queensland woman who worked as a travelling bush nurse before being sent to work on the 'Dark Ships' that slowly steamed between England and Australia during World War I. After the war Sister Kenny dedicated herself to combating the waves of polio infection that pulsed through the 1920s, 1930s and 1940s.

While physicians and researchers studied the pathology of the disease, Sister Kenny concentrated on methods that would ensure mobility after the disease had run its pathological course. At the clinic she established in Townsville she fine-tuned techniques of limb manipulation, hot packs and stretching.

Eventually Sister Kenny's results became near miraculous. Many children whom physicians had expected to be crippled for life travelled to Townsville and made a full recovery.

The Australian press claimed erroneously that Sister Kenny was 'curing' polio in Queensland, and that was the start of a lifelong conflict between male physicians who claimed that her treatments didn't work at all, and this headstrong, largely self-taught Australian woman who knew that they did.

By the time I was in hospital it was known that Sister Kenny's techniques worked, but they were not widely known nor practised in New Zealand. I was incredibly lucky to end up in a hospital where one of the doctors had previously worked at clinics in America where Sister Kenny's recovery techniques were wholeheartedly accepted.

The rehabilitation method was effective but excruciating. It required vigorous stretching of limbs that pained me to move at all, but today I couldn't be more thankful to the staff who administered the treatment. Without them I wouldn't have lived the life I have.

I spent some months in hospital and after I had read *The Adventures of Huckleberry Finn* perhaps half a dozen times I desperately wanted to go home. I was no longer contagious, I knew the exercises that I was required to do, and I was slowly but surely getting better. I wanted my family and I wanted normalcy. The doctors told me I could leave as soon as I could walk out.

The first time I tried to walk I fell on the floor. Some days after that I managed to circumnavigate my bed, always making sure I had an arm on the mattress or frame. A few days after that I could go from bed to bed, and a few days later I made it out of the ward and along the hallway, which had a railing all the way to the hospital exit. A few weeks after that I walked out of those doors wobbly but unaided.

It was wonderful to go home; to be with my mother and father and brothers, one born shortly before I became sick.

My mother told me about the devastation of the polio epidemic. A cousin of mine had died in Australia, his best friend was a permanent cripple. The boy I sat next to in assembly had been in hospital and then released. The boy I sat next to at Sunday school had been in hospital and died.

I tried to go back to the life I had been living before polio, but that proved impossible. I was a different girl and I had come home to a different world.

Teachers and students pitied me. I was 'The Girl Who Had Polio', awkwardly dragging my stiff leg from one class to the next. I had missed months of schoolwork, and I fell further behind academically. I spent two hours of every day but Sunday receiving treatment at the clinic at Hutt Hospital. I also fell behind socially. When I left school for hospital the girls around me were girls, with naked faces and a lack of interest in (perhaps even contempt for) boys, but when I came back they were young women wearing lipstick and nail polish.

I gravitated to the younger girls at school, those who had not yet become intrigued by boys and make-up. A local girl, Joan Bognuda, was the younger sister of Tonia who had been my friend before I became sick, and she now became my best friend.

My mother bought me a simple pair of rollerskates that could be strapped to the bottom of my shoes. She rightly thought the exercise would be more helpful than just walking. But I was out of step in more ways than one. The interests of the other students were not mine. I was less interested in the walled garden of my teenage life than the huge expansive worlds revealed in the books I had read. They hinted at a much larger world, full of monsters, heroism, monumental quests and true, enduring love. All far more exciting than geometry and young boys.

Even when I had recovered my strength and mobility and was back to a full class schedule, I preferred my books and my imagined adventure to socialising or studying. My mother would tell me I really should be more concerned with conformity, but I found it boring. Books had shown me another life far more interesting than the one around me.

I was what I was and I wanted what I wanted. Polio and the attendant pain had changed the way I looked at the world. I just didn't know how to find that other life – the adventure I dreamed about.

I was a student who always had my nose in the wrong book, so my grades were not exemplary. On the Friday after my fifteenth birthday, my mother told me it was time to leave school and enter the workforce. I wasn't unhappy with her decision.

After borderline disasters working at a nursery and a department store I applied to work at the New Zealand National Film Unit on the Miramar Peninsula in Wellington, and there I discovered my place in the workforce. I was born with a particular talent: I could draw. If I could see it, I could draw it.

I was assigned to an animation studio tasked with creating educational films. They first had me fulfilling the most elementary animations, such as water dropping from a swan's wings, but increasingly I was entrusted with more difficult images, such as the creepy-crawlies that ended up on a little boy's unwashed hands when he came to dinner.

Who knows, if I had stayed in that job I might have been animating the boys and swans themselves, but my father had decided it was time to return to Australia.

I would miss my animation work, but I didn't mind the move at all. Six years earlier we had holidayed in Australia, and I knew wonderful things awaited me: cousins to play with along the Murray River where my uncles grew grapes on fruit farms, gorgeous beaches, and much larger and better-stocked sweet shops full of new flavours and tastes.

After all, just because I was no longer a schoolgirl didn't mean I wasn't still a girl.

I had a boyfriend then and I was sad to leave him. He was a Maori boy named Johnny, who danced very well, was nicely mannered and kind. We stayed in touch over the years, and he still visits me every Easter near my holiday house north of Sydney. Shortly after I left, Johnny told me that he and my friend Joan, who used to tag along on our dates because she had no boyfriend, were now an item. I was very happy for them, and continued to stay happy for them as they married and raised four children.

After a short stint in Kogarah, our family settled in a waterfront house on Port Hacking, fringing the sparkling blue waters of Burraneer Bay. As a girl who could not yet swim well, I would only splash around in the water outside the front of the house, mostly with family members, but over time that would all change.

I found work in Sydney's central business district, illustrating for Press Feature Services, a company that employed several artists. My job was to convert American comic strips, such as *Li'l Abner* and *Daffy Duck*, into an Australian context. This wasn't because the comic-consuming public was then such a patriotic bunch, but because the Menzies government was so adamant about the protection of Australian jobs that all international comics had to be redrawn and resituated for Australian consumption.

It was a fine job and one at which I was quite adept, but I wasn't particularly happy. There was only so much a single woman was allowed to do in that period. I could work and spend time with the family, and I enjoyed both of those activities, especially when we visited our cousins, aunts and uncles who all had fruit blocks growing mainly grapes; my relatives were very religious and would not allow their grapes to be used for wine, so instead the crops were dried then sold.

Joan's sister, Tonia, lived with us for a few months, and that meant I could attend the dances at Rockdale Town Hall. I enjoyed the dances, but when Tonia went home my permission to be out after dark left with her.

Until I started modelling.

It wasn't something I had ever thought about doing, and the opportunity presented itself quite unexpectedly. I didn't preen and primp, nor was I concerned much about my clothes or my figure, but money was money, so when I was offered four pounds an evening to sit and do nothing, I couldn't turn the opportunity down.

The offer came while I was studying lettering at East Sydney Technical College. My boss had sent me to do the course, which ended with one of my teachers asking if I would be interested in modelling for the evening portraiture class.

'You have a good head,' he said. 'Good bone structure.'

It was easy, lucrative work and the continuation of a routine that was already permissible: a walk to East Sydney Tech after work, class, then a train to Woolooware and a short walk home where my mother and a reheated dinner awaited me.

It earned me money and it gave me a new, different situation to any I had previously experienced.

One night class ran late, and when I realised I wasn't going to make my train, I looked for a public phone booth so I could tell my mother to expect me home later than usual. I found one on Burton Street in Darlinghurst, only a little way down the road from the college.

Now, to understand what happened next, you must see in your mind what public phone booths were like in the 1950s. The best way to explain is that they were a hybrid of the full enclosed booths that still exist around the country today and the open, exposed public phones that you might see inside a train station. They had a door and full, 360-degree protection but only from the top down to waist height. I suppose one might say they looked like an overgrown glass mushroom with a light and phone inside.

I called my mother, and while I was on the phone with her a group of men appeared; about half a dozen, I think. I talked to my mother as I waited for them to walk past. They were quiet as they approached, but they didn't walk on, instead they stopped and crowded around the booth. One held the door shut by leaning against it, another reached into the booth, pulling my dress up and my underwear down.

I screamed, without thinking that my screams were being transmitted to my poor mother. I reached down in an attempt to pull up my underwear but my hands were fought back by other hands – more hands, stronger hands.

The assault continued. I continued to scream, stuck in a phone booth with no escape as they laughed and grabbed my thighs, some repeating a phrase to each other, *Yalla, yalla.*

A passing taxi driver stopped, got out of his vehicle and chased the men away. He took me to the police station, where I reported that I had been assaulted by what looked like Greek men; it would be decades later that I found out that the word *yalla* was not a Greek word, but Arabic.

I caught the train home without any problems, but my mother and father were shocked and angry. They and the police agreed that a young woman should not be out on the streets of Sydney alone at night, and I must say after what I had gone through I think they had a point.

That was another pivotal period in my life. If polio had taken the bumpers off my life, the incident in Darlinghurst could quite easily have put them back on. I could have become timid, but it was not in my nature to be nervous. I wouldn't allow those men who assaulted me to change my life.

The world is large and fascinating, but it contained restrictions and danger, more so for a woman than a man. This may not be fair but this was our world. Many of the doors of life would only be open with a husband; the right husband. That's why I thank God that I met Ron.

CHAPTER TWO

Love and other adventures

Returning to live in Australia meant I was close to the water and the ocean and I could sit on the sand, float in the ocean, paddle our canoe. The call of adventure would never allow me to be still. I had learned how to dog paddle in New Zealand, and in Sydney I learned to swim – at the Sans Souci baths – if what you could consider what I do now swimming. Fortunately I could float very well, and although my breaststroke needed a little polish it allowed me to move through the water nicely.

As soon as I could swim competently I started to snorkel, usually in the water out the front of the family home and always with a hand spear ready to kill whatever we could eat. My father needed to eat fish. War wounds came in all shapes and sizes, and my father's were internal, suffering from the effects of chronic lead poisoning for most of his life. This meant he could no longer stomach meat, but he could eat fish. There was no point buying fish when an abundance of it was there for the taking in front of our house.

One day as I was spearfishing along the rocks near our boatshed, I was spotted by another snorkeller spearing fish. Brian McKenna, known to his friends as Bruno. An experienced spearfisherman, Bruno was a garrulous man with curly, sun-streaked hair and a ready wicked smile. He approached me and told me he was the president of the nearby spearfishing club, the St George, and suggested that I should join him at the next weekly meeting for two reasons: one, his club was having trouble finding female members who were good at spearing fish, and two, I might enjoy it.

I was happy to attend. I still didn't know many people in Sydney who were young and interesting and weren't part of my family. And I would be lying if I didn't think about the possibility of finding a boyfriend at the club. I had been hoping to meet a suitable young man for some time. I had met many boys but somehow they were not quite right.

The club members made me welcome. They were a fit and adventurous group. Spearfishing was their love and they did it as a club almost every weekend. There was one man in particular, their champion spearfisherman, whom I found not just charming but wholly intriguing. I would sit behind this man at meetings and stare at the back of his neck, tanned and long, and at the fall of his hair, thick, black and shiny. Unlike Bruno who loved the limelight, this man was quiet, never wasting words. However, when we entered the water he was all efficient action; holding his breath around two minutes every dive, spearing with unbelievable accuracy.

That man's name was Ron Taylor.

I liked the club, the community and Ron. In my young mind, he looked to me what a hero might look like out of the pages of a book: strong, handsome and capable, with an adventurous spirit. He seemed to have little time for me, however, and I had little time in the club, because my entry into the spearfishing world coincided with my short-lived career as an actress.

The first commercial television licences were granted in Australia in 1953 but it took a few years for the medium to prove itself as more than a scientific curio and become a dominant force and a potential earner.

My employer, Press Feature Services, had decided that they were going to try to take a slice of the revenue that television presented, offering animated advertisements for any client who wished to be a television early adopter. The in-house artists such as myself, who drew comics and cartoons, were quickly trained to become animators. It was easy for me, because due to my training at the New Zealand National Film Unit I already knew how animation worked. When we finished a set of cells I would deliver them personally to Artransa Park, a multi-purpose film studio in Frenchs Forest, where the images would be photographed against a slow-moving background. And that's where my acting career started.

I was out at Artransa delivering the latest animated story to be filmed when I saw a crowd of women roughly my age. I asked one of the producers who the women were and why were they were milling around the studio. He told me a producer was looking for talent to appear in a television advertisement for the Australian chemists' guild. I asked if I might be included in the casting, to which he said it was no skin off his nose.

My audition was very different from those of the other models. The script required the character to come home to a cup of tea and the newspaper after a long day at work. Most of the girls did the aforementioned actions with affected and ladylike grace. I did not. I slumped on the couch, slurped my tea, cracked the paper open and went straight for the funny pages, laughing gleefully. This was, after all, my experience of coming home after a hard day.

My acting career had started. I was employed to appear in a series of commercials advertising the chemists' guild. That advertising job generated more on-camera work, almost always at Artransa Park. My long blonde hair led to a series of Silvikrin shampoo ads, and I also had nice hands and so did a series of Kraft cheese ads in which I cut the cheese, placed it on crackers and handed the plate around to a room full of guests. It was easy money, and I enjoyed being on camera. Not being trained as an actress, I simply played myself. I was comfortable in front of the camera, had a clear speaking voice and was keen to try almost anything.

One day out at the studio a man approached me; a strong-jawed, blond-haired vision of masculinity.

'Are you here for today's *Whiplash* shoot?' he asked.

I told him I was not. Afterwards I asked around about this man and this *Whiplash*. I found out that the man was an American television star named Peter Graves, and that *Whiplash* was the show in which he starred. *Whiplash* was Australia's first television drama, an adventure series based loosely on the life of Freeman Cobb, the man who established Australia's first stagecoach line. Graves played Cobb. There was plenty of action. Also it was a thoughtful series based on fact, with many of the scripts written by an American writer named Gene Roddenberry, who would later create the TV series *Star Trek*.

I was intrigued by the show, so I hunted around until I found the *Whiplash* casting director. I asked her how I might join the *Whiplash* cast, and she told me I should supply her with my acting CV, which I did. It was almost exclusively an invention; mostly fictitious acting jobs in New Zealand that I was betting she would never be able to verify.

A week later I was on the set of *Whiplash*, in an insignificant three-second role. After that shoot I continued to get work on *Whiplash*, juggling my obligations at Press Feature Services. My role on *Whiplash* was not as an actress, but mainly as a sometime double for one of the lead actresses, Annette Andre, first as a stand-in and later as a so-called stunt performer.

My stunt work started with horse-riding. The director asked if I had any experience with horses. I told him I did, which was not a complete lie; I had been led on a tame pony once. I held on as they filmed and shot the scenes that were needed. I found the galloping horse easy to ride – it was when she slowed down that I became uncomfortable.

The director again came to me, this time asking if I could paddle a canoe. As I had a canoe at home I could honestly say yes. Approaching a waterfall in my canoe, I wondered if I had perhaps bitten off more than I could chew, but I just held on and persevered and everything worked out beautifully. It was more rapids than a waterfall. The canoe did all the work – I just hung on waving the paddle like an expert.

I managed to maintain my job at Press Feature Services throughout, and even into my next acting engagement, a several-month job on stage that cured me once and for all of any desire to tread the boards.

The job came to me after I saw a notice on the board in the offices of *Whiplash*. Hayes Gordon, the notable producer, director and actor, was looking to cast a production of *The Seven Year Itch* at his theatre, The Ensemble, in Kirribilli.

A hugely successful play by George Axelrod, *The Seven Year Itch* had recently been turned into an even more popular film by legendary director Billy Wilder. It featured an American everyman actor, Tom Ewell, and a blonde bombshell named Marilyn Monroe.

The role Ewell played, that of a middle-aged publishing executive, had been filled in the Hayes Gordon production, but they were looking for someone to play the Marilyn Monroe role, who was written very much as an idealised male fantasy and simply known in the text as 'The Girl'.

Along with several girlfriends I'd met through my time on *Whiplash*, I auditioned. I thought it would be a bit of a giggle, but to my amazement Hayes gave me the role. Soon my life was very full, working days in the city and then being required, without fail, to be at the stage door of The Ensemble at 6 p.m. for hair and make-up preparing me for the night's performance.

There was not much I enjoyed about being an actress on the stage. The people I worked with were fine, but the work was repetitive and restrictive; the same thing over and over again. I took the role because I was always looking for something different, but I stayed in the show purely for the fun of being part of a group of very interesting people.

I would have been perfectly satisfied if the show did not become a success, but it was quite a big one. The play opened on 28 June 1961 and many months later we were still performing. It had been a difficult year for theatre, with many blaming the advent of television for the medium's decline, but there had been two hits in Sydney that had bucked the trend in 1961: a production of *Lock Up Your Daughters* at the Palace Theatre, and our play.

For me, one of the few redeeming features of being in that show was Gary Shearston.

When I met him, Gary was an actor, folk singer and guitarist who regularly played gigs at hotels around the city. Then twenty-two, Gary worked at The Ensemble in various front-of-stage and backstage roles, but his dream was to record albums and tour the world as a singer.

I suspect Gary took an instant shine to me when he saw me at the theatre, and it didn't take much time for me to be intrigued by him also. He was very kind and very thoughtful, and that man really knew how to play his guitar and sing. All the girls liked him, including me.

One day Gary asked me to go to Manly with him for ice cream. He brought his guitar and, as I held both the ice cream cones, he played the English folk song 'The Riddle Song' for me. I was enchanted, and I moved from my parents' home to his rented apartment shortly afterwards, with the approval of my parents thanks to the tacit understanding that he and I would soon marry.

I'll never say a bad word about Gary, but we were never a good match, a fact that was only really revealed after *The Seven Year Itch* finally ended.

Gary was a musician and artist, heart and soul. He gravitated to people who were similarly inclined, and he and his friends spent a lot of time playing or writing music, drinking coffee, talking music, all indoors. I liked to be outside, and ideally in the water. I'm not sure Gary really understood that there were wonders in the ocean.

While living with Gary I used to spear fish for our supper, snorkelling out from the harbour beach near Gary's place in Balmoral after work. I'd do it for the fish, but I'd also do it for the joy of being underwater; a place of increasing wonder for me.

One afternoon I was spearfishing off Balmoral beach when I saw one of the most wholly unexpected things I think I shall ever see in the water. I had launched myself from a jetty near the southern end and, as I usually did, after spearing two fantail leatherjackets, I decided to head to the rocks near HMAS *Penguin*, the naval base on Middle Head, where past experience told me there was a chance of finding a crayfish. Gary loved crayfish. Mask down in the murky harbour water,

I was looking for crays when suddenly I saw a strange shape, and I swam over for a better look. The thing was big, huge, black and flat like a wall. I was puzzled and moved around it.

There was a number in white: '571'. Just then, two SCUBA divers appeared. SCUBA diving was still very unusual in 1961, so I was surprised to see them and waved. They did not wave back – instead they grabbed me roughly and dragged me to a pier at the naval base. Seamen were waiting. A couple had guns, a couple had the insignia of seniority.

'Take her weapon,' one of the officers barked. The gunmen took my spear and my sack, the contents of which were disgorged: two fantail leatherjackets. The SCUBA divers took an order and disappeared back into the water.

'What is this all about?' I demanded, feeling a bit foolish.

It seems the officers were to be the ones asking the questions. As the divers disappeared, the officers interrogated me, asking questions from the banal (Where do you live? What's your name?) to the ridiculous (Have you ever been part of the Communist party? How do you feel about the Soviet Union? Do any family members come from Russia?).

Eventually the SCUBA divers returned and reported to the senior officer that they had found no evidence of listening or sabotaging devices. After a time, and in lieu of knowing what else to do with me, the men drove me in their jeep to the gates of the base and left me and my spearfishing gear on the other side.

After a long, humiliating walk home in my swimsuit, I prepared the fantails – lightly fried, with chips. I told Gary my story, but he seemed more interested in the fish.

Sometime later I found out what I had seen in the harbour: it was the USS *Nautilus*, the world's first nuclear-powered submarine. It had come to Australia from the east coast of the United States through the Northwest Passage, under the Arctic ice. It was the first vessel to ever do so and was visiting Australia under a veil of complete secrecy.

* * *

After *The Seven Year Itch* I was offered another acting role immediately, in another production at The Ensemble. The money was reasonable, but I simply couldn't do it. I wanted my life back, and to be able to choose what to do with my time. I wanted to swim and dive, I wanted adventure.

After two years it had become more and more apparent how different Gary and I – and our ideal lives – really were. The expectation that soon Gary and I should be married was an idea that had come to fill me with apprehension. Gary was completely engaged with his music, as someone should be when they have a real passion in life. The problem was, I wasn't musical at all. Gary's people were musicians, specifically a troupe of folk singers called The Kingston Trio with whom he played, and that group's coterie. He was part of a community of music lovers and players. I was not a player nor was I a lover of that style of music. I appreciated it, but I didn't love it.

Gary was a lovely man but I feared for the life we would have together. Some women's version of adventure did coincide with the life I might have had with the notable musician that Gary was becoming, but not mine. Gary was an indoor man and would have lived an indoor life. That was not what I wanted.

I told Gary that, as soon as I really knew myself. When I told him I was moving out his heart was broken, and it pains me to remember that period and his many beautiful mournful letters, some of which I still have.

Gary died in 2013, having fulfilled many of his dreams, releasing thirteen albums, touring the world and having chart hits in Australia and the UK. For many women a life with Gary would have been wonderful, but I wanted a different life. I needed a chance at the adventure I had always dreamed about.

When I moved back home with my parents I once again started attending meetings of the St George Spearfishing Club, and it was in that period that I started competing in spearfishing competitions.

Spearfishing as a competitive sport was gaining popularity in Australia in 1962. Quality rubber masks and flippers were becoming commercially available and clubs were popping up in many of Sydney's coastal suburbs. Spearfishing looked set to be included in the Olympic Games (in 1968 the IOC held a vote to choose between synchronised swimming and spearfishing for Games inclusion and chose the former) and unified associations and rules had recently been settled.

I was back in the ocean and immersing myself in all aspects of the club, including competition spearfishing. The goal of a spearfishing competition was to find the largest example of each edible species at any given location and kill it, presenting all your kills to the judge after the allotted time. If you established yourself locally, there were state championships. Win there and the male winner could aim to compete at the national championship, and with success there, the next step was the world titles.

The competitions were very enjoyable. During summer, weather permitting, on the weekend I would join the other members of the club and drive to a marine location close to Sydney – some rocks or an island – and set up camp. Then, before the competition, we and those from the other clubs would march through the main street of the hosting town like an invading army, wearing our wetsuits and carrying our spears on our shoulders.

A spearfishing competition is really a slaughter of fish for sport. Each competitor would kill the first fish of each edible species, then look for a larger specimen. If they found one they would simply throw away the smaller fish. It was a sport that required an ability to control one's breath, understand one's prey and be efficient with the spear.

Although there were fish species I could not kill because they were so friendly, I thought nothing of spearing most good eating fish. I was living under the misconception that the ocean has an endless capacity to replenish itself. We never thought for a moment that the fish struggling on the end of our spear might contribute to a permanent depopulation around offshore reefs and headlands.

It saddens me to think that almost no one reading this book will even know what kind of sea life used to exist off the New South Wales coast. At the time, though, we thought nothing of it. We were happy as spearos (as spearfishermen and women were known); ignorant about the changes we were making in the local fish populations.

In the relatively small field of female spearos I established myself as very good, but Ron Taylor quickly became known as almost supernatural. Ron moved well and had a steady hand, but what really made him exceptional at spearfishing was what also made him exceptional at so many other aspects in life: he was fit, meticulous, cool-headed and nothing short of an analytical genius.

As Ron and I travelled together for state and national titles, often in his old Volkswagen, I learned a lot about the man who would become my husband. Ron worked as an apprentice at a printer's shop, doing work he hated. What he really wanted to be was a professional photographer. He had applied to be a photographer for the *Sydney Morning Herald* but there were no positions available. He took other work, but told me of his desire to build a career as an underwater photographer, something that was then still some years away from being possible. He said he was developing an underwater housing for a friend's camera that he could borrow.

It was apparent to me that Ron was a genius. He had worked as an electrician with his uncle when he was just a child, and he used to build his own toys and even rockets. He had passed his pilot's licence before he was eligible for a driver's licence and had already built his own makeshift darkroom. He was one of those technical people who could figure anything out, from washing machines to family cars, just because of his understanding of logic and his ability to reason. I had no doubt that Ron would do everything he said he would do.

Ron was so very different from Gary. Gary was highly emotionally intelligent and totally focused on his music; Ron was technically brilliant. Gary let his heart live on his sleeve; Ron's was buried deep in his chest.

I think I fell in love with Ron far earlier than he did with me, although I'll never really know.

Ron and I would camp close to each other on our way to and from spearfishing tournaments. We would share food, cooking it on a single portable cooker. We would gravitate to each other like a positive proton and negative electron. The problem was, I couldn't see him having any interest in me other than in my function as travel companion.

I did everything I could think of to attract Ron's attention and wondered why he did not notice me as a potential romantic match.

When Ron did notice me, it was when he needed me as a model for his camera.

It was late 1962. Ron and I had travelled to Norfolk Island, a place we had visited in the past mainly because Ron could buy camera equipment there duty-free. We also used to snorkel in the lagoon taking photos. We knew the tragic story of the wrecking of the supply ship *Sirius* but nobody seemed to know where it was. One day our friend Carl introduced us to his grandfather Daddy Bell, a truly delightful old man with white hair, blue eyes and very dark skin, a heritage from his Polynesian ancestors. Daddy Bell claimed he knew where the *Sirius* lay. He took us up a hill and pointed out to an offshore hump in the swell. 'There she be,' he said. This excited Ron. He decided we should snorkel out into the open ocean and try to find the ship. The idea was to me a bit scary. I was used to snorkelling along reefs, over sand, not straight out into the ocean.

The following day Ron took the lead as we battled our way through the break into the open ocean. After what seemed like half a day but was only about half an hour of hard swimming over huge swells with no bottom in sight I saw the ocean floor rise up – then suddenly, there it was. A giant anchor, handmade in some long-forgotten foundry, marking the grave of that unfortunate ship. Ron took some photos, then we swam towards the island. There was the second anchor, this one lying down, then further in through the white water of waves breaking on the reef we saw the remains of the *Sirius*.

Back on shore we told the governor of the island what we had found. He did not believe us, so, the next day he had a crane lift the glass-bottom tourist boat from the lagoon into the open water and, with Ron directing, we took the governor to the wreck site. He was truly amazed. After we left he had the anchor lifted and placed on the lawn in front of Government House. More than thirty years later other divers claimed to have found the wreck of the *Sirius*, but we knew we were the first.

Ron was now shooting still photographs and film underwater and had started selling his photographs to overseas spearfishing magazines. What Ron really wanted to do, though, was to make his own documentaries, like

Hans Hass, an Austrian biologist and adventurer whose work could sometimes be seen on Australian television.

When Ron started getting grabs of 16-millimetre movie film underwater, a minute at a time before having to surface again to wind his camera, he quickly realised something about the viewing public: they would most likely prefer watching footage of a young blonde woman swimming with fish over footage of fish swimming alone – and if that fish was considered dangerous, all the better. (This was true then, and a quick scan of Instagram will tell you it's also true today.) And that's where I came in.

It was in that period that Ron and I first became collaborators, and an interesting time it was for me. We worked very well together. It was also in that period that I had my first foray into SCUBA (Self Contained Underwater Breathing Apparatus) diving, which was very much a novelty in Australian waters then. It was by good luck that I ended up being a SCUBA diver so early.

Next door to our family home lived a man named Kyle Kobson who owned a ship chandler business. An American company called Healthways had sent Kyle their latest product, a commercially available SCUBA kit. The gear was his to keep and they simply requested that he consider buying some of the SCUBA equipment for sale in his business. Kyle had no interest in the kit. SCUBA had no buoyancy control then, nor even a back plate for the tank. Compressed air that you can breathe safely was very difficult to source, and Kyle considered the whole thing more effort than it was worth. In fact, not only did Kyle have no interest in purchasing any

SCUBA equipment, he didn't want the equipment cluttering up his Sydney store.

Over the years, Kyle had seen me often in and out of the water in front of his house, so he gave the equipment to me. I was delighted. With my brother Greg, we figured out where compressed air was available, then we taught ourselves to dive off our parents' pontoon. Probably what saved us from serious injury was the fact we never went deeper than about four metres.

The equipment, while almost weightless underwater, was quite heavy out of it. It was a huge annoyance to carry the steel tank everywhere we went, but even then I thought the potential of the technology was obvious. The SCUBA tank was to become a useful tool in following and photographing marine animals, something I was helping Ron with. SCUBA even became a category in the spearfishing national championships in 1963, held in Denmark in Western Australia.

In 1963 Ron and I were the New South Wales state spearfishing champions and so we were given five pounds each to pay for our passage to Western Australia, which was very different then from how it is now.

Before the Perth British Empire and Commonwealth Games in 1962 the road between Adelaide and Perth received no more than a dozen or so cars a day. Most of the traffic was trucks, and that meant the road, which was then just a dirt track, only received maintenance about once a year. The wrecked cars and destroyed tyres marked the most used path across the desert. The Empire Games traffic tore the road up so badly it became a very perilous passage until the road was sealed in the 1970s.

It took two days to reach Adelaide, then five more red dust–filled days following bullet-pocked signs and broken-down cars for us to get to Perth. Evenings we spent under a canopy of stars, talking about spearfishing before retiring into sleeping bags.

I won the SCUBA section of the competition, which was a fairly minor affair, and I came second in the open competition. I think I would have won but for the fact that the winner was hunting in tandem with a man, permitted to be in the water by the rules of the competition if the female claimed to be scared in the water. Also because I had no idea which fish in the Indian Ocean were good eating, a requirement for a fish to be counted.

Ron won the open competition, as he usually did, and we travelled back east together, this time by rail, using the prize money to book his car and us on the train and thereby coming back in relative comfort.

Sometime after we returned I decided it was time to issue Ron with an ultimatum. If he didn't ask me to marry him, he would lose me to the singer. That's what he called Gary – 'the singer' – somewhat derisively, one of the few indications that he cared for me. One thing I did know was that Ron would have hated to lose me to the singer, and he also knew it was no idle threat.

Up until then, Gary had not left my orbit completely, even as I was off with the spearos. I knew he would still have married me and, were it not for Ron, I would quite possibly have eventually married him.

Marriage wasn't then the game that it can be now. It was expected and necessary, especially for a woman getting to the latter stages of her twenties. If you wanted to have any life as a woman, you needed to be married, and the idea of having sex outside of marriage was unthinkable.

Perhaps a decade later a woman could be single in her thirties, in control of her own finances, her own living situation. Perhaps a decade later again the prefix 'Ms' wouldn't bring too much societal pressure down to bear on her. That revolution may have happened somewhere in 1963, but it hadn't come to Australia yet.

Ron finally agreed to marry me late in 1963, just before we were preparing to travel to Kangaroo Island so Ron could defend his national spearfishing title.

'That can be our honeymoon,' he said, and it all sounded wonderful to me.

We went to the registry office a few days before we were due to leave for South Australia, accompanied by our mothers, and there we were married. I don't remember it much; there was minimal fuss. Which was as Ron and I liked it.

On Kangaroo Island, Ron and I initially scandalised the tournament by disappearing into the same tent at the end of the first day, until the news started to spread that we were married.

That year, Ron won another national spearfishing championship, the third of the four consecutive national titles he would take, one of which would lead to his inclusion in the world championships in Tahiti, a competition he won by many thousand points.

I had also taken a national title, and I think we were perhaps the best spearfishing couple in the world, but our interest in that sport started to wane in the face of another, similar interest that we felt had the opportunity to pay us more than just a few dollars and travel money.

After we were married we bought a house under the flight path in Mortdale. It was all we could afford and I hated it. Ron and I had saved £2000 each, and the house, a fibro box, was £5000. We were looking for ways to quickly pay off our £1000 loan.

Ron had started to make his own short underwater film clips, and Movietone News had shown interest. Television was then like the internet is now, a dominant force becoming more dominant every day. That didn't mean the previous media forms were dead. In the way that terrestrial television is still limping along now, the theatres that played the news of the day on a loop were still peppered across Australia and across the world. Movietone News, the biggest supplier of newsreel packages, was still paying £25 an item; what we considered then to be pretty big bucks.

The Movietone people were very interested in Ron's footage. The underwater scenes were like science fiction without the cost of special effects; a huge and alien world the likes of which very few had ever seen. The encouragement was all Ron needed.

He started producing specifically for Movietone. Each news story needed to be two to three minutes long, then Movietone added narration and an orchestral soundtrack capable of presenting a newsworthy story, a formula that had been honed during the war.

With war stories, dark and dramatic music would play as Nazi or Japanese forces were shown. A narrator would describe a threat, often in an exotic location. That footage would give way to vision of some plucky Allied soldiers. The music would change and the narrator's tone would too as he wished the men on camera good luck. There was often a moment of whimsy accompanied by a joke from the narrator to break the seriousness of the situation. Perhaps there would also be a resolution, good triumphing over evil. The best and most popular reels did.

By the time Ron and I were delivering packages the Movietone style of presentation hadn't changed very much: we divers were obviously the heroes, the locations were all exotic and there were exciting extras, from eels to rays to large groupers.

That just left the villains; the mysterious danger lurking, ready to strike, accompanied by ominous music and a sense of trouble about to happen. Movietone would edit the piece for the most dramatic effect.

For that there was only one choice: the shark.

CHAPTER THREE

Escaping a bad choice

Telling a life story is a strange thing. The important moments are more easily recalled. And there are memories that perhaps are better not told. But to understand me, I think I should share this. I married, briefly and very poorly, before Ron came into my life. It was to a man I'd known in New Zealand who seemed a suitable match in the period I needed a husband.

He was not lovely like Johnny had been. He was a wrestler, with a good frame and nice teeth. I found him attractive, for a while.

We were engaged without knowing much about each other, which was not unusual for the time. He came to Australia, where he thought new prospects for him would exist. We married at the registry office and then, the next day, moved into my parents' boathouse.

There I very quickly started to understand the true reality of what it meant to be a wife.

To be a wife was to have a second job and perhaps even a third. Meal preparation, shopping, darning, gardening, washing, cleaning – these were all tasks I was expected to do, in addition to my full-time job. My life was filled with undesirable tasks.

My husband had time to sit and read and enjoy unencumbered hours with his mates. He had money to spend outside of what was spent on meals and essentials. I never had either. He had a subordinate, attending to any task he saw needed attending to, but I did not. I was that subordinate.

This man and I didn't share much in our short marriage, except a bed and the smell of his old socks. It didn't take long for me to realise I had made a mistake. I saw before me an uninteresting and disagreeable life, but I had no idea what to do.

Then, one night, the situation resolved itself.

After a day working, I was at home cooking mutton chops, one of the few meals we could afford. When my husband returned home from work he was instantly disappointed. He wanted steak, a luxury we could only intermittently enjoy. I told him that at least there was a tasty dessert ahead, indicating a pot of rhubarb I had grown myself and had been stewing, sending a wonderful scent of peppery sweetness through the house.

He was not interested in the rhubarb. He was not interested in the economic reality of our lives. He was uninterested in me as anything but a utility. The only thing he was interested in was steak. I had bought myself a jar of cold cream, which he considered a waste of money.

He was being unbearable, unfair and nasty, and I lost it. To my amazement I picked up the pot of rhubarb and tipped the lot on his head.

I thought he might hit me, he let out such a yell and rose from his chair.

The argument before I dumped the dessert on him had become petty and hurtful in the way that only a mismatched husband and wife arguing can be. Wounds had been exposed and I knew I had hurt his ego even before I had inflicted on him the ignominy of being doused in stewed fruit.

I had long thought he had violence in him, and when he didn't hit me immediately I ran scared out the door on our balcony and jumped into the bay. Being a boathouse, our house sat over the water. I held my breath and dived under the water, swimming as far away as I could manage without surfacing.

When I emerged I went straight to my parents' place and, after a while, called the home I had just fled. There was no emotion in his voice, and I did not feel apologetic. I told him our marriage was over. He agreed and said that, in return for giving him all our savings, he would be gone from our home when I returned from work the next day.

He was true to his word, and then some. When I returned home the next day he had stripped the place of anything that had any resale value. That was fine by me. My adult life could start anew. No more demanding husband.

Even now I shudder when I think about the life I might have endured. I thank the stars for the pot of rhubarb and the bay in which I was able to escape.

But the truth was, at that time, a woman who craved adventure was going to find an easier path if she had a man with her on the journey. As wrong as that may be, it was a truth I had to live with. And with Ron, I was well and truly taking an adventurous path.

CHAPTER FOUR

Movietone sharks and Ron Taylor Productions

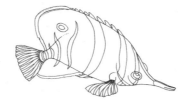

The first sharks I saw were often a species that was then widely considered to be a threat to human life, but actually posed no threat at all.

I remember one of my first interactions with a shark. My brother Greg and I were snorkelling at Bundeena, just a short paddle from our parents' home, when we were confronted by a grey nurse shark. I say confronted with the shark's presence, but in reality we meant almost nothing to a grey nurse when in the water with it.

The grey nurse is an easy shark to confuse with something dangerous: a threatening profile, sleek skin, a long, lean body and sharp, pointed teeth that I now know are for catching and eating fish. That first time, however, I had no idea the shark was completely uninterested in me; the media had most people believing grey nurses were dangerous. I thought the grey nurse would like nothing better than to strip the flesh from my bones and leave my desiccated corpse on the sea floor.

After seeing that shark, Greg and I swam to shore as fast as our flippers could take us and then told whoever would listen our breathless tale of escape from certain death.

When Ron and I started travelling the country for spearfishing competitions, sighting grey nurse sharks became a relatively common occurrence, so too whalers, which we called bronzies, and sometimes even bull sharks, which can actually be quite dangerous, but we almost always confused them for bronzies.

Some of our interactions with sharks were confrontational. Sharks would swoop in, with bared teeth and hungry intent. This behaviour would often be characterised as an attack but the reality is the sharks were far more interested in what was on the end of our spears; bleeding, fleshy and vulnerable.

Human deaths from sharks were very rare even then, but our friends were sometimes bitten, and those injuries helped push the narrative that sharks were aggressive killers, ignoring the fact that most bites were due to the spearos getting between a shark and their food.

Spearfishermen and women hated sharks, like the ocean swimmers, divers, board riders and even thousands of Australians who never ventured into the ocean. Sharks were evil killers and they had no right to be in our waters; everyone knew that. Sharks killed for food but it was also believed they killed for fun; everyone knew that. The only good shark was a dead shark; everyone knew that.

The sharks were there in the water, where we speared and where we swam, but the animals didn't show much interest in Ron and me, and in turn we didn't take much notice of them – that was, until we realised we could make some money filming them for our Movietone clips.

As we travelled around the state and country for spearfishing competitions we started taking notes of which reefs and points had the largest shark populations, as well as details of behaviour, in general and species specific. We took these notes like an army building up a dossier about the enemy.

In one of our popular early Movietone clips I speared a whaler shark in northern New South Wales.

'A vicious man-eater, over eight feet long,' the narration chirped as the shark swam away terrified and bleeding. 'It won't be long till this whaler becomes the only good shark we know, a dead one.'

We made Movietone clips about all kinds of underwater adventures in the first couple of years of the 1960s, from the perils of a sea snake to the domestication of two giant crayfish that we captured and kept in the saltwater pool at my parents' Cronulla house. What Movietone liked best, however, and apparently what the public also liked best, was the seemingly deadly sharks.

At the Australian spearfishing championships in Western Australia we became friendly with a man who, a few months after the competition, would actually dance the dance and become the subject of one of our most popular early films.

We met Rodney Fox when he was a 22-year-old South Australian insurance salesman. He was a kind and adventurous soul with a great talent for spearfishing, and we quickly befriended him. We were especially intrigued to hear about the Eyre Peninsula in South Australia where he mostly fished, and the great population of sharks that lived there.

We compared notes about the shark populations in New South Wales and it seemed they were similar to the South Australian populations, except that South Australia had another shark rarely seen in New South Wales waters, known as the pointer, white or great white.

That shark was very large and seemed quite energetic, but none of us really understood how different the white was from the grey nurse until, to bend a phrase, it jumped up and bit one of us.

It happened only a few months after we met Rodney. He was competing in a spearfishing competition at Aldinga Beach in Gulf St Vincent, roughly an hour's drive south of Adelaide. He had seen a large fish in the water that he liked the look of. He dived down, fired his gun and pierced his target. The vibrating fish, along with blood, sent out signals of distress – and a moment later he was riding in front of a freight train. That's how Rodney described it, anyway.

Rodney flew through the water with terrifying and confusing speed. He looked around and saw he was wedged in the jaws of a great white, perhaps five or six metres long and weighing around 1000 kilograms. The animal's teeth were embedded in his abdomen and his own blood was pouring out, clouding the water.

Rodney says he instinctively reached down to try to free himself from the jaws but his hand just ended up wedged into the beast's mouth. After he managed to yank himself free his hand hung limp and bloody, shredded from the wrist down.

Rodney says the only reason he survived the attack was because the shark adjusted its bite, which resulted in Rodney's speared fish – the thing that had attracted the shark to Rodney in the first place – ending up in the shark's mouth, and Rodney's body out.

Rodney required 462 stitches to repair his torso and hand. Young and strong, he recovered fully, with a hell of a story and some very photogenic scarring. We used both in one of our early films, *Revenge of a Shark Victim*.

The film, which we shot at Seal Rocks on the mid north coast of New South Wales, a beautiful and abundant place we had become very fond of, starts with Rodney. As he takes his shirt off and reveals scars from the bottom of his rib cage all the way up to his neck, the narrator explains the attack and then says: 'Today the tables are turned, the hunted becomes the hunter … A one-man war against sharks.'

A smiling Rodney enters the water with his powerhead, a then popular one-shot, direct-contact underwater firearm that fires .303 bullets and shotgun shells – a favourite for killing sharks.

'Movietone underwater cameraman Ron Taylor takes us down to look over Rodney's target area,' says the narrator, and a scene that could never be seen in Australia these days appears: dozens and dozens of sharks, all grey nurse, milling around the ocean floor. 'They look like they're in battle formation,' the narrator continues, and they do somewhat in the black-and-white footage; dark and foreboding against the light white sand.

Rodney swims up to one of the sharks, a five- or six-foot whaler, who takes almost no notice of him. He fires a single round into the shark's head, killing it instantly.

'And that's the only good shark. A dead shark. Hats off to Rodney Fox, a man on the vengeance trail.'

Another television classic.

Most of our early films were shot in New South Wales or in southern Queensland, on extended weekends where we spent more time driving than diving. I remember those trips fondly, but I also remember them as being quite frantic, requiring not just filming and diving, but hustle.

At the time we were filming a minute of footage per free dive, with each reel requiring the housing to be cleaned, opened and the film changed before Ron could go down and film again. The nature of the animals we wanted to film and the conditions they lived in meant we would often go to a location and return without anything usable in the can.

We would never know when we would have enough footage to sell, and with our regular salaries paying only for our Sydney lives, we had to make these trips pay for themselves. We would spear fish and sell or trade them when we could, often grouper in exchange for a meal at a Chinese restaurant or fuel at a petrol station. I can see in my mind right now

John Harding, a friend who often helped as an assistant for the trips, with his fingers in the gills of speared fish selling them around the camping area, his voice explaining to the campers how the fish could best be cooked. John was a fine diver and photographer. Like us he was always looking for the new and exciting, which is probably why we worked together so well.

We would also sell wetsuits that Ron made from sheets of neoprene. He would cut and glue to measure. It earned enough money to keep film in the cameras but not much else.

Ron had bought a Siemens projector to review our footage some years before, and the idea came to us that perhaps we could project our footage onto the walls of sheds, halls or barns, and charge the locals two shillings for the privilege of watching. We would show our best footage in the towns and cities we visited, a practice we came to call 'barn-walling'.

Like most things worthwhile, we started small and then grew. Ron built a reel-to-reel editing machine, and he started cutting our films, setting the images to music we played on a record player, and adding narration that Ron and I wrote. We started travelling into the towns a day earlier, in order to stick up posters advertising our screening and to plan a publicity stunt for the benefit of the local newspaper and radio.

In one instance, we saved a turtle from the shark nets off the local baths; in another we found a very young white shark and handed it over to the local Porpoise Pool. At the end of each story, print or radio, we would tell the readers that if they wanted to know more about the aquatic world on the shore of their town, they should come along that night to see our film.

Interest in these film nights grew and so too the size of our venues; from barns to university theatres, churches and halls. Interest in us grew also.

In those early years, it was rare for us to come back home with more money than we spent, but with a small following starting to build around us and our films, we had started to glean that there were more opportunities out there than we first realised. It was obvious that those opportunities were in television.

Television had been little more than a technological curio in Australia until 1956, and broadcasts of the Melbourne Olympic Games, but in that year TCN-9, a Sydney-based broadcaster and HSV-7, a Melbourne-based broadcaster, started transmitting. Those two stations would later become the Nine Network, and the Seven Network.

From 1956 into the early 1960s, the scope of television broadcasting grew in Australia, all the way to Perth, but the content was usually sourced overseas. Series such as *Whiplash*, shot and set in Australia, were the exception on Australian screens until a 1963 senate select committee convened for the 'encouragement of Australian productions for television' and brought forward a series of recommendations and incentives to promote more local production.

It was in this environment that we first sat down with Bruce Gyngell, the son of a flying circus owner/operator and the man hired by newspaper and magazine baron Frank Packer to run his new venture, TCN-9. Bruce was Packer's television right-hand man, but also the man in charge of okaying the purchase of footage for TCN-9, including news footage. Then, as it has largely remained to this day, footage was chosen because of its visual excitement, often regardless of news value. Bruce was interested in our stories, especially stories about sharks. We didn't have to worry about the news angle on the stories, they'd figure that out. It seemed sharks were news by themselves, so Ron and I started hunting for sharks to film every weekend.

At first we provided dramatic footage for Channel Nine News, but soon enough we were delivering documentaries, the first of which, *Shark Hunters*, an hour-long program in black and white, was an exceptional success.

Utilising a great deal of archival footage that Ron and I had shot over the years, featuring some of the first underwater images of sharks in Australia, and a lot of marine death, the film was shown multiple times on Australian screens and even made its way to the United States, being bought by NBC.

We were happy with the film's success but we could see that television's future was in colour, not in black and white, and we knew the public would be interested in the brilliant fish and picturesque corals found in Australian waters, specifically in one place that we both dearly loved and couldn't wait to see on Australian screens: the Great Barrier Reef.

Ron and I had started visiting the Capricorn Bunker reef area a few years earlier, travelling to Queensland for the Heron Island Dive Festival organised by the Poulsen family, who had leased the island. Sitting as it does on an immense platform of coral, Heron is a true coral island, and it was a mecca for free divers and photographers.

None of the facilities on the island that exist today existed then. Visitors slept in accommodation built for workers at the now-defunct turtle-soup factory. Years earlier the workers on the island were tasked with grabbing the female green turtles that came to lay their eggs, stunning them with clubs, boiling them in water and then canning the soup, to be sold as a delicacy.

Now people were starting to come to the island and the nearby reef to observe the beautiful coral and the marine life it supported. We went there to film and spearfish for the resort's kitchen. The cook paid sixpence a pound for good eating fish gilled and gutted. Selling fish to the island helped defray our expenses.

It was an enjoyable time at the dive festival. I was the twice-winner of the beauty pageant that was the social centrepiece of the festival, which required me to be ogled in my bathing suit, but also to complete an underwater obstacle course as quickly as possible – a task that the other entrants sometimes found a little difficult.

The real attraction of the festival, however, was the Great Barrier Reef itself, a true wonder of colour, shape, excitement and, above all, fish.

Our second documentary on the marine world that screened on Channel Nine was called *Slaughter at Saumarez*. Ron and I had a very reliable tinny that we towed everywhere when we went to dive. It was not a suitable vessel for the 400-kilometre return trip to the Coral Sea, so instead Ron hired Wally Muller and his tuna boat the *Riversong* for the journey. A tuna boat, with its lack of privacy and ablutions, was not thought of as a place for women, and so I was not permitted to take part in that trip. Instead Ron took along John Harding and fellow spearfisherman Bob Grounds to fill out the crew.

The central premise of the film, and the on-screen slaughter, was a competition between the spearos and Wally, the line fisherman, which would happen at an untouched paradise, filled with marine life. After a few amusing asides on a World War II wreck and among the birds at a coral cay they anchored off Saumarez Reef, and the competition was in play.

About 400 kilograms of top-quality fish were killed in one day, with Wally Muller accounting for most of the haul. The real action in the film happens near the end, when the men try to retrieve their anchor and find that not only is it stuck, but it is being circled by sharks that have been attracted by fish heads and offal dumped off the deck when Wally cleaned the catch.

John Harding is seen preparing his powerhead with .303 ammunition.

'John prepares for battle. He's an expert when it comes to clashing with these denizens of the deep. If he can kill a few, perhaps the rest will take fright.'

Ron goes down and films John shooting grey reef sharks and a tiger shark and dusky shark. Those were the money shots, and likely what sold the film. Channel Nine bought the documentary and we established a deal with them that would become standard for the years to come: they would have rights to the footage for three years, and then it would revert back to us.

Ron wrote the narration for that film, which was performed by Channel Nine stalwart Chuck Faulkner, accompanied by a jaunty jazz soundtrack composed by another Channel Nine favourite, musician Geoff Harvey.

The film was proof positive that Ron Taylor Productions could produce full-scale, end-to-end broadcast-quality productions, and in that capacity we were hired to make another short film for the Queensland Tourism Bureau. The film was called *Skindiving Paradise*, and it took us back to the Great Barrier Reef.

That film featured me, my long blonde hair and my yellow swimsuit, quite heavily.

Ron became increasingly interested in great white sharks after we shot *Revenge of a Shark Victim* with Rodney and he thought that, while there was a possibility that the other sharks readily found close to Sydney would become less interesting to the viewing public, the elusive great white shark, with its fearless energy and immense size, would keep its on-screen value.

When Ron set out to produce *Great White Death* no one had ever filmed a great white swimming underwater.

Again Rodney would be our on-camera talent, this time joined by Brian Rodger and Henri Bource, both divers who had also been attacked by a white. Brian was bitten on the thigh in the same area that Rodney was attacked, and Henri lost his leg from the knee down while snorkelling with sea lions off Lady Julia Percy Island. These men told a similar tale to Rodney's: the shark had appeared from nowhere and struck with the power of a thousand-pound bomb. The speed of the hit was immense, the sharpness of the teeth like a razor, the injuries were devastating.

Another uniform characteristic of these attacks was that they happened in the peninsula off South Australia, so Ron headed there in search of this great white shark, travelling out on a fishing boat with Rodney, Brian and Henri. Rodney also arranged for another man to join them – a man who has put a larger hole in Australia's white shark population than any other individual in history: Alf Dean, the self-proclaimed world's greatest shark hunter.

More shark hunter than game fisherman, Alf Dean, then in his sixties, claimed to have killed a hundred great white sharks over 1000 pounds, and it was no empty boast. Everyone in the world of spearfishing would have seen a photograph of Dean dwarfed next to a dead shark on a dock, hung out in its giant glory. I had certainly seen enough, including a famous image of Dean in Denial Bay in South Australia next to a 1200-kilogram great white, killed by Dean with rod and reel.

While they were out on the ocean Dean explained to Ron where great white sharks could be found, and the techniques most likely to attract them. The sharks Dean attracted helped Ron become the first-ever cameraman to film a great white shark swimming underwater, which he did by dipping his head, shoulder and camera in the water as the whites attacked baits.

I'll never forget the respect and gravity in Ron's voice when he returned and spoke about the sharks he'd seen in South Australia.

'That is a very, very dangerous shark,' he said.

Shortly after that trip Ron signed himself up for a course in aluminium welding, and when he finished he started building cages in the backyard of our home. The cages were designed to be lowered from a boat to protect a diver against the bite of a large great white. Rodney had two more cages made in South Australia.

As dangerous as the shark was, it was even more photogenic. When we saw Ron's footage shot during the Alf Dean trip in South Australia, we knew that the public would want more images of this magnificent fish.

We decided to ride another wave of interest starting to swell at the time: surfing.

A documentary film from director Bruce Brown came out in 1966 called *The Endless Summer*, and in Australia it packed out every cinema it played in. Many board riders would go in to one session, and as soon as that ended, they would come out and immediately buy another ticket for the next session.

The idea of us making our own surfing film came after a conversation we had with the editor of a national surfing magazine. He spoke of an incredible but largely inaccessible surf break a little way north of Maroochydore in Queensland. He had seen it from a light aircraft when flying along the Queensland coast.

Ron and I contacted Paul Witzig, a cameraman who was well known in the surfing community, and who had contributed footage to segments in *The Endless Summer* that had been shot in Australia. He'd heard of the break and was interested in working with us, and even suggested which surfers we should take with us: Russell Hughes, a Queensland phenomenon who was introduced to Witzig after leaving home at fourteen and arriving at Witzig's door asking to help him make a career out of surfing; Robert Conneeley, a former world junior champion; and perhaps also Kevin 'The Head' Brennan.

The 'perhaps' was because Brennan was a wild card and well known as a 'bad' kid. He was the youngest of the group that Paul suggested and perhaps the most talented, but also the most rambunctious. At fifteen he was already junior and senior NSW surfing champion, but he also had a history of larceny and substance abuse, having grown up rough in the Sydney suburb of Bondi, then known as 'the seaside slum'.

Ron and I were confident we could handle the young man, especially when we heard that the teenager was the size of a boy many years younger. We asked Paul to arrange for all three to go with us to Queensland. We also asked a beautiful actress and surfer named Tanya Binning to join us so she could bring some sex appeal to a film we knew would be mostly watched by men. We wanted her to fulfil the same role she had taken in the famous 1962 Italian exploitation documentary *Mondo Cane*.

I saw the opportunity for a film like this to be sponsored, then had a novel idea. One day I caught a North Sydney bus to visit the offices of Speedo, a well-known swimwear company.

The receptionist seemed hesitant when I asked to speak to the man in charge, but she made a phone call. A friendly man arrived. I told him who I was and about the film we wanted to make, and that I'd like some money, please.

Another man arrived and they convened a meeting there and then in the boardroom. Eventually we emerged. I could have my money, as long as everyone in the film wore Speedo clothes.

That was fine by me.

I don't think either of them could quite believe what they were seeing; a young woman fronting up on their doorstep asking for money, and quite a lot of money too. I think they accepted in no small part because they were just tickled by the whole thing.

We drove from Sydney to Queensland in two cars – Paul's station wagon and Ron's old Volkswagen – filled with boards, cameras, surfers, tripods and provisions. Trailing behind the vehicles were our fourteen-foot aluminium de Havilland runabout and a rather leaky plywood runabout with a thirty-five-horsepower engine.

When we got to Maroochydore we rented a huge house right on the sand, which cost us a pound a week. We spent the first three days filming our stars riding the local break. By the fourth day the wind had switched to the west, which made perfect conditions for an open-ocean trip in our small craft. We set off immediately on our first voyage to the unsurfed break.

As soon as the boys saw the waves they started whooping and hollering. We dropped Paul off on a rock nearby with his camera and tripod, then Ron started shooting from our tinny as we rode waves next to the board riders. John Harding handled the motor with his usual skill. It was great fun. We were all yelling and shouting with joy and excitement.

Each shooting day we would come back to the house in the dark, exhausted but happy. Every night I would cook a meal, usually a roast. Bread-and-butter pudding was everyone's favourite. They needed energy for the next day's surfing.

I was taken aback by the way Kevin 'The Head' Brennan responded to each home-cooked meal. Every dinner, even if it was just a simple roast and vegetables, introduced The Head to something new. It seemed for fifteen years of his life he had only ever eaten the simplest of foods or, when he had money, pies or fish and chips.

He was intriguing, The Head. He was perhaps the most talented surfer of all of them but would allow himself to be bullied horribly, and slept most nights in a baby's cot that was in the house after the other boys laughingly suggested it. He could be incredibly standoffish sometimes, but in one instance, when I put my arm around him to stop him shivering from cold, he acted like a scared dog, jolting away before slowly coming into my embrace; fearful but with a child's desire for touch.

I think The Head was as unaccustomed to human touch as he was to roast dinners.

The film, entitled *Surf Scene*, was a success, not so much on Channel Nine but at our barn-wallers. Each night we would show four or five of our documentaries and when *Surf Scene* was on the bill a troupe of board riders would be in attendance, leaving immediately after that film ended.

We planned to make another surfing film one day, but as our marine and shark films became more and more popular, we never seemed to have the time. We did see the people we made *Surf Scene* with around the place though; everyone except The Head.

I would hear stories from time to time about him; that he'd gone to the northern beaches and then to Darlinghurst. I'd hear that he'd been beaten badly or that he'd ripped someone off. Later I heard he was in Kings Cross, on the streets and addicted to heroin. Then one day I heard that Kevin had died of an overdose. I never heard anyone say his name again.

Around the time that *Surf Scene* was finished, Ron finally realised his dream of working exclusively on his films.

With more and more work coming in from Channel Nine, Ron Taylor Productions had a full-time staff member, but only one. We weren't in a position for both of us to leave regular employment, so I kept on drawing, for Press Feature Services initially and later for a Jesuit magazine called *The Messenger of the Sacred Heart*. It was work I liked, but I did fantasise about the day my only office would be the ocean.

In addition to the documentaries and fully delivered news stories we made for TCN-9, we took on underwater contract work too, such as filming Murray Rose as he swam in a Sydney pool for a news story, and also underwater shots for a ground-breaking new Australian kids' show about the adventures of a young boy and his pet kangaroo shot in and around a New South Wales national park. The series, *Skippy the Bush Kangaroo*, became an international success.

As had been the case at Artransa Park, I found more work for myself when I arrived on the set of *Skippy*. I made myself available for any work they needed doing and when the producer Lee Robinson asked if I had any experience doing stunts I wasn't lying when I said I did.

It was in this capacity that I was given the most beautiful view of the Hawkesbury River – as I dangled on a rope below a helicopter. I remember it was a cloudy day, and they wanted me to fall into the river, but not until the sun was shining. I must have hung there for half an hour until they told me to drop, but at that stage we had veered over a muddy bank. Drop I was asked to do; drop I did, plummeting into the muck. As I was wading my way out, Tony Bonner, one of the stars of the show, bounded over to 'save' me. I waved him away, I was fine. The shot ended up being used, and that's all that mattered.

The male stars of these shows always wanted to 'save' someone, except for Tony's co-star, Skippy.

There were actually about nine Skippys, usually six on the set, and each lived in a bag hanging on the wall like a giant pouch. Different kangaroos were called up when the story coincided with their particular skill. The Skippy who had no interest in saving me was the swimming Skippy. We had been put together in a small boat in which we were to sail down the river until a rogue wave turned us over. I was to be stuck under the dinghy in the water unable to escape, and Skippy was to swim to the shore and bound away for help. However, when we upturned our craft we both ended up stuck under the boat, and the unhappy soaked mess of marsupial would not leave her air pocket.

The cameras were ready to roll, but every time I tried to push Skippy free, she fought hard to stay with me under the boat. She was a fine swimmer but would not allow me to pull her underwater. I realised I was going to have to wrestle the kangaroo free so she could swim for help. It was a bit of a struggle but eventually the little marsupial was on the outside of our dinghy and, as expected, she swam to shore.

I had a few scratches but I didn't mind. Get the shot; that's all that mattered to me. That's what I'd learned above anything else over the past few years of filmmaking with Ron.

When I heard that the producers of *Skippy* were looking for story outlines, and paying handsomely for any that went into production, I saw no reason I couldn't do that too. The first storyline I wrote involved a beautiful, blonde marine biologist who was visiting the national park to study grey nurse sharks; of course it required a lot of lovely underwater photography. After that storyline was bought, Ron and I were brought in to take the underwater shots. Seal Rocks north of Sydney was the ideal place. We knew the local reefs and marine inhabitants well.

On arrival we checked in at the small general store, as we usually did, only to learn that another underwater filmmaker had arrived just before us; a man who is still alive to this day and therefore cannot be named, but who was then deeply jealous of the amount of work that we were getting.

At the store we were told this guy had been out to Seal Rocks, where we all knew a large shark colony existed. These sharks were essential to our story, and so, worried by this information, Ron and I jumped in our tinny and motored out to the rock. When we arrived we were greeted by our worst fear: there, drifting dead in their own blood like massacred shadows, were twenty-two grey nurse sharks, all killed with a powerhead; one round each to the brain.

The entire colony had been massacred to stop us filming the sharks.

I was sad that we would no longer be able to film at Seal Rocks but, more than that, I was desolate because of the useless slaughter. I could see in my mind how they would have died. Our understanding of the grey nurse had evolved since we first filmed them. I knew they were a placid fish, completely uninterested in humans, and would have not thought anything about a diver swimming up, powerhead in hand. The grey nurse might look dangerous but is actually one of the quietest, most peaceful sharks along our coast. Night hunters, they gather in communities to rest during the day. There was a well-known shark gutter out from the lighthouse where the grey nurse sharks drifted peacefully, and it was these sharks that had been an essential part of the story. We moved to another shark location and completed our work.

In our spearfishing days we had always been told that the ocean could replenish itself endlessly, but experience was starting to show us that this wasn't true. Even here, in Seal Rocks, over the dozen years we had been visiting, we could see that some species were becoming rare. Now these gentle sharks were suddenly rare too.

When I saw those slaughtered sharks I thought about Alf Dean, the hunter of great whites, and this man who had killed so many of the grey nurse sharks at Seal Rocks, and I couldn't help but wonder if sharks might too one day become scarce in our waters.

I resolved to never again kill a shark, and to this day, I have saved several but not harmed any.

CHAPTER FIVE

Discovering paradise

If, in the 1960s, sharks were seen as the dark, malevolent villain of aquatic Australia, then the counterbalancing hero was probably not an animal but an area: the Great Barrier Reef.

Australians were perhaps more parochial and patriotic then than they are now, and while we had no great church or tower or coliseum we had near incomparable natural icons: we had Sydney Harbour, we had the Rock (Uluru), we had the Great Barrier Reef, a living underwater monument to Australian glory. All were known, all were revered.

Even so, very little was understood about the reef then. Few people visited it, except for some divers and an unknown number of sports and commercial fishermen. In 1967, Ron and I formed part of the largest (and possibly most extensive) expedition ever undertaken on the reef. Much of

71

the understanding of the remote parts of the reef had been gleaned from the previous scientific expedition, undertaken by English marine zoologist Maurice Yonge in between the two World Wars. The biggest difference was that Professor Yonge's exploration was all above water, yet most of the reef and its inhabitants live under the surface.

We now know, however, that human knowledge about the reef is as old as the reef itself. There is a story told by an Australian Aboriginal group whose land is close to the reef that tells of an ancient fisherman who once, thousands of years ago, accidentally speared a sacred and godlike ray mistaking it for a fish. The aggrieved ray started waving its fins and didn't stop until he had raised the ocean to the peaks of some nearby mountains. All of the coastal land below, full of the best animals and plants and seeds to eat, was sacrificed to the oceanic realm. This was now the domain of the sacred ray. The ray built a new home for himself and his friends; a huge, oceanic wonderland stretching north and south as far as anyone had ever travelled.

When I started going to the reef in the late 1950s we had no idea that this story was the closest to accuracy of any that was being told about the history of the reef. Scientists now believe the reef was made possible after the last Ice Age dramatically raised the level of the sea. In fact, in many consecutive years, hundreds of metres of coastal land was claimed by the ocean each year.

Eventually a very wide, very shallow seabed was established just off the coast of what is now Queensland, a fertile area with plenty of light ready for the acceptance of life – and oh did life come. Tiny coral polyps built their limestone homes in the warm, shallow seabed. The coral polyps multiplied and thrived like in no other place on earth, and in their coral home colonies of tiny fish and crustaceans appeared, a food source that attracted larger fish including grouper, tuna, sea turtles, sharks and of course all types of rays, the most beautiful being the manta.

Scientists have now established that coastal inundation happened between 11 000 and 14 000 years ago and that the Great Barrier Reef was built relatively quickly after that. All of this happened after Queensland's Aboriginal peoples settled on the coast, so it seems that Indigenous Australians had been telling the story of the reef for thousands of years before science caught up.

When Ron and I arrived at the Great Barrier Reef in 1967 for a six-month scientific expedition taking in the full 2300-kilometre length of the reef, we knew the history and the place as well as anyone else, which is to say we knew very little indeed.

We had previously travelled to many parts of the Great Barrier Reef, spearfishing and filming. Our visits had given us a serviceable understanding of the behaviour of many reef dwellers but we had little understanding of it holistically, nor of the creatures who were rare or even unknown.

We, like many of the Australian and international scientists with whom we shared six months, jumped at the opportunity to be involved in the expedition, but unlike many of the Australian and international scientists with whom we travelled, we were primarily doing it for the money.

Ron's and my true appreciation of the significance of the place and the journey would only come later.

* * *

We first learned about the expedition after the phone rang in our house in Mortdale. An accented voice, that of a man named Pierre Dubuisson, was on the line, saying he had seen our work and wanted to talk about a project he was planning. He was hoping to make a film epic in scale and artistry and he wanted Ron and me to help him make it.

This man said he was backed by the University of Liège in Belgium and we would work as part of a scientific expedition on an unprecedented scale. We wondered if this was all hot air, until one day Pierre arrived at the doorway of our fibro box in Mortdale, very young, very blond and rather aristocratic.

We had met few Europeans then, and certainly no European aristocrats. We didn't know what to make of this man, elegant and handsome, as he stood in great contrast to the humble surroundings of our house under the flight path next to the industrial area. Dubuisson had no film credits, and was only in his mid-twenties but carried himself as a man of importance. He spoke as though he was undoubtedly making a great film, and while we had no idea whether Dubuisson would be a great director, it quickly became apparent that he had access to great money.

Dubuisson told us he had recently seen the James Bond film *Thunderball* and was inspired by the film's underwater sequences, especially the epic final underwater battle between James Bond and the CIA and SPECTRE. He was so inspired, in fact, that he contacted the producers of that film so he could purchase all the equipment used for the underwater sequences: the red wetsuit and SCUBA equipment used by Sean Connery, the 35-millimetre underwater camera and housing as well as the lights and tripods.

We had not used 35-millimetre film before, and the prospect excited us greatly, especially Ron. Dubuisson said we would be hired for six months, earning a daily fee as we travelled from the southern end of the Great Barrier Reef to the northern end, and reimbursed for any expenses. Dubuisson asked if we could help with Australian marine logistics, and when he said he was bringing a large vessel from Europe as the main platform for the journey, Ron explained that he would need to include a secondary vessel and a local captain to navigate the trickier parts of the reef.

It was agreed that Wally Muller and his tuna-fishing boat the *Careelah* would be hired for the shoot: a man and vessel Ron was especially familiar with having already made a number of filming trips with Wally on that boat.

Wally, like many of the best captains at the time, liked a drink, and even though we knew he would drink rum all day (in a mug with a splash of Coca-Cola) he was still the best man for the job. He was an excellent seaman and after decades pulling fish out of these reefs to sell at markets across Queensland he knew the most about the area we would traverse.

Wally and the *Careelah* would have many uses but none more essential than as a pilot ship for the main vessel when navigating the treacherous Swain Reefs, then a lesser-known part of the Great Barrier Reef and often a ship's lament. To that end we knew we would wind up using the most complete charts available at that time: those of Captain James Cook himself, who 'discovered' part of the reef by running his vessel the HMS *Endeavour* straight into it.

Dubuisson said he would arrange a 35-millimetre camera and housing for us to use, but Ron asked instead if we could defer part of our fee and have Dubuisson purchase a French 35-millimetre camera that we would keep afterwards. After our handshake agreement, Pierre left for Belgium to make his great preparations.

Even with the camera payment we would walk away with enough money to pay off the house, buy a new car and pocket some money for whatever we wanted to do next. We were excited to begin this job that would make us truly independent.

We wouldn't see Pierre again for more than a year.

The expedition's mothership, *De Moor*, planned to make passage to Australia from Belgium via the Mediterranean, the Red Sea and the Indian Ocean. Prior to leaving, however, they discovered that the Suez Canal, the only passageway between the Mediterranean and the Red Sea, was closed.

Israel and Egypt, where the Suez Canal flowed, were having one of their innumerable wars and both the entry and exit of the canal were closed but for those fighting. It was unknown how long the conflict would continue, so the Belgians decided to forgo the Suez and instead steam across the Atlantic to South America where they could use the Panama Canal to access the Pacific.

This extended the journey to Australia by some months, but ended up being a very wise decision. The fourteen European ships and one American ship stuck in the Suez when the conflict started stayed there for eight years.

When we heard that the Belgians were getting close to Australian waters, Ron and I stuck our de Havilland tinny on the back of our 1960 Volkswagen bug, filled it with diving equipment, locked our front door and headed north.

The expedition was to start at Heron Island on the southern end of the reef, where a tiny research centre had been established by the Queensland government and the University of Queensland. Behind the research centre, a dormitory had been built for visiting scientists, which is where Ron and I stayed while we waited for Pierre Dubuisson and his floating film and research vessel. There we were kept company by a man named Sandy, who I recall was the director of the Heron Island research station. He was with us on the shore when the Belgian ship came into view, rising over the horizon and revealing its formidable size.

A British-built Algerine class escort ship, the *De Moor* had recently been decommissioned by the Belgian Navy and was now fitted out to be the home of Pierre Dubuisson's venture into the world of feature documentary. Displacing more than 1000 tons and with a length of seventy metres, the *De Moor* was to host around twenty scientists, perhaps four filmmakers and a crew of seventy-five sailors. This was truly a ship and expedition befitting a great man, and we felt rather privileged to be included in the scientific adventure.

We would find out later that the *De Moor* and the funds for the trip had been procured by the Belgian crown under the direction of the king himself, who was doing a favour for the rector of the University of Liège, a close personal friend of the king and the father of budding filmmaker Pierre Dubuisson.

There were indeed scientific motivations for the trip, but it quickly became apparent that the primary purpose of the trip was to fulfil Marcel Dubuisson's son's desire to kick-start the underwater photography career he desperately wanted. Pierre was planning to do with money and a naval corvette what Ron and I were attempting with ingenuity, perseverance and a tinny.

Ron, Sandy and I watched the *De Moor* drop anchor in the Heron Wistari Channel a few hundred metres off the shore. A ship's tender was lowered, and as it came closer we saw two rows of stern-looking uniformed sailors, mostly former navy, flanking Professor Albert Disteche, apparently globally renowned (within the world of oceanic studies) for his ability to measure the pH level of seawater at depth, and the ranking scientist on the expedition.

The difference between open-water seafaring and the kind of reef-hopping that we were going to be doing on this trip became apparent before the men of the *De Moor* even reached the pass. As the tender got closer a prevailing wind pushed it slowly and inexorably towards the reef. We waited for the men in the tender to correct their course, but due to either a lack of capability or understanding of their potential fate, they motored closer to the coral ledge. The tender hit the reef with a loud crunch, ejecting two sailors and their passenger into the ocean.

Sandy turned to us with a look of resignation. 'Well, good luck to you,' he said, and wandered off back to his papers and experiments.

Ron and I were given quarters in the *De Moor*, but we soon discovered they were less than desirable. The Belgian and Australian scientists were an amiable bunch, and the sailors had no animosity towards Ron and me, but it seemed many hated each other, which created an air of tension. We started to understand that there was a cold civil war happening on the boat; 'on one side the Belgian crew members with Flemish as their native tongue, the other side those speaking French. Some time ago the captain had decided to settle the matter, ordering that neither Flemish nor French be spoken throughout the trip, and decreed instead all must speak English.

This was no problem for the officers, all of whom spoke good English, but it struck many of the enlisted men all but mute. It did not cause the desired effect among a group of young, angry men who had already been at sea for many months and had many more ahead of them.

After a few nights on the Belgian ship Ron and I decided that we would be happier on the *Careelah* bivouacking on a bench and a bunk, than in a bed in a cabin on the *De Moor*. The food was far superior on the *Careelah* too, which was a great surprise because I was the one buying and cooking. I don't claim to be a great cook now and was worse then, but I cobbled together edible meals, sometimes by way of searching on the ship's radio for other fishing boats and asking how I should prepare and combine the ingredients I had.

The question of how the well-funded Belgians could produce such disgusting meals hung until we learned later that the *De Moor*'s cook was jailed for pocketing much of the money he was given for fresh produce, instead using the stores of old tinned food. This might account for a good part of the tension on the ship, actually. In my experience, there's no quicker way to make a man insufferable than to serve him inedible meals at sea.

Before we started work Pierre gave us a shot list that was far from exhaustive, but it was not difficult: he wanted turtles, fish, sharks eating and searching for food, as well as beautiful coral and giant clams. It seemed a bit boring to us. We knew we could tick off this list in a matter of days, but we also knew there would be so much more to film.

I think we entertained the idea of Pierre being the great director he wanted to be pretty much right up until it was time for him to direct.

When we arrived at the first reef we were, as usual, working from our de Havilland. Ron quickly assembled our dive gear, we did our checks, loaded the 35-millimetre camera for which Ron had built a very special waterproof casing, and we were ready to dive.

When Pierre arrived at the reef, however, it seemed he had come to slowly colonise Queensland. In his Hercules launch Pierre had boxes and boxes of equipment being handled by a large crew. Eventually the boxes disgorged all of the cinematic equipment bought from the producers of

Thunderball – tripods, cameras and huge banks of lights as well as an industrial generator.

The generator stayed on the ship's tender, bleeding a cable down to power the lights. Everything else had to be arranged on the sea floor, powered up and prepared before Pierre could shoot. Once his lights were illuminated, the scene was as bright and hot as a midsummer carpark. It took about ten minutes before the coral started oozing a horrible slime, and another ten minutes for it to appear rather distressed. The dying polyps became clouded in a fine white mist and when that happened Pierre had no chance of shooting anything useful. He would simply move his equipment to another location with attractive coral. He seemed unperturbed, though. He also attempted to film fish but he lacked the skill needed to approach them without sending his would-be stars fleeing. After that happened Pierre, stuck behind a tripod-bound camera, had no chance of following them.

There is very little need for a tripod in the ocean because the natural buoyancy helps every camera become a steadicam. In fact, a tripod is a great hindrance when shooting fish that cannot be blocked, directed and told to repeat an action. Pierre could not be told. He was committed to being a waterlogged Cecil B DeMille with a camera in front of him, giant lights beside him and a crew behind him.

The plan was to collect each day's footage and deliver it to the *De Moor*, then at the end of ten days it would be sent ashore for processing – but Ron and I became concerned about the ability to get usable footage. We knew the film would have the type of action needed, but we were apprehensive. After all, this whole circus, at its core, was happening so Pierre could make a film. We wanted him to be happy with the end results.

We stopped being concerned, however, when we were invited to the *De Moor*'s makeshift screening room to look at the rushes. The footage that was screened was excellent, as we expected; full of colour and activity – and quite obviously shot by Ron. But when a shark would appear and attack a fish, or when the camera followed a green turtle in its serene meander, or when a giant grouper peered into the lens, those in attendance would uniformly cheer: 'Bravo, Pierre, bravo!'

Pierre Dubuisson would duck his blond locks in a small bow of humility, taking the merest shine off the praise he hadn't earned.

'Bravo, Pierre,' we would parrot. 'Bravo.'

We never went back to see rushes again. We knew our stuff would continue to be good. Pierre would continue to get the credit. We had no problem with this state of affairs because we had no rights to any of the footage. It meant nothing to us for Pierre to get credit – after all, his desire to be an underwater cameraman had given us a fabulous job on a marvellous reef full of excitement and wonder. Our best efforts were for sale, and with it any glory that accompanied it. Like most talented people, Ron was content. It was a high-paying job and, most importantly, we were learning about the Great Barrier Reef, far more than anyone before us. We did not realise it at the time but at the end of our six months of diving and filming we knew more about the reef than anyone else in the world. We saw this wonder of nature before the destructive human hand changed it forever.

Our life on that trip was marked in fortnightly cycles. We would spend ten consecutive days at sea, slowly working our way north, dropping anchor every day to film, then we would have four days ashore. In those four days we would all be concerned with the resupply of the *Careelah*. Ron would be primarily focused on film and camera equipment, Wally on fuel and rum, me with food and fresh water.

The *Careelah* was only able to carry a small amount of fresh water, and after the drinking water and water used to clean the camera and equipment, there was almost none for washing ourselves. This became more of a concern when the manifest of the *Careelah* grew. A Belgian able seaman named Will Rummens, who was often tasked with liaising between the *De Moor* and *Careelah*, was given approval to be our assistant and sleep in the saloon of Wally's boat. He was a particularly personable bloke (and someone I speak to via email every few days even now) and we were happy to accommodate him. After Will, two more people came to the fishing boat; not quite as personable but whose company we couldn't refuse.

Pierre Dubuisson had decided to fetch his very lovely, very young girlfriend from Europe. When she arrived, she did not feel particularly comfortable cohabiting with a hundred young men thousands of miles from their wives and girlfriends, so she and Pierre ended up crammed into the tiny forward cabin normally used for storing equipment. We didn't mind having her on board, because all she did was sun herself in her bikini, and we couldn't mind Pierre even if we wanted to.

We were all in our own little world on the *Careelah*, only hearing about the Belgian tribulations when officers came over to see if they could find deserters (this happened twice) or when the impact of news was big enough to vibrate over to us. One such instance was when one of the scientists took his own life after discovering that his family had died in a car accident.

We became something of a temporary family on the *Careelah*. Pierre would never be the great director he hoped to be, but he did learn as we worked our way north. I'm not sure anyone would choose any of Pierre's footage over ours in a blind test, but one would certainly choose his later footage over his early work. This rate of improvement was not seen in the capabilities of the *De Moor*'s sailors, however. It seemed that no matter how much time they spent on the reef, their shallow-water seamanship just never got better.

Three times Pierre and his crew lost a boat full of filming gear, turning their inflatable Hercules boat over and sending expensive equipment into the water. And three times Ron, Wally and I had to spend hours retrieving any equipment that didn't float. Fortunately the cameras were always in their waterproof housings and quite safe.

From memory it was also three times that Wally Muller correctly predicted at what point the Europeans would capsize.

'Just wait,' he'd say. 'It won't be this wave, nor this one … *this* one.'

Hurried shouts of '*Merde!*' and '*Putain!*' would be heard before all in the Hercules ended up in the ocean. It seemed the crew of the *De Moor* would never learn the difference between the lee side and the windward side of a reef.

It was frustrating, but they were set in their way of doing things, which I suppose was understandable. Ocean-going sea journeys required a strict rigidity in the conduct of the enlisted sailors. 'Captain's order,' is the most common answer to any question in the open sea, and usually the correct one.

This unquestioning rigidity didn't really apply to us when we were on the *Careelah*, but it did when we were in the water. Regardless of visibility or weather we were obliged to dive whenever Pierre did, and this meant many an instance when we were sent down to film in murky water or turbulent seas. That was the job, though. Every day underwater we exposed film and handed it over to be developed. Pierre and the scientists could view the work once it was developed. We fulfilled the shot list of special scenes, corals, molluscs and fish. As we predicted, it was not too difficult.

There were also truly wonderful parts of that journey. When we were close to Heron Island, we saw familiar wonders but as we travelled further and further north, a whole new underwater world was revealed.

We saw and filmed species of eel, shark, fish and sea snake we had never seen before – likely no one had ever seen before. In one instance I even ended up nose to nose with a pod of pilot whales. It happened north of Lizard Island. I had been chasing a small tuna with my camera and got a body-pulsing shock when a huge mouth appeared and engulfed the fish. It was one of six whales, so close I could almost touch it. I had been diving for many years at that point, with many large and wonderful marine animals, but an encounter like this, with a whale hunting, was beautiful and transformative.

We had adventures above water on the reefs, the cays and the islands too. Once Ron and I walked up to Cook's Look on Lizard Island with Sir Maurice Yonge, who had joined the expedition for a spell, and he told me stories about his ground-breaking expedition undertaken a few years earlier.

And then there was Waterwitch Pass, a place as close to Papua New Guinea as Cairns, and one of the most northern parts of the journey. This was an aquatic empire the likes of which I had not seen before, and only a few instances have I seen since. Waterwitch Pass revealed to us an explosion of life – every type of animal, every species. It was immediate action: fish, reef sharks and two manta rays. This pass offered so much colourful marine expression and interaction I think perhaps even Pierre Dubuisson's fixed-point filming would have been useful.

I also think it was there, with one vista showing almost the entire cycle of life, from the smallest animals to the largest, that I truly started to appreciate the balance and delicate beauty of marine ecologies.

It was only a few years earlier that Ron and I had produced *Slaughter at Saumarez* and a few years before that *Revenge of a Shark Victim*; films concerned with the conflict between humans and the aquatic world. After our journey through the Great Barrier Reef I didn't think I would be able to consider underwater journeys of 'slaughter' and 'revenge' ever again.

It was at Waterwitch Pass that I started to understand how all the pieces mattered. One extreme and memorable example was seeing the devastating effect that a plague of crown-of-thorns starfish could inflict on a coral reef. This thorny but seemingly unthreatening animal was sucking out the living polyps, leaving a dead white reef in its wake. Like a rainforest, a coral reef supports millions of marine animals – when it dies, so too do they.

On this expedition were scientists who were studying the crown-of-thorns problem.

They were taking cores showing ancient reefs up to 600 years old. There had been similar plagues before but it seemed nothing as vast as the destruction we were seeing now.

The effect of this starfish was stark and shocking. In great contrast to the many coral-rich locations of activity and diversity, the areas where the crown-of-thorns had taken over were drab, pale and nearly completely lifeless except for the starfish. The limestone homes of the polyps were still there, but they were dead and as white as snow or grey with algae.

Those reefs were a depressing sight. And a warning of what happens when balance is destroyed.

A number of the scientists on the expedition were looking at the rise of this starfish, concentrating on chemicals and pesticides in the water soiled by agricultural run-off, but Ron and I had our own ideas about the source of the infestation. We had discovered that the triton's trumpet, a large sea snail with a beautiful shell, was the natural enemy of the crown-of-thorns, after we had put a triton near a crown-of-thorns and seen the snail attack the starfish with rapidity and vigour. The market for this triton shell was strong – Thursday Islanders commercially collecting trochus for button-making would always take a triton for sale to collectors or in the tourist shops – which meant that collectors were harvesting them, therefore reducing the population of the only large predator able to impact the crown-of-thorns starfish population.

The scientists later confirmed that this shell-collecting, among many other, man-made causes, was a contributing factor in the crown-of-thorns infestation. This was in the forefront of our approach when we helped the scientists from the *De Moor* turn coral plates back over the right way on reef flats after the crew, at low tide, had disturbed them while hunting for shells to take back to sell in Europe.

Ron and I changed during that trip, and we both ended up with a greater understanding of how humans affect the marine world. This is a well-understood concept now, but that was not the case in the 1960s, with the word 'environmentalist' in few vocabularies. If, when we took that trip, you asked a hundred people which animal was a greater threat to marine life, humans or sharks, most would have chosen the latter.

I knew it was the former, but I had no idea just how great was the extent that humans were affecting the balance of life.

Whereas Ron and I had been spearos, seeing the marine world not just on the Great Barrier Reef but in all the ocean as a place that was one-part shooting range and one-part supermarket, only concerned with what we could get out of a reef, now we were thinking of the ocean quite differently. We no longer saw the marine environment as something for us to exploit at will. It was a living, breathing collection of a million life forms, all part of the planet Earth.

Me and my little brother Greg when we were youngsters in New Zealand. In our teenage years in Australia, he and I spent a lot of our time together in the blue waters of Burraneer Bay.

A photo of me and my pet cat, a few years before I was struck down by polio. When I came out of hospital, the cat was gone.

Publicity photos from my acting days. It was typecasting. I just played myself in *The Seven Year Itch*. The play opened in June 1961 at The Ensemble Theatre in Sydney. I was offered another play, but after months on the stage I knew I did not want to be an actor. Far too repetitious and boring.

Me with Fred, my pet possum (*above*) and (*right*) with Crabby, one of my two pet crayfish. I had them for years.

As part of the Heron Island Dive Festival, I was twice the winner of the beauty pageant, which required me to be ogled in my bathing suit but also to complete an underwater obstacle course as quickly as possible.

Ron Taylor was almost supernatural in the water. He was exceptional at spearfishing, fit, meticulous, cool-headed and nothing short of an analytical genius. He was also extremely handsome, and I fell in love with him. I got to know him well as we travelled to spearfishing competitions together, and were male and female champions. We married in 1963 at the Sydney registry office, accompanied by our mothers. There was minimal fuss. Which was as Ron and I liked it.

Out from Heron Island, I met two moray eels, whom I named Harry and Fang.
I have been visiting them for decades, and they remember me. I consider them friends.

Ron and I (*above*) are taking the temperature of a live great white. Dr Samuel H. Gruber, an American marine scientist, wanted to know if great white sharks were warm-blooded. To our surprise we discovered they are. We also tagged the shark. She was caught by a fisherman six months later and the tag returned.

When I was a spearo, I was living under the misconception that the ocean has an endless capacity to replenish itself. I know now how wrong I was. Not many years later, I became active in trying to save our marine life. This gruesome photo shows the horrendous reality of the shark fin trade. The scale of the harvest is horrifying for anyone who cares about shark conservation.

Above: Bruno Vailati was an Italian writer and director whom Ron and I worked with on a documentary he made about us.

Right: Ron and me at one of our favourite places, Seal Rocks on the New South Wales mid-north coast. We knew the local reefs and marine inhabitants well.

Left: Ron and I wanted to find a way to make a living travelling the world and exploring the ocean. Filmmaking was something we were passionate about but also something that opened up marvellous opportunities. And a blonde woman in a wetsuit was far more marketable than a man in the same situation.

Below: We discovered a large family of potato cod and we went to great lengths to ensure their location remained a secret so they weren't targeted by game fishermen. These magnificent fish live in family groups.

For a young woman who craved adventure, Ron Taylor was the perfect partner – and my goodness, we had a wonderful life together, from discovering First Fleet artefacts (such as the anchor from the wreck of the *Sirius*) to astonishing marine life and exotic places. We saw so much natural wonder.

That idea came to a head one day when we travelled to a sand island. We found that all the clams had been gutted for their meat. This was not a surprise – we had seen the effects of illegal clam-fishing across the reef; hundreds of giant clam shells that had been alive when Captain Cook first discovered the reef by running into it – but amid the tragic killing of the clams we found something even more distressing. On one island was a large pelican colony, which is to say there had been a large pelican colony. Every bird, small and large, had been slaughtered in their nests. Hundreds of birds, each death purposeless. This confounded and disgusted me. I had killed, for sport, for food and for what both Ron and I thought was safety, but there seemed no point to this. There was nothing to take from these deaths but the sadistic joy of killing.

When we finished that long job we thanked Dubuisson and took our reward, which we used to pay off our house and buy a new car. We never saw Pierre Dubuisson's final product – titled *Le Grande Barrière de Corail* – though we were told that the entire cost of the expedition was recouped from public showings. We never had much interest in the end result. For us the highlight was the expedition itself – seeing a marine world we never knew existed and one I will never forget. Given that we never heard of Pierre again in a film context, I assumed he didn't become the great director he wanted to be.

Years later Will Rummens, the able seaman whom I still email to this day, told me he heard that Pierre was working in transport. Someone else said he had tenure as the Belgian ambassador to Korea. Either way, I hope he had a lovely life. He gave us an excellent professional opportunity and was a nice young man.

* * *

Three years after returning home from our epic voyage through the Great Barrier Reef, we accepted a job that took us back there.

In 1970 Lee Robinson and John McCallum, the creators of *Skippy*, asked us to run the underwater unit on their latest dramatic television show, which was titled *Barrier Reef*. The show, an action–adventure series detailing the exploits of a marine expedition studying the reef, was an all-Australian production but the producers had designs on overseas sales, trumpeting at every promotional turn the fact that the production was to include 'extensive colour underwater scenes of the Great Barrier Reef', which was what they saw as the best chance to achieve international sales.

When we arrived for that job we were to be based out of Hayman Island, but Ron explained to the producers that the visibility at Heron would be far greater and the fish life much more spectacular. Eventually they relented, moving the entire underwater unit there for the six-month duration of the production.

The series was mostly based around the adventures of the crew of the *New Endeavour*, a replica of Captain Cook's ship converted, in the fiction of the series, into a modern scientific mothership. Living on Heron Island, we only saw that beautiful ship once, when she called in to Heron Island on her way to Sydney. As soon as I saw her I was transported back to an experience in my youth in Wellington sitting on the deck of the *Pamir*, a German square rigger that was captured by the men working on the wharf when she sailed into Wellington Harbour with a broken radio. Only when the ship arrived was the captain informed that war had broken out and he and his crew were now the enemy. The *New Endeavour* reminded me of the glory of square-rigged sailing ships, and my resolution to, at some point, sail on one. We never boarded the *New Endeavour*, but she is a beautiful vessel still sailing around Australia.

To help us with the shoot we had four divers and the use of a cutting-edge, Japanese-made barge with a two-person open submarine, generator and compressor. Knowledge we'd gleaned on the Belgian expedition was extremely useful. Ron had no problem finding the locations and animals the producers needed.

In one instance, in an episode named 'His Majesty Regrets', they required a loggerhead sea turtle in multiple shots, so we befriended one such animal by feeding him fish from the barge. We made a sling for the turtle so he could be transported to where we were shooting, and fed him fresh fish as a reward when we returned.

That turtle became something of a mascot for us on that shoot, and it saddens me to think of our turtle trying to keep up as we moved the barge to a different location. I know that the turtle was likely just following a source of food, but my affection for him was real.

In 1970 the reef was a different place from the same reef today. Fish life clouded the water or watched from small coral caves. It was a kaleidoscope of movement and colour. The reef is still beautiful, but for me who knew it so long ago, like a flower in the sun it has faded, its former glory lost to a modern world.

Many fish, such as the Queensland grouper and Maori wrasse, have been harvested into rarity, and other species have succumbed to overfishing, and sharks to finning.

It occurred to me recently that Ron and I were some of the only people to see the reef in its original glory. Before we dived the length of the reef, technology required for such an odyssey mostly did not exist. A few years afterwards the marine ecology started to degrade. Perhaps I should be thankful for having had the opportunity to see something that so few ever saw.

The thing is, that's not how I feel.

CHAPTER SIX

An unusual office

I never liked our house in Mortdale, even when we owned it outright. In fact, it's not too strong a statement to say that I hated it. It was perfect for our purposes then; with space for a workshop and room for a boat and vehicle, and we did what we could in the living spaces to make it our own ... yet it never really felt like home.

I suppose I was uncomfortable there, and accordingly the smallest things would aggravate me. One instance that comes to mind involved something seemingly small and insignificant: a peach. Whenever Ron ate a peach he would leave the stone for me to pick up; often the one blight in an otherwise perfectly clean house. It was a very small thing, but it aggravated me and is embedded in the folds of my memory, even now some fifty years later. I would calmly and silently pick the stone up and would, for some reason, think about a time in the future when we might move.

The reality of the matter was, however, that we were barely in that place after the Belgian expedition. Jobs filled the calendar throughout the late 1960s and early 1970s with wonderful, globetrotting opportunities. It was a busy time and a special one; a dream that eventually became reality through Ron's and my hard work.

The ocean was now our office, a camera the tool of our trade.

Ron had conceived a life, including the tools he would need to create. There was no such job as 'underwater moviemaker' when Ron decided to head on this unbeaten path. He picked up all the skills required to beat that path, as well as a partner in this unique professional journey and in a unique life.

I was always grateful to Ron and his will to succeed as an underwater cameraman. I don't diminish my role and capacity, which became greatly expanded later in our professional lives, but I don't hesitate to say that those professional lives were launched off the back of Ron's ingenuity.

Ron was unlike anyone else; with a brain working in a rare and incredible way. Cameras for him were not just a medium of art but a mathematical language, an equation with myriad variables that when mastered would produce magical results. Ron understood camera housings, aperture, shutter speed and lenses, but also light and colour and composition and the other non-linear variables of photography.

If Ron was an artist, as I consider him to be, he was more like Turner than Picasso, perhaps even like a minor Australian

Leonardo da Vinci, marrying the technical and the artistic in his own way. All the more impressive that, like da Vinci, Ron was never trained, and instead just saw possibilities in his head and also the steps to make them become a reality.

That technical element in Ron was an essential part of him, but also a private part that I'm not sure I ever completely understood. Throughout our lives, Ron would disappear for hours into a workshop or editing room and exercise his capacity for technical creation. It wasn't always cameras, equipment or housing, sometimes it was the fridge or the car. If something didn't work and Ron didn't understand why, he would take it apart, in a meticulous and logical deconstruction, until he did understand why it was not working, and remedy the problem. Nothing was ever thrown away, everything could be fixed or perhaps would discover a secondary life elsewhere as a door handle or a part of an engine.

I have no hesitation saying that Ron understood cameras and photography in a way I never did, but I suppose I understood marine animals in a way he never quite did. Ron and I were very different people, but that's often the basis for an effective and productive partnership. Together we brought a broader spectrum of capacities to every challenge than either of us could individually. Together we made a team that worked well and was perhaps the main reason for our success.

I suppose it's true that we wanted different things, also. Actually, it's more appropriate to say that we wanted different aspects of the same thing. The marine expeditions that we went on were for me the realisation of an ambition I had craved since I was a little girl: adventure, breathless and in technicolour. Ron's ambitions were different. He was far more goal-oriented. He was always inventing new equipment, testing the pressure his latest housing could handle, the controls on a camera, diving in good weather looking for sharks or unusual fish. Always filming footage that might be of use later.

Ron was a dedicated and taciturn man, a man's man. He was very slow to anger, but also not nakedly exuberant in his passions either. There was no malice in him and no ire, except when expectations were unmet in those he trusted.

Ron had admirable discipline in his life, which necessarily extended to me. He had a distinct role in our marriage and in our professional partnership, and so did I. You might read some of this book with modern eyes and think some of what you read is unreasonable, but always remember that I was, if nothing else, the product of a very different era.

As you've already read, if I wasn't happy in a marriage, I would have left (with or without turning a pot of rhubarb over my soon-to-be ex-husband's head). The truth of the matter, though, is that I very much loved Ron, always and forever. I loved him and I admired him. Sometimes I would be struck as I looked at him, thinking how beautiful he was, how incredible he was. Sometimes I still am today as I watch an old film or look at a photo.

There was never a time that I didn't love Ron. He was the most impressive and gorgeous and lovable man I ever met and yet, even now, I can't help but wish he would have picked up those damnable peach stones.

CHAPTER SEVEN

Blue Water, White Death

Blue Water, White Death, a documentary about searching for great white sharks, is an exceptional film, and ended up creating quite a wave in the international film industry.

There were sharks in the film, obviously, and incredible locations above and below the water, but I think interest in the film was primarily because of the creatures who were in the wetsuits, not in the water; the divers and camera operators, the people who became a part of the vanguard of an underwater subculture yet to explode, or should I say the English-language vanguard because French pioneer Jacques Cousteau had at that point already been an underwater adventurer and filmmaker for more than two decades. And Austrian Hans Hass two decades before Cousteau.

There was an interesting mix of people involved in *Blue Water, White Death*, and a decent representation of the types of people who had the means, capability and desire to dive in the late 1960s; people who were moneyed, who wrote or filmed, or had served in the armed forces – or in some instances all three, such as Stan Waterman, a bald-headed and barrel-chested war veteran and American pioneer in the diving world.

A unique individual, Stan was a Dartmouth alumnus and spoke in a lyrical but also very American way, turning colloquialisms into elements of vernacular art. It came as no surprise to us later when Stan told us that at university one of his lecturers was no less an orator than poet Robert Frost.

Stan was someone Ron and I didn't initially comprehend, as he would build elaborate fabrications by way of humour, but once we realised what was real and what was whimsy we both appreciated his quirky humour and we became great friends. Stan is a wonderful man, who is still kicking strong today as he creeps towards his hundredth birthday, but was then a powerful man in his late forties.

A crew member much younger than Stan was Tom Chapin, who mostly worked as part of the surface crew, and who was also a wonderful folk singer. A good-looking, hard-working fellow, Chapin brought on board a moustache, a sweet nature and a guitar; these are three of the things I best recall about him, but I was reminded of him a few years later when his brother, Harry, had a hit with the song 'Cat's in the Cradle'.

Tom contributed some original songs to the film, but I remember he would also play folkloric ditties. When we boarded the ship that became the home base for the shoot, he played a song written by American humorist Wallace Irwin called 'The Rhyme of the Chivalrous Shark', which also seemed to be known by Stan Waterman, who sang along with Tom.

The famed American writer Peter Matthiessen joined us on the shoot for several weeks. Like Stan, Peter came from old east coast money and had served in the navy, later revealing that he also worked as a clandestine CIA agent. Another very intricately spoken man, Matthiessen would later win the National Book Award three times, but not for the book he wrote about the expedition, which was called *Blue Meridian*.

The expedition's writer didn't feature on camera, but the still photographer certainly did; a relatively young, slightly doughy New York society boy named Peter Lake. Lake had a very beautiful and very rich wife named Candy, and he acted as though he had few cares in the world, mostly because he didn't. He was an amiable character, and enjoyable enough below deck, telling stories and sharing cups of coffee, for us to forgive what he did while we were diving. Almost.

Then there was Peter Gimbel, the director, the star and the most memorable and essential of the filmmakers. Gimbel was like Pierre Dubuisson in that he yearned to be a great director and, as the heir of the Gimbels department store fortune, he had the knowledge and knowhow to arrange a grand marine expedition just as Dubuisson had. Comparisons to the Belgian, however, end there.

Gimbel was a very capable diver and filmmaker, but his confidence and daring extended even further than his capability. A lion of a man, Gimbel had a touch of the salesman to him, a touch of the madman and hint of the son trying to move out of his father's shadow.

Ron and I very much liked Peter. He was also intrepid, inventive and dynamic and would never ask his camera people to do anything he wouldn't first do.

Gimbel, like Stan Waterman, had served in the US military, but being a couple of crucial years younger than Stan, he had missed out on the fighting, instead being deployed to occupied Japan. Like Waterman, Peter Gimbel had an Ivy League education, studying finance and business at Yale, and had worked as an investment banker for almost a decade until his twin brother, David, died of stomach cancer when not yet thirty.

Gimbel left Wall Street after the tragedy and went back to university, where he studied physics and zoology. He was born to money and had made money and now he wanted something else in his life: adventure.

By the time we shared that particular adventure, Gimbel had already had a few, including parachuting into the Peruvian jungle in search of Vilcabamba, the lost great Neo-Inca city, and diving into the icy depths of the North Atlantic Ocean in search of the sunken Italian luxury liner the SS *Andrea Doria*. The former adventure was a failure, the latter a success, but both looked good on screen when he turned them into documentaries.

None of his films, however, would ever be as well received as *Blue Water, White Death*.

The idea was simple: to find the biggest great white sharks and film them in their environment. In preparation

Gimbel had done a global tour of coastal regions, looking for locations and interviewing those who lived on the sea about their interactions with the sharks.

He had decided to start this adventure in South Africa, where he thought he was guaranteed to find both great whites and also dynamic, violent footage. Whalers had told Gimbel that after harpooning a whale they commonly saw great whites feeding on the carcasses.

Durban was the centre of whaling activity in South Africa for most of the twentieth century and this was the place we all met up and began our adventure.

The nasty business of whaling in Durban was primarily done by the Union Whaling Company, a Norwegian/South African company then hailed as having the most technologically advanced land station in the world. A crisis was coming for Union Whaling, though; they and other large global whaling companies had gone through a boom after World War II, but had been too successful, too rapacious. The humpback, blue and right whale populations had been hunted near to extinction, and populations of sperm and sei whales were very much depleted as well.

After those statistics were revealed, international conventions had been brought in that limited the species and size of whales that could be hunted, and that meant open-ocean whaling had been mostly left to Russian, Japanese and Norwegian operators, who largely ignored the international rules.

Union, having sold their huge factory ships a few years earlier to the Japanese and Russians, were now limited to coastal hunting, finding mostly sperm whales, which are smaller with less flesh, blubber, oil and ambergris to be harvested, and so therefore less profitable.

It seems that Union Whaling was on the verge of extinction also, not that Ron and I understood this when we arrived in South Africa. Now it occurs to me that this was likely how Gimbel managed to procure the cooperation of Union Whaling, and the rental of one of their whale-catching ships, the *Terrier VIII*, for the duration of the shoot.

The *Terrier VIII* was a standard Norwegian whale catcher. At five hundred tons with a length just under fifty metres, the ship had a large, dark smokestack, a deck low to the water and a high bow so that the gun would have an angle of attack on whales who were close to the ship. It was very much a working ship with few luxuries but, although rusted and barnacled, the *Terrier VIII* was in good shape and quite powerful, which Ron and I were reminded of every time we walked along the gangplank suspended over the huge, loud and powerful brass pistons to our tiny cabin.

The ship had a crew of no-nonsense but amiable and efficient African men, who were generally better company than the disaffected sailors of the *De Moor*. Usually they were Union Whaling's men, but for the next six months they were employed by Gimbel, in the service of filming wildlife, not killing it. The *Terrier VIII*'s gun was removed, and it was stipulated that no one from our ship could help the whaling fleet in their terrible work even though we would be closely following Union Whaling's fleet in search of sharks.

As soon as we were on the open ocean it took very little time to find whales, and what followed was as horrific as you can imagine.

I can still hear the *THUNK* of the fleet's guns firing, and the heavy line spooling out towards a fleeing animal. I can hear the echoes of the hunters whooping, and the noise of a whale in shock and pain as its lifeblood stains the water.

If I lived a thousand years I would not be able to forget the cry of a dying whale. It goes through you and embeds in you. It has been speculated that a whale's mating call can cut through an entire ocean to another whale near another continent, but the sound of a whale dying can also cut through time. Here, now, in 2019, I can still hear the agony of that dying whale in its death song. I can hear its heart and soul. Not a beautiful sound like the song of a humpback, but a deep rumbling groan.

It was a terrible business, this killing of a beautiful, intelligent animal for commercial gain, but there was little time after a kill to ruminate on it. Ron and I had been brought on board to do a job, and the job started as soon as the ocean was stained red with blood.

The crew told us that whenever there was a dead or dying whale in the water, there would be sharks, and they were right. Sharks, especially open-water species, can smell blood one part in a million and sense vibrations over two kilometres away, especially the vibration of a dying whale or fish. Instinctively they know what the heartbeat of a whale in distress means.

Sharks are nature's garbage men. They cull the old, sick and unwary, keeping the ocean clean and the species strong.

A dying whale means food for the shark; the predator's call to a feast.

For us, it meant dive time. We on the *Terrier VIII* sprang into action. The divers would suit up, cameras would be strapped into the custom-built cages that Gimbel had designed and built, so strong they could probably withstand a Sherman tank running over them. Compared to the simple cages we used in Australia, these were true state of the art. Not only were they super strong, they could be raised and lowered independent to the ship.

We were all professionals and in the water very quickly. The cages were fastened to the whale so we could stay close to the action. Once submerged we were treated to a scene of carnage unchanged in a million years. They came from the deep, beautiful sleek fish, perfect predators. There were not just dozens of big sharks down there but hundreds, gliding through the water like supple torpedoes. We filmed, then watched these perfect creatures as they plunged into the whale, tearing great lumps of flesh from the giant corpse. The clear ocean became clouded with blood, reducing visibility to a few metres before a swell would flush it away.

In filming terms it was a wonderful start, with good shark action in the first week. The oceanic whitetip sharks were all big, handsome and known man-eaters. They are the shark that attacks airmen in downed planes and seamen in sinking ships. Oceanic whitetips have killed and eaten more humans than all the other dangerous sharks together, and here we were watching a scene more horrible but also more exciting than I had ever imagined.

Peter Gimbel had divided us into diving pairs, and he requested that I be his dive partner. Ron and I understood Peter to be very competent in the water, so neither of us had a problem with that. When we were down in the cages I found him to be an excellent diving partner. He was also something of a daredevil. He was not happy just shooting through the bars of his custom-made cage – he would open the door and hang out into the open water trying for shots without showing the cage bars. I noticed Ron and Stan doing the same. In one such instance I was rather alarmed when an oceanic whitetip shark swam from a cloud of whale blood through the open door and into my cage. I hit the floor as quickly as I could and watched the shark thrash around as it tried to find the exit.

Poor thing, it was just as terrified as I was.

Back on the deck of the *Terrier VIII* we were excited, with undoubtedly a great deal of incredible footage already in the can. There were a lot of big sharks and three different species, but none of the sharks that had come to feed were great whites.

The scene was repeated a number of times over the next four weeks: the bang of the gun, the vibrations of a dying whale; frantic activity on deck as the cages were lowered and we suited up; and then a bloody frenzy below. Sometimes the bigger sharks would test the cage, bumping the aluminium bars hard. Peter Gimbel would test himself too, putting arms, cameras and in some instances his whole body out of the cage. I was always behind him with a shark billy (a 1.2-metre long club with a blunt end), but had he been grabbed, there would have been little I could do.

Not once, as far as we could tell, did a great white appear.

Peter Gimbel couldn't understand why they weren't coming. The whalers had promised him great whites. The mystery was solved one day, when on the deck of the ship a large blue shark arrived and the crew excitedly pointed to it, shouting, 'White! White!'

It seemed the whalers, who only ever saw the sharks above the water, confused the sleek and slick blue with the muscular, snow-bellied, black-eyed great white.

Gimbel's effervescent demeanour sagged momentarily after he realised the mistake. These men had never seen a great white, they were simply trying to be helpful. They were whale hunters not shark experts, so how could they know the difference between shark species? Peter became somewhat despondent as the weather closed in. Under stormy skies that were first grey hours, then grey days that rolled into a grey week, the *Terrier VIII* was forced back to shore. As we cruised closer to land, we saw the most powerful Union ships towing the day's catch into the flensing station: maybe fifteen harpooned whales that had been pumped with air and hung along the sides of the catchers. To me it was a tragic sight. Whales are wonderful animals; intelligent, peaceful, an important part of life on this planet, yet we slaughter them without remorse for a few tons of oil. All had terrible wounds, they had fought and lost a battle for life against a metal ship with an exploding harpoon and a trained gunner to fire it.

After docking, the film crew took the opportunity to get footage of the surface station where the whales were butchered, broken down and boiled. Strong men using huge saws, pulleys and machines carved the dead whales into lumps before sliding the blubber into the underground boiling vat. Most of the whales killed had been females, some pregnant. To my further dismay, I saw a perfectly formed, blood-soaked foetus lying on the slipway. A pregnant carcass had somehow given birth, the foetus a perfect little whale. Another tragedy in the story, the purpose of which I didn't want to speculate about. I felt that in one blood-soaked panorama I saw all of humanity's capacity for industry, greed and cruelty.

In Durban I also saw that man's cruelty wasn't confined to other species, but stretched to other races also, particularly in this time of apartheid. Once, in between bouts of inclement weather, Peter Lake and I were driving through Durban with an African woman who had been on the boat with Peter, when we were pulled over by plain-clothed white policemen.

Ignoring the African woman's cries and protestations, they took her away and threatened to arrest me when I started asking questions. It was only when Peter Lake told them (somewhat spuriously) that I was the star of a major film happening here in South Africa and that to detain me would be a grave mistake that they backed off. The terrified woman was paying the price for spending the night with a Caucasian.

Despite the dismay that filled me at this incident and the scene in the whaling station, I rather enjoyed South Africa.

The crew on the *Terrier VIII* were full of wit and wisdom, the cities were exciting, and the scenes on the street were so different from Sydney, a ribbon of colourful women, jewellery and music. I think I enjoyed it all so much because it felt a lot like the adventure I'd been craving since I lay helpless in Wellington Hospital as a polio-ridden child.

When the weather cleared, Peter Gimbel, still hopeful of finding great whites in the killing grounds, had the *Terrier VIII* back out with the Union fleet. Ron, a man who knew as much about sharks as anyone on board, told Peter he was surprised they hadn't arrived when the whale blood was drifting for miles in the current.

It was somewhat ironic; we were hunting for the great white mostly because of the public perception that this shark is the most dangerous to humans, but as I mentioned the reality is that no shark has killed more people than the oceanic whitetip surrounding us down in the South African waters. A large shark, with some reaching over twelve feet (3.7 metres), the oceanic whitetip is usually a slow-moving animal but one attracted to any unusual disturbance it senses in the water and capable of working itself into a wild and vicious frenzy when feeding on helpless prey.

As we steamed out of Durban I read a story about oceanic whitetips in an old copy of *Reader's Digest*. The story was about the sinking of the RMS *Nova Scotia*, a British troop ship torpedoed close to her destination of Durban in 1942. The captain of the German U-boat that sank the *Nova Scotia* and crew members of the doomed ship contributed interviews to the story – and what a tale of chilling terror it was.

Three torpedoes hit the *Nova Scotia* early in the morning on 28 November, and minutes later the ship started to list as the hull filled with water. Most of those on board managed to get into lifeboats or rafts that the crew had launched before the *Nova Scotia* sank. The U-boat captain surfaced, watching the scene from the deck. Before the Nazi submarine submerged again it rescued two Italian officers floating among the wreckage in an attempt to discover what had been destroyed. The captain was dismayed to find that most of the men in the water were his allies – the ship he had torpedoed was carrying about eight hundred Italian prisoners of war, and they represented roughly seventy-five percent of the men in the water.

When out of the range of Allied sub-hunters, the Nazi submarine re-emerged and reported events to Nazi command, which contacted neutral Portugal. A day later a Portuguese frigate was at the site of the attack.

The scene was gruesome. Amid the flotsam and exhausted but frantic survivors crying for rescue were corpses, perhaps hundreds, many half-eaten or torn to pieces.

The Portuguese rescued nearly two hundred men. These survivors described what it was like once the ship sank. They explained that it took a while for the oceanic whitetips to come, and when they did the sharks initially just circled, likely confused by the mass of kicking legs, rafts, dinghies and life rings. However, as the day dragged on the more curious sharks quickly became aggressive. They would glide in from the depths, bumping the legs and buttocks of the men in the water, and if they weren't bumped back they would feel with their teeth, causing the victim's blood to flow. Blood in the water is a great shark attraction – it gives the predator a desire to feed – and so the helpless men floundering in the water, some wounded and bleeding, would have seemed a feast to these hunters from the depths. Throughout the night the sharks dragged the men under, tearing at their flesh. Not all of the 858 men who died were killed by whitetips. Some probably drowned or died of their wounds, but most died because of the sharks.

Almost to a man the British survivors described being bumped, responding with aggression and then seeing the shark back off. This seemed to be the key to survival: meeting aggression with aggression. There were no stories about men being bitten or dragged down without first being bumped. The British sailors had their captain and officers telling them to stay off the lifeboats and fight off the sharks, whereas the panicking Italians, without their officers to lead them, tried to climb into the already overloaded lifeboats, overturning the bleeding wounded passengers into the water.

This story was one that matched our experiences. While we had been filming, the oceanic whitetips were mostly concerned with the dead whales, but a few had broken off from their feeding to investigate us. Whenever they did, they led with their noses, bumping the cage or diver, seemingly gauging resistance, and when they were challenged they became cautious.

This behaviour quirk was the thing that Peter Gimbel cited when he suggested that perhaps we could dive without the cage around the carcass of a dead whale. It seemed a mad idea. Stan thought it could be a little risky.

We looked to Ron, the man less likely to be caught up in a moment of reckless bravado. He said that if we maintained hierarchical supremacy in the water and met every aggression with aggression, then we should be okay. He then stroked his chin, considering the variables for a while before speaking in his quiet but confident way. 'I think we could get out,' he said.

That was it. We would get out of our cages. The men were confident and therefore I was also. I had been starting to suspect that Gimbel had something of a saviour complex and that this was why he chose me as his dive buddy. It seemed he very much wanted to save the only damsel diving from distress and asked me several times was I okay. I would have been concerned that Gimbel was taking on unnecessary risk in diving cage-less just so he could have a chance to come and save me from danger, but when Ron said it should be okay, I thought it probably would be.

'The crucial thing is that when they bump us, and they will, we should react strongly,' Peter said before we dived. I felt he was loving this devil-daring.

That dive ended up being a little more than okay. There was no chance to be terrified or wonder what we might have for dinner – it was full-on unadulterated, exciting action; I think far more so than any of us had expected, but also glorious and exhilarating.

The plan was to keep the sharks in front of us, and this would be achieved by diving in pairs with dive buddies facing away from each other, effectively giving us collectively a 360-degree field of vision. This meant any time a diver was challenged from the front, they could hit back, and if they were bumped from behind, their partner could respond.

Before we were to pair off, though, we would try to get a close-up shot of sharks tearing the flesh off a whale carcass, and that would require our best combined efforts. The closer we swam to the whale the faster the action around us would become.

Peter's plan was that three divers would create a triangular formation, with Gimbel at the point, and we would protect him as we got closer to the stomach of the whale where the sharks were feeding. The sharks, however, had other ideas. As soon as we approached the whale we started to understand the difference between being in the water with sharks while they were eating, and getting between the shark and their food. The sharks became more aggressive and more confident when we were almost to the whale, where in the water nearer the carcass stained by blood we lost visibility.

Because we were close together I could see Stan and Peter, but otherwise I oriented myself by shapes and shades – light and red was up, dark and red was down, the long blue oblong smudge marked against the light was the whale. Sharks appeared suddenly and from all angles, and disappeared just as quickly. I had a moment of horror when a large whitetip pushed behind me and shuddered against my side as its teeth sliced into the whale.

It didn't bump me; it just came straight in and pushed me. I was of no interest other than being in the shark's way. I held my place next to Peter as he filmed the shark's teeth sawing through blubber. I was certainly aware of how helpless we were, but in what seemed only seconds the shark, hunger sated, slipped away as suddenly as it had appeared.

I had rarely been so ill at ease in the water or felt so helpless. For a few minutes we were truly at the whim of these animals. Still, there was a job to do. The blood cleared for a few seconds and I could see that Peter and Stan were still very close, and I let Peter know all was well. He seemed to like it there in the blood and gore. Eventually he gave me the 'film's out' sign. I had a short metal stick for gill striking but had not used it. It wasn't necessary. It appeared to me the sharks had come to recognise us as other marine animals attracted to the banquet.

A famous German general once said that no battle plan survives contact with the enemy. I might not have realised it before the dive, but submerging into that mob of feeding sharks was definitely making contact with a potential enemy. We divers were too few, and the sharks too many for us to have any control over them. It was like shark soup; they came from front, back, above and below. The water was very clear, and as far as I could see were sharks, some carrying bleeding lumps of flesh, others sated but unwilling to leave the feast.

We were all bumped like the survivors of the *Nova Scotia*, many times. For my part, I had a whitetip come and investigate my head, nibbling daintily at my ponytail. I darted around and attempted to strike the animal on the nose, but it was already gone.

Fortunately, Ron filmed it.

I would find out later that we all had some close calls, and Ron's was the most concerning. He'd been shooting stills and, while his eye was on the viewfinder, a shark broadsided him, bumping him in the temple with a great deal of force. His mask was knocked sideways and his regulator pulled out. He said he was close to losing consciousness and could feel darkness stealing his vision, when he tumbled against the cage. He grabbed the bars and dragged himself in, where he was able to recover. Not one for hyperbole, Ron said if there had been a few more pounds of force in the shark's strike he would have been unconscious, with no regulator or mask, and on his way to the seabed two miles down. The BCD (Buoyancy Control Device) had not yet been invented; we were all diving overweighted so we could stand without moving when in the cages – so, Ron would have sunk.

No one saw Ron being hit. No one had seen much except sharks, sharks and more sharks. Stan, Peter and I were busy in the blood while Peter filmed close-ups. Ron was below us, alone. There were dozens of huge predators, perhaps hundreds. The buddy system fell apart almost from the get-go and when we left the water, we climbed out in ones.

Back on deck my excitement just bubbled. We had done something no one else had dared try; I loved it. Any concern I might have had melted away and all that was left was adrenaline and excitement. The emotion can be seen on my face in the film. I had an ear-to-ear grin and could barely articulate my pleasure.

'It was … fantastic,' I said while drying my hair. 'Fantastic!'

I didn't know what else to say. It had been in many ways the ultimate dive; one unlike any I had experienced before or would experience afterwards. Perhaps that dive was ill advised and even foolhardy, but it was pure, concentrated excitement; an experience like no other.

'While you're doing something like that you convince yourself that there is no danger ... and when you've done it, you wonder how you got out of it alive,' Ron said afterwards. It was the ultimate adventure. To me it was going back in time. We had entered a world unchanged in millions of years, and survived to tell the tale.

Sadly, there can never be a repeat of that day. The whales have gone and the sharks finned into rarity. The only proof of that incredible dive is a strip of film projected onto the silver screen.

When we reviewed the footage we saw that it really was some of the most incredible and hair-raising underwater footage ever seen. It also confirmed to us that it would be very unwise to dive out of the cage again while large sharks were feeding like that. We all agreed that we were lucky no one was bitten and that perhaps it was time to move on to another location. After all, this film was about finding great white sharks, not about possibly being eaten by oceanic whitetips.

Gimbel decided that the *Terrier VIII* would now steam across the width and length of the Indian Ocean to Batticaloa in Sri Lanka (then Ceylon) where, he had been told on his preparatory expedition around the globe, he would find great white sharks – and not just that, he would find them swimming around the wreck of a sunken aircraft carrier several kilometres off the coast out from Batticaloa.

Sri Lanka is only a few hundred kilometres north of the equator, and Ron and I thought it very unlikely that we would find great whites there, but Peter was steadfast in his belief in what he had been told. Like Stan, Peter was worldly but naïve, never cottoning on to the fact that when he arrived in a poor coastal village and asked if they had great white sharks off the coast – and if they did he would spend some of his production money in their village – they were always going to say yes.

Ron and I knew where Gimbel could find great whites, and that place was South Australia, but as we were hired camera people, not directors nor producers, we stayed quiet, took our orders and prepared to see a bit more of the world. We travelled to Kenya, stopping at Madagascar for fuel then visiting Grande Comore, a French island where the local divers had convinced Peter we would find not only great whites but also the incredibly rare coelacanth. I knew we would not encounter great whites, but to see a coelacanth alive in the water would be an amazing event. Unfortunately, the local divers seemed more interested in joining us on our adventure than finding a shark or fish. We did try once at night and once during the day but the current and bleak conditions made it all too hard.

We disembarked in Kenya. Peter wanted to fly to Colombo and meet the *Terrier VIII* there. He felt we needed some time on land. Life on the *Terrier VIII* was becoming tiring: the food was dreadful, fresh water always a problem and we desperately needed a change of scenery.

There was an interesting incident en route to Sri Lanka when we boarded a plane filled almost exclusively with

Chinese agents doing business and spreading the good Communist word across what was then the graveyard of European empires. We called them 'Mao's Men' and they were everywhere we went in the subcontinent: on the street, at the temples and shopping strips, and on our plane.

They were a curiosity to me, both male and female all dressed the same, with identical haircuts and clothes. There was a oneness about them with their little red books that they dipped into every hour as though refreshing their loyalty, and the shiny pin badges of their great leader they all wore.

They seemed a reticent but amiable enough group (one even swapped his Mao badge for my QANTAS kangaroo badge), until we heard the news that 380 000 kilometres away another American-led adventure expedition had achieved more success than ours. The *Apollo 11* spaceship had successfully travelled to lunar orbit, and the leader of that mission, Neil Armstrong, had walked on the surface of the moon.

A patriotic soul, Peter Gimbel was ecstatic. He saw it not only as a great feat for the United States, but a great feat for all of humanity. In a plane full of Chinese Communists, he stood up, called for attention and then told all assembled what had just happened out in space.

There was a silent beat while the Chinese leader translated this information, then, uproarious laughter from men who were obviously unaccustomed to mirth. Mao's Men had been told to be very careful about the things they read and heard when out of their country, and this claim – that the decadent West had managed to travel to the moon – was clearly an absurd lie.

They pointed at Ron and me too, laughing a spiteful laugh and joking among each other. Of course it meant nothing to us to be mocked by the ignorant, but it was an interesting time to be out in the world.

When we landed in Colombo, we waited for news from the *Terrier VIII*, but none came. On the day the ship was supposed to dock in Colombo Harbour, there was no sign of her. This state of affairs was not cause for panic – in the late 1960s, communications were far from being what they are today. A few days' delay could be expected, but the ship's non-appearance was one that did raise some concern.

As the days dragged on without contact, Peter Gimbel asked me to travel to Batticaloa and prepare for the arrival of his ship and the rest of the crew while he, Stan, Ron and Peter Lake sought to find out what had happened to the *Terrier VIII*. He also asked that I look after another terrier, his much loved Norwich Terrier puppy, Billy.

Still in Peter's employ, I was more than happy to agree, and I must say I had a delightful time travelling through the country with Billy. On the way to Batticaloa, Billy and I visited the temples of Anuradhapura and the King's lakes, which were usually best taken in while sitting at an English teahouse, eating cucumber sandwiches and drinking tea.

Billy was usually excellent company, but his curiosity sometimes got the better of him. The most extreme example of this was when, at one of the most delightful little teahouses, he became very interested in a group of Mao's Men who were eating lunch. Billy ran over to the group and yapped at their feet begging in a friendly fashion. Obviously annoyed, one of the men picked the dog up and hurled him into the lake. I had to launch myself over the railing, down a large pylon and into the water to save the floundering puppy. The men didn't even look up when Billy and I returned to the teahouse; me angry, Billy terrified and both of us dripping. There was nothing I could do but slop to our car and leave my cucumber sandwich and the teahouse.

When we arrived at Batticaloa, Billy and I installed ourselves in the hotel. Peter Gimbel had rented every room. Billy and I spent the time sightseeing but I missed Ron, the diving and even the uncomfortable *Terrier VIII*. A week later our ship arrived, and a day after that we were ready to dive again.

Our destination was the HMS *Hermes*, a British aircraft carrier sunk by Japanese Zeros just a few months before the sinking of the *Nova Scotia*. Before we joined our whale catcher we visited the fishing village just seven or so kilometres from where the *Hermes* lay. There, a pastor claimed to have seen the battle between the *Hermes* and the Japanese planes from atop a nearby lighthouse. At the village, Peter Gimbel once again asked the locals what kinds of sharks they had seen when fishing near the wreck. Once again they said that they had seen sharks that were 1800 kilograms, which could only be great whites. (I must add here a great white of that weight would be as big as a small whale, but Peter seemed to believe them. The average weight of the great whites I have seen would be, at a guess, 1000–1500 pounds/450–680 kilograms.) The water was warm enough to dive in without a wetsuit, and there was none of the oceanic life – such as sea lions and seals – that is the normal prey of a great white. Even so, we said nothing. This was Gimbel's train set.

We shackled the *Terrier VIII* close onto the bow of the carrier, which sat in 180 feet (55 metres) of water, and proceeded to undertake some very trying dives over a number of days. The dive site was striking, full of small sea life. The dead aircraft carrier, still almost intact, sat on a plain of sand. Unfortunately it offered very limited visibility and had sunk in an area of great current. Not just that, most days we were unable to dive at all as storm after storm came in. This put a lot of pressure on the dives that we did manage. We did not see any sharks, not even any tropical species. The wreck was interesting but hard diving, and we could see the detrimental effect this enterprise was having on Peter.

On one dive Peter Gimbel suffered from the bends, a malady that some divers experience when nitrogen builds up in their bloodstream due to pressure, and can't dissipate because of too quick an ascent. I have never suffered from the bends and suspect that I may be un-bendable. Hundreds of Japanese hardhat pearl divers working the Western Australian pearl fields, however, died from the bends; their graves can be seen in the Broome cemetery. Both Ron and Stan suffered as well but not as badly as Peter. They decompressed for about an hour longer than usual, but Peter was in serious pain and it was almost dark by the time he could surface. I was on the same dive but suffered no ill effects.

It took a full-ship effort to bring Gimbel up as slowly as was needed to keep him from suffering permanent damage, requiring many hours and many tanks of air. In those hours of desperation, you can learn a great deal about the people around you. I was not surprised to find that Ron was endlessly cool and useful, but I was disappointed in Peter Lake who was frantic and unfocused.

Peter Gimbel ended up being fine. In fact, I would say the person who went closest to death while diving the *Hermes* was Peter Lake, who was starting to get on my nerves not by dint of his personality but through his carelessness, which led me to decide I would stab him with my diving knife.

It was after a dive during which, in a moment of extreme clumsiness, Lake kicked my mask and regulator off and then swam away without offering assistance. This is not just a breach of diving etiquette, but an invitation to calamity, injury or worse. This was a time before octopuses (as second-stage regulators are known), and my only chance at 170 feet (52 metres) down was to find my regulator again, air being my first priority.

Fortunately my mask was pale blue and I could just see it on the sand at 180 feet. I found my regulator, then dropped down and recovered my mask, which I cleared, and began to surface. I was furious as I stopped at each of the safety stops to burn off nitrogen, but as I thought about Lake's mindset I decided he wasn't being spiteful, merely mindless – and to me, being imperilled because of someone's stupidity was even worse than being imperilled because of someone's malice.

On the deck I waited for Lake, saying nothing but drawing my knife. The surface crew saw that. Jim Lipscomb picked up his camera and Tom Chapin, who was on sound, tried to talk me down.

'What are you going to do with that knife, Valerie?' Tom asked.

'I'm going to kill Lake,' I told him. I remember how calm I was, and how dedicated to the task ahead.

'You can't kill anyone, Val, even Lake.'

It took a long time for Peter Lake to surface, and in that time Tom got the knife off me. I stayed annoyed for several days but understood that senselessness isn't always a choice; some people just naturally have it in them. I was always wary of Lake afterwards, though, especially when diving with him.

Eventually we got some interesting footage on the *Hermes*, but of course not of any great whites. The Sri Lanka visit had been a failure in Peter Gimbel's eyes. He was understandably disappointed. Ron and I had enjoyed seeing Sri Lanka and diving the *Hermes* but the lack of sharks of any kind was a real disappointment. We still had to return the *Terrier VIII* to Union Whaling, and Gimbel held out hope that on the way he would find his shark.

On our return voyage after several weeks in Sri Lanka we visited other islands, where we found incredible animals, including one giant and very friendly fish with distinctive markings. We were filming around the uninhabited island of Europa. When we surfaced Stan said, 'All that fish and no potatoes', and I told him the 'potato' was on its skin: it was the potato cod. You can tell an Australian named it. Only Australians call groupers cod. It was three years later that I took on the Queensland government, National Parks and game fishermen after finding this same fish at Cormorant Pass in the Ribbon Reefs, but that is another story.

After that dive Peter asked me to go back down and kill one of those very large, very placid fish as he filmed. He thought the sharks in the area would be attracted by the death throes. But there was no way I would kill such a delightful fish. I did spear a jack, which was taken from my hand by a caranx who became my best friend for the rest of the dive. But there were no sharks.

We visited several more islands after Europa, perhaps the most interesting of which was Aldabra in the Seychelles, where we encountered a huge tortoise and thousands of nesting gannets. The only other place I knew of with these huge reptiles was Galapagos in the eastern Pacific.

As we made our way around these breathtakingly beautiful islands our tenure in Peter Gimbel's employ was coming to an end, and we still hadn't filmed any great whites. Ron and I had already committed to another project, but we told Peter that after we had completed that job he should bring Stan and Tom – and Peter Lake if he must – to South Australia, where we had worked with great white sharks with wonderful success. We could have our old friend and collaborator Rodney Fox organise a boat and baits, and then all go out to the reefs to find the shark Peter desperately wanted to film.

A new contract was drawn up and, as soon as we finished filming the second and final season of the *Barrier Reef* series off the Queensland coast we travelled south to meet Peter Gimbel and the crew in South Australia. It took a few days at sea and a ton of bait, but we found the great white sharks we had promised. Although a blue shark or a bull shark, or an oceanic whitetip, can kill a man, they're nothing like a great white, which is so much larger, and completely fearless. Peter and Stan were equal parts exhilarated and astonished. When we got back to shore, Peter Gimbel was a man relieved. He finally had a successful ending to his film.

* * *

A year later, Ron and I travelled back to South Africa for the premier of the film *Blue Water, White Death*, a grand and lavish affair with open-top cars parading us and the other stars of the film through the streets of Durban until we arrived at a grand cinema and the stirring sounds of a full Scots band.

There we watched the final production. So many adventures were missing. A seven-month adventure whittled down to a ninety-six-minute film; a requirement of the producers, National General Pictures, likely so it could fit in a two-hour commercial TV spot. Peter Gimbel had called from New York saying the film had been fine cut and was four hours long. He asked if Ron had time to fly to the United States to give advice on what best to edit out. Peter claimed there was enough good footage for two feature films. Ron and I were busy preparing for a TV series of our own and had no time to travel anywhere unless it was to do with our own production.

It is only with the perspective of time that I can see that film as others do. It's a story as much about people as it is about sharks, and has the lovely cadence of a travelogue. Although it seemed far less exhilarating than actually experiencing the underwater sequences they are thrilling and unique in retrospect, especially when we dived cage-less with hundreds of oceanic whitetips.

As Ron and I watched the film, we could only think of all the footage that hadn't been used; all the storylines that had not been explored. Once again we wondered if, at some point, we might be in charge of our own filmmaking destiny, in control of the camera and the edit on a large-scale production.

After Durban we went back home and looked at the calendar, filled with work on our own series. *Blue Water, White Death* was just another filming job, a very exciting one but nonetheless we could think only of the future, not the past. The film, however, had other ideas.

Blue Water, White Death was fast becoming a success in American cinemas and beyond, both critically and commercially. As the box office gross grew, there was also a growing suggestion to producers and creators that there was a global desire to see more of this great white shark.

One viewer of the film was Peter Benchley, a then 31-year-old New Jersey native who was making a living as a freelance feature writer but dreaming of becoming an author. Benchley had suggested a few non-fiction ideas to a few publishers, but they weren't particularly interested. After seeing *Blue Water, White Death* he thought that perhaps he could write a fictional thriller, featuring a rogue great white shark terrorising the north-east coast of the United States.

Benchley went through a few working titles for the book, including *The Jaws of Leviathan* and *Silence in the Water* until, after some consultation with his agent and publisher, he decided to go for something short and snappy.

Jaws.

CHAPTER EIGHT

Jaws

Jaws started as just another job. No one involved could know how our sharks would become international superstars, changing not just cinema but people's perceptions of the ocean in a drastic way.

Ron and I took our work as seriously as ever, and though we suspected the film we were working on would be forgotten after a short run, we had a job to do and would give it all the energy and talent we had. The young director Steven Spielberg wisely wanted the live shark footage in the can before going into full-scale production, and we had made a promise of sharks that we intended to honour.

The great white shark is not my favourite aquatic animal, but with its ruthless locomotion and violent virility, it is a fish that has long fascinated me. There are no boring dives with a great white shark nearby.

It was on the third day of our expedition that our guest came, gliding through a slick of taste and smell that stretched all the way to the horizon.

Ron, our long-time South Australian collaborator Rodney Fox and I had been taking turns out the back of the *Trade Wind* for the past three days, watching seabirds feasting on the drifting chum, stringing bloody offerings along the sunny side of our vessel always watching for the telltale fin to cut through the slick. Waiting as we had so many times for a guest that dictates their own hour of arrival. All we could do was send out an invitation to a party that couldn't start without them. In this instance the invitation was slicked whale oil, desiccated tuna and a dismembered horse offered up close to a colony of Australian sea lions and their unsteady pups; a favourite meal of the great white.

When our shark arrived, it was my turn on deck. As I dribbled minced tuna into the water I saw a ripple that disappeared as quickly as it came. Calm returned. The chum bobbed, the bait bled, the sun bore down. As I considered telling the men below what I'd seen, the ocean exploded.

The huge shark erupted through the slick – mouth agape, arrowhead teeth bared ready to grind our bait into mince right in front of me. The monstrous jaws of the great white snapped down while still in the air, then with bloody tuna oozing between its teeth it disappeared. This shark was energetic, huge and magnificent. Only the red around the stern was proof of its appearance.

* * *

The first step down this path started six months earlier, when galley proofs for a book by a first-time author named Peter Benchley arrived at our house, along with a letter from film producers Richard Zanuck and David Brown asking our opinion on whether we thought the book would work well as a film.

The pair had already produced a crime film called *The Sugarland Express* with first-time director Steven Spielberg and things were going so well, they were looking for a second project to attach him to. After seeing *Blue Water, White Death* they were considering adapting Benchley's novel *Jaws*, the film rights of which he had offered to the producers cheaply hoping the film could promote his book.

Ron and I read the galley proof. It was the story of a giant rogue shark terrorising a resort town in New York state and the three men – policeman Martin Brody, marine biologist Matt Hooper and professional shark hunter Quint – trying to catch and kill it. As I read, I saw the scenes play out in my head. It was a work high in tension and cinematic value, and I thought it would make an enjoyable feature. The producers also sent us a copy of their film *The Sugarland Express*, and we agreed it was a very impressive and entertaining production.

Ron sent a letter telling Zanuck and Brown that we believed *Jaws* could be an excellent film but stressed that it was impossible to script a shark, that they are very dangerous and unpredictable animals and that the on-water and underwater photography would be the key to success in making the fish look real.

The producers agreed and sent us a rough plan of the aquatic shots they wanted, and asked us if they were viable, and how much we thought it would cost to shoot them all. One of the shots they wanted was a man in the jaws of a great white, and we told them that was impossible, but we thought we could get the rest of the shots for around $2 million.

The producers told us that this figure was impossibly high – after all, *Jaws* wasn't budgeted as a blockbuster full of stars like *Cleopatra*. Ron explained to them that they couldn't just order up great white sharks like they do camels or elephants. They are wild, dangerous animals that live in an unpredictable habitat. To get all the shots they wanted, we suspected that we would have to be out in the ocean for more than a year.

Richard Zanuck and David Brown wondered if there was another way to work and eventually it was decided, in consultation with Spielberg and Ron, that they would build an animatronic shark to use for some of the shots where the animal would interact with a human. Ron went over to Los Angeles to help in the design of the artificial shark and I prepared for the trip we would take to film live animals, which would still be an essential ingredient for success.

The company ended up building multiple fake sharks, which had hydraulic cables attaching them to the surface. There was a left-to-right shark, a front-on shark and a right-to-left shark – but every time a whole shark fills the screen, it's an Australian great white and very real.

Ron and I arrived in South Australia on 12 February 1974 where we met Rodney Fox, who had already hired a boat and ordered fish baits. We were to go out in two vessels, the main craft being the chartered thirty-five-foot *Trade Wind*, and Rodney's nineteen-foot abalone boat *Skippy*.

The American contingent had arrived in Sydney a few days earlier, but one of their number, an art director named Frank Arrigo, had a heart attack almost as soon as he arrived in Sydney and had to fly back home to Los Angeles immediately.

Production coordinator Jim Hogan arrived in South Australia with actor Carl Rizzo, a small and gentle man who had been a jockey in a previous career and still raised and trained horses in the American west. Carl was to be our stuntman; an experienced diver, we were told. Because of his petite size he could wear a child's-size mask, SCUBA rig and wetsuit, and be placed in a miniature diving cage in order for us to create the illusion of him being menaced by an enormous shark. This was necessary because Benchley's book *Jaws* starred a great white shark described as roughly twenty-four feet in length, which is on the very limits of what nature can produce, and it was highly unlikely we would find a beast of that size. Instead, we would rely on a few tricks – Carl, the miniature props and a smaller boat, namely the *Skippy*, to double for the fictional marine researcher hunting an over-sized shark.

We had stressed to Zanuck and Brown that anyone diving with us would need prior experience, and they assured us that Carl would be prepared and experienced. Experienced he was, having worked in Hollywood for many years and had even doubled as a pre-teen Elizabeth Taylor in the film *National Velvet*. Prepared, however, he was not. His diving experience was all very recent – in a pool in sunny California. Now we were planning to put him in a cage, tie bait to that cage and then lower the whole thing into the icy and turbulent Southern Ocean.

We expressed our concerns about this plan to Jim Hogan, a fast-talking, chain-smoking coffee addict whom we all liked immensely. He told us not to worry. We had a contract, we had insurance, and we had a willing professional actor. We had everything we needed except a shark, but Jim was quite sure we would have one in a few days. We liked his positive attitude. It was Carl's lack of experience that was a worry.

My concerns only heightened when, on the day we were ready to leave port, Carl Rizzo asked to be taken to his stateroom.

There were no staterooms on the *Trade Wind*, in fact there were no rooms at all except the galley, hold and the toilet. Ron and I planned to sleep behind the anchor alcove in the bow, but everyone else had to find space in the saloon. Carl ended up sleeping on a shelf, but not before voicing much consternation.

Before we set off into open ocean we thought it prudent to test the diving ability of our human star Carl Rizzo, who we had been told was a proficient diver but we knew would be tested to the limits when thrown into the frigid tumult of the Southern Ocean alongside an 800-kilogram apex predator.

In calm shallow water next to a rocky shore we attempted to get Carl swimming in his SCUBA apparatus, but it was nigh on impossible. Just getting him in a wetsuit was a chore, and when, not without some difficulty, Ron managed to get him into the water, he claimed he wasn't getting any air through the regulator. We checked his equipment and there was no problem. All he needed to do was breathe, but even in shallow water we could not get him under. He would cling to a rock, with his face in the water, and refuse to let go. I tried coaxing him from the rocks and Ron gently encouraged him from where he was standing in the water, but Carl would not let go.

Ron, Rodney and I were very concerned about what would happen once we got Carl into the cold agitated water with a shark swimming around, but Jim Hogan told us that when the time came, Carl would perform as per the stipulations of his contract.

'Isn't that right, Carl?' he said to the man who was shivering like a wet cat, cold and unhappy. (My gift to the perpetually cold actor was a handmade tea cosy. Carl was delighted with the unusual hat. It kept his bald head warm but he looked a trick with one ear sticking out the spout hole and the other through the handle hole.)

When Jim spoke, Carl nodded, mutely wearing the look of someone caught up in a stream of terrible and irreversible momentum.

Once we got out onto the open sea we solved the problem of Carl's inability to breathe from the tank on his back by feeding an air supply from a hookah on Rodney's abalone boat into Carl's mouth. With him no longer able to claim he couldn't get any air, we did get him in the cage and just under the surface. Unfortunately, Carl was also unable to clear his ears, so just under the surface was as far as he could safely go.

We never would have forced Carl under the water, but any time Jim told us to proceed we would look to Carl, who would nod whenever Jim told him it was time to get in the cage.

Jim was no seaman, but by force of personality and drive he was comfortable wherever he was, as long as he had access to cigarettes and coffee. Ron and I figured he would be great company as we headed east, and we were right.

A hundred and seventy years before we set off into the Southern Ocean, Captain Matthew Flinders had done the same journey as part of an expedition mapping the south of the newly seized land he liked to call *Terra Australis*. When Flinders saw a ribbon of jagged, spray-smashing granite boulders thirty kilometres east of what would become Port Lincoln, he named it Dangerous Reef to serve as a warning for whalers, sealers and other mariners who would soon use the port.

Decades later, when the reef was far from established shipping lines, the name retained its utility as a warning for fishermen of submerged rocks and the concentration of great white sharks that congregate in the area attracted by the sea lion colony.

Experience had told us that the cold, windswept water around the reefs was one of the great areas in the world to find large, strong and active great white sharks. This was where we were planning to find the star of *Jaws*.

Our skipper dropped anchor in thirty-seven feet (eleven metres) of water. It was an uncomfortable anchorage, with a bitter south-easterly wind whipping the ocean into a choppy carpet of white and blue. We slicked the water with whale oil, lowered chum buckets, strung horse parts across the hull in an appetising fashion and waited. That was all there was to do; a great white is a guest that's never early, or late, it will arrive when it chooses to arrive and that will be when the party starts.

In the way that not all humans are great performers, not all sharks are destined for the big screen, but our first shark of that trip looked like a star. As soon as Ron saw it he ran for the cage strung with baits, dumped it off the stern of the *Trade Wind*, then grabbed his wetsuit and 35-millimetre Cameflex camera. The Cameflex also shoots techniscope. The only commercial housing available for the camera was very heavy and hard to handle, so Ron had made a special perspex housing for his camera.

All on deck were full of purpose and activity, working towards a common goal, except for poor Carl who looked like Somerset Maugham's Mesopotamian trader who had just seen Death on his way to Samarra. I doubt the man had ever seen a shark before – and seeing a great white feeding is a rather alarming introduction. After asking for his agent, Carl succumbed to fear and seasickness.

Jim Hogan, on the other hand, simply stared, coffee in one hand, cigarette in the other, at our underwater star. He was in awe, perhaps of the power of the beast, perhaps at how this shark might look across a wide screen.

The shark seemed to be a good performer, happy to tear at the baits and swim close to the boat constantly bumping the stern with its nose. We pulled the baits above the surface, keen to keep our potential star eager for more not full, happy and no longer interested. Ron climbed into the cage, which floated next to the hull. With our shark performing beautifully, Ron filmed a good four hundred feet of excellent footage sometimes in and sometimes out of the cage.

The script called for several clear sequences without bars in the frame, so whenever possible Ron worked outside the cage. This could only be done because there was one shark around. It would have been far too dangerous if there had been more than one. Also, the script called for just one shark.

With Carl so reluctant, we decided to pick up the over-the-shoulder shots of Hooper, the marine biologist, later played by Richard Dreyfuss. In these shots I doubled as Hooper, so I changed into my black wetsuit and slid into the cage with Ron, who was to film from Hooper's point of view. In that sequence we used a shot of my hand reaching from the cage and touching the shark. It was my big scene in *Jaws* – in fact, my only scene.

The surface conditions went from bad to worse. The cage was tossed to and fro, so getting steady, usable shots was very slow going. By the time my tank was empty and I was back on the deck of the *Trade Wind* I was thoroughly drained. Bouncing around in a cage is rather unpleasant. It would have been calmer at depth, but Ron wanted good light and the script called for open ocean as a background not kelp or rocks.

Sometime in the late afternoon our shark became bored with us, or perhaps was full of tuna, and disappeared. As usual Ron and I were anxious about the day's footage. We had been damned with difficult conditions but blessed with an excellent performer. Ron was quite confident there were not just usable shots, but some that were exactly what the script asked for.

As the sun waned and the deck cleaning started, I, being the cook, was thinking about what I might put on the table for the men at dinnertime but also about Carl who was in the galley with me. Today's shark had been roughly thirteen feet (four metres) long, and the star of the Benchley book was roughly twice that size. I figured if we got a shark at about sixteen or seventeen feet (4.9 or 5.2 metres), it would be roughly sixty-five percent of the size of *Jaws*. Was Carl roughly sixty-five percent the size of the men in the movie? I mentioned this to Ron, who said that because there was no background, size would not be a consideration.

When dinner came, Carl ate nothing. The rolling boat had taken its toll, and the seasickness tablets he had taken were making him drowsy. I don't think he even noticed when we started talking to him. Jim noted that despite Carl's reaction that day he would get into the ocean the following day, should we be lucky enough to get another shark to act for us.

When we all looked to Carl he nodded slowly, his face a portrait of bland resignation below a warm but silly-looking cosy hat.

It seemed to me that any resistance in Carl's body and mind had disappeared.

Unfortunately, the next morning was one of consistent rain, wind-tossed waves and grey sky, but to our great excitement it also brought a visitor. As we teased the shark closer to the boat with baits, Ron went down in the cage. This shark was nowhere near the performer the previous day's shark had been, but it stayed around and Ron filmed what he could.

As the morning went on, the waves built and an icy wind from the South Pole blew through us. Our shark was unaffected by the conditions and patrolled the baits close to the boat. Around midday the sun came out and Ron decided it was time to get Carl into the water.

I had to pull Carl into his wetsuit – and if you've ever tried to dress a small child, then you know what it was like for me as I tried to prepare Carl. Eventually I got him into his wetsuit and SCUBA equipment, and onto Rod's abalone boat where the smaller cage hung over the side. Although we were rushing to get more shots before we lost our shark or the sun, there was a pause before we lowered Carl into his cage. Ron and I were still unsure of whether it was a good idea. Jim Hogan, however, had not a doubt in his mind, motioning with his hand that wasn't wrapped around a coffee cup for us to send the stuntman below.

Three times Rod tried to get Carl underwater where Ron waited, and three times we failed. In each instance Rod gave him the regulator and started to lower him down under the choppy surface, and in each instance he started spluttering and gasping for the surface air. Carl claimed that there was no air coming from his tank, and that his mouthpiece was filling with water, but after checking and checking again we found no evidence to support his claim.

I don't think Carl was lying, I just think he was incapable of reaching the minimum level of calm required to actually breathe. Eventually Ron decided we weren't getting any shots with Carl, and we called it a day, letting our low-energy shark go back to its regular shark life.

Later, when we had some quiet time with Jim Hogan we gave him some solace, telling him that the conditions we were sending Carl under in were exceptionally difficult for a diver with almost no experience. There was every chance that when the conditions improved and we got another shark behind the boat, we would be able to get Carl and his cage below the surface, far enough to get the shots that the script called for.

It took a week for us to lure in another performer.

After puttering around here and there to nearby anchorages we returned to Dangerous Reef and Australian sea lions with their pups that looked at us with what felt like familiarity. We dropped anchor on a sunny, calm day in the lee of Dangerous Reef and sat down for sandwiches. After I had finished mine, I took to the deck and threw some minced tuna into the slick. Only a few minutes later I saw a shark gliding to and fro, its fin cutting through the burley.

I yelled, 'Shark!' and reached for a bucket of minced fish, which I dumped into the water. Our new shark, mouth wide open, swam through the blood seeking the source. It was all-round action stations. Two cages were lowered, and Ron with camera went down to wait for Carl. Carl was helped into his smaller cage, and I had a tense moment when our stuntman disappeared below the surface, but telltale bubbles flowing from the cage to the surface were proof he was breathing, maybe not happy but alive. Using his abalone winch, Rod lowered the cage about a quarter of a metre under the surface.

It was heartbreaking to find that while our human co-star was now pliant, our star was not. This shark would be kept close with the promise of food but would not approach close enough to either cage for truly useful footage.

Ron did his best with passing shots, but there was no excitement in the shark. It simply swam slowly around looking but not giving a useful performance. Eventually Ron resurfaced, immensely frustrated that he hadn't been able to successfully film the type of action required on the shot list.

We winched Carl up, and the frustration was mitigated somewhat when we found that he was partially restored by the dive. He had managed to do what he thought he couldn't do, and we all congratulated him on his courage. Perhaps with calm conditions, and a shark that was a good performer, we would get the good action shots the script asked for after all.

We were on deck for only a scant few minutes before another shark arrived, much larger than any that we had seen so far, but more importantly it seemed like a virile performer, attacking the baits, approaching the boat without apprehension, lifting its head above the water to watch us. Australian great whites are unlike any other shark we have seen in that they lift their head above the surface to observe the unusual. The fact that this shark was watching us was a good sign.

Ron hustled to replace his air tank, yelling for us to do the same for Carl. I did so and kept an eye on the animal, who started attacking the flotation tanks on Ron's cage, making it leap and dance. This was our shark, sleek, beautiful and a good performer.

As soon as we had replaced Carl's tank I loaded a .303 army bullet into our powerhead and put my mask next to it. There wasn't just one shark with us now, there were several. Perhaps two, perhaps more. With Jim Hogan adamant that we get as many shots as possible without bars, Ron, his cage suspended well below the surface, was spending a lot of time outside the protective bars filming, concentrating on one shark while at the mercy of the most dangerous shark of all; the one you had no idea was there. If Ron were to have any problems with an out-of-control shark I would jump into the water and help with the powerhead.

We moved Carl to the *Skippy* and attempted to get him back into his cage, but his fear had returned – with such a magnificent shark around, I didn't blame him. This shark was a performer, banging the cages, the boat and reaching up for baits; all noise and motion.

'I don't like this,' he said again and again as Rod attempted to coax him into his cage.

We tried to comfort him, promising that the cage was the safest place he could be, telling him that we had all done hundreds of dives in the cages and they were as safe as houses, and reminding him how well he had done on the previous dive.

Rodney was fitting Carl's mouthpiece when our new shark swam around the boat's stern, cut close to the hull and bumped the cables attaching Carl's cage to the abalone winch. In an instant we were all spiked with adrenaline. The animal rounded the stern a second time and banged harder into the cage. Feeling an unfamiliar sensation – its nerve-packed nose had struck the coarse and unyielding cables – it panicked and leaped over the cage, wedging itself solidly into the cables that tethered the cage to the winch. The small abalone boat tilted violently as it suddenly took the immense weight of the thrashing shark.

The animal, which weighed at least half a ton, exploded with incredible energy, using all its terrifying power to try to free itself from the cables and get back to the safety of deep water. All on the boat were flung violently as the animal used every sinew, every muscle to escape, its great tail sweeping across the deck. The beast nearly stood on its head, the most vigorous action being the last, snapping the cables with a loud crack. Rodney pulled Carl back as, in a fountain of spray, the shark, the winch, the cage and part of the boat disappeared.

From action and noise came stillness and quiet.

As we slowly regained our senses, we started to perceive the reality of the situation. Carl should be dead, drowned, or with his brains dashed against the cage, or perhaps even a combination of all three – but instead, he was standing stunned, staring at his feet.

'Are you okay?' Rodney asked him. 'Carl, are you okay?'

It took some time for Carl to realise that Rodney was talking to him. When he did he spoke in a detached and awkwardly deliberate voice, as though he hadn't spoken for many years.

'Am … I … wounded?'

'No, Carl, you're not wounded,' Rodney reassured him.

'This is ... my ... blood?' Carl asked, looking down at the red liquid in which he stood.

It wasn't his blood; it was hydraulic fluid, running from a severed hose smashed by the shark's tail when the frenzied animal broke the cage and winch from the side of the smaller abalone boat. It seemed Carl's reticence had saved his life. If he had been in the cage when the shark and the boat tangled, he surely would have drowned or been injured. Drowned most likely, because although he wore a perfectly good tank of air he still seemed unable to use it. Carl had a physical reaction to all the excitement and back on the boat rushed to the deck locker-cum-toilet. His private moments were being exposed, however, as the sliding door opened and shut with the swell. Seeing this I jammed a screwdriver in the door to stop it opening, then went back to the others to assess the situation.

The cage was gone, and the shark for the moment also. At least we had some dynamite footage, with Ron having filmed the whole scene underwater. We now had to find the cage. Ron said it seemed to be falling off the shark as it swam in a tangled, swirling mess towards the bottom.

Ron sank to the sand in his cage, put his legs through the bars and walked, with the cage around him, away from the boat to rescue the small cage, which he found some distance away. Ron tied the small cage to his larger one and, still wearing this cage like a skirt, walked them both back to the mother ship. A second shark, more curious than aggressive, watched Ron as he walked the cage. The small cage looked rather bent as it was hauled over the stern. While that was all happening two large sharks appeared, showing interest in the boat and baits.

Once Carl's damaged cage was dragged onto the deck, Ron submerged again in his cage to get footage of the circling sharks before the light disappeared.

At twilight Ron brought his cage to the surface, handed up his camera and climbed out. It was only when Ron returned that I realised I had forgotten about Carl. I rushed to the door of the head, yanked out the screwdriver holding the door shut, and slid the door open, where I was greeted with a scene of capitulation. I started an apology but as his eyes met mine, I stopped. Carl was a mess mentally and physically. He said nothing, probably because he had shouted himself hoarse trying to get our attention. He just stumbled into the saloon, put on his tea-cosy woollen hat and lay down.

When dinner came Carl ate nothing. He was ill from spending an hour or so in a small lurching room cold and seasick; an experience that would dampen anyone's spirits. A conversation started between Ron and Jim about the shots still to capture. Carl barely noticed, he seemed unable to think about anything but his terrifying experience when the shark broke away the cage. I don't think he even noticed Jim telling us that despite Carl's frightening experience earlier that day he might have to get into the ocean, possibly tomorrow, should we be lucky enough to get another shark to perform for us.

The meal we ate that night was large and the mood was celebratory. I brought out a box of wine to toast the day's success. We became a very merry little group. The incident with the *Skippy* wasn't on our shot list, but Jim Hogan appreciated any action he could get, and Ron said he would be surprised if Spielberg didn't make use of that very dynamic footage.

We were happy that we'd managed to deliver sharks to Jim, and Jim was happy that he would return to Hollywood having completed his task – perhaps not getting every shot he envisioned, but a lot of excellent action.

When we eventually returned ashore Jim and Carl went immediately to Adelaide to catch a flight to Sydney. Jim was anxious to get his footage developed, and understandably Carl was anxious to escape home before Jim thought of any shark scenes he might have missed. Before we parted ways I thanked Carl for attempting a task that was obviously very difficult for him. By way of appreciation I gifted him the little tea cosy, with the spout and handle holes that perfectly fit his ears.

He thanked me for my understanding, and I think his thanks were sincere.

A few months later we had all but forgotten *Jaws* and Steven Spielberg until a letter arrived in the mail. Inside were two first-class tickets to Los Angeles and then tickets on to Massachusetts where the principal photography on *Jaws* had begun.

When Ron and I arrived in Martha's Vineyard, a resort island in the northeast of America, we did so ready to work but were quickly told we would not be allowed to be part of the filming crew due to the Teamsters' strict union rules.

Richard Zanuck and David Brown explained that we had been invited as guests, and we were welcome to enjoy the beach and sit in some scenes as extras if we were so inclined.

Ron and I had a truly wonderful time on the beach, spending lots of quality time on the sand with the film's stars, especially Roy Scheider, who was a former boxer and air force officer, and was very intrigued about diving and all things aquatic.

I did wonder why the actors had so much time on their hands, until director Steven Spielberg, a man who looked like he was straight out of college and was, in fact, only a few years removed from dropping out of California State University, confided to us that the animatronic sharks that Ron helped design kept breaking down and halting production. Ron had only been required to help with the look of the shark not the mechanics.

When neither Spielberg nor Zanuck and Brown were around, I heard some extras laughing about this 'shark film'. I felt a bit sorry for Steven and his uncooperative mechanical sharks, but he seemed confident this problem would be rectified, and of course it was.

Later, when we were invited to the Sydney premiere of *Jaws*, we were unburdened by great expectation but greeted by a film that was undoubtedly a modern masterpiece, and something we were instantly proud to have contributed to.

The power of the film was not the volume of shark photography as we might have imagined, but the scarcity. It was the quiet before the action, the music and the tension that made *Jaws* stand out, a tension that was multiplied when coupled with kinetic moments of action, such as the attack on the *Skippy* and the shot of my hand touching one of the unafraid sharks swimming by.

As we watched, Ron and I agreed that we were seeing a star in the making; not our friends on Dangerous Reef but the director himself.

Even now when I watch *Jaws* I am reminded not of the frantic moments or the difficult conditions we worked in once we had a shark, but the still moments; the pregnant moments staring at a slick of taste and smell stretching to the horizon, waiting for a visitor from a cold alien world. Nature's perfect creation: the great white shark.

CHAPTER NINE

Inner Space

I can remember the incident vividly. It was a bunch of drunken football players wanting to have a bit of what they termed fun with the other passengers. They were coming for their so-called bit of fun. And there was nothing we could do about it.

It was late at night; black and quiet outside. Ron and I were in bed and I had locked the flimsy door of our cabin. That door wouldn't hold; it could be easily forced. I could hear them coming for us. Their voices had fallen quiet and there was silence, but then the voices rose again.

They'd already dragged all the other passengers from their cabins. We were the only ones left.

A fist smashed on the door. There were yells for us to come out, the end of each word slurred with drunkenness.

'Get it over and done with,' a drunken voice yelled.

'I'll go,' Ron said steadily. He hadn't said a thing while it was all happening, but of course he was awake throughout. He went out and there were cheers and jeers.

They left but I could hear what was happening. There was fear. I'm not often fearful and I hate it when I am. I cursed the men who were doing this; these drunken idiots Wally had invited onto his boat.

The men were professional rugby league footballers enjoying their off season, swimming and fishing and seeing the delights of the Queensland coast during the day but at night they were drunken louts and all on board had to be pawns in whatever stupid, violent game they wanted to play. Tonight the game was to pull everyone from their bed and throw them off the top of the boat.

Ron and I had always wished that we could afford to charter the whole boat when we worked, but never more so than on that night.

I hoped that throwing a reluctant Ron over the side would be enough, but of course it wasn't.

'Mrs Taylor,' I heard them yell to each other. Then I heard them coming.

When I realised there was no defence I could mount, I rushed to my clothes, hoping to put something on that wasn't my nightgown before they got to me. I was too late. There were hands on me. I struggled but was easily overpowered. Ron was still in the water along with two other passengers.

I was dragged onto the back deck, all the while trying to pull my nightgown down as it rode up. Someone poured a can of beer over me then suddenly I was flying through the air. I struck the water, left ear first. I was not prepared for being thrown; my hands were busy keeping my nightie in place. I hit the water with a horrible smack.

Under the water it occurred to me that the impact seemed far greater than it should have been; something was wrong. I tumbled and swam and searched for the surface but couldn't seem to find it. I spun in the cool darkness wondering if I'd ever emerge into the air again.

When I did, I felt sick and disoriented. I was dragged aboard and as my vision came back to me I saw them all staring at me.

'I thought we'd lost you there, Val,' someone slurred.

The next day everyone acted as though nothing untoward had happened the night before. It was just a bit of fun. But I was hurt. I had pleaded with these men to stop but I couldn't pretend I hadn't been injured. I knew my eardrum was not just punctured. It was gone. I could pour water into my ear and down my throat. My diving days looked over. I had punctured my eardrum in the past but this was something far worse.

We all wanted to continue with the trip, but I simply couldn't. I was in constant pain and felt intermittent nausea. When Wally agreed to take the boat back to shore there was a general sense of annoyance from the men, but no one said anything directly to me. I was annoyed too – in fact I was much more than annoyed, but there was no place to vent except in my diary.

It took three long days to return to shore and when I got to see a doctor I found out that I had lost one-third of my eardrum. He told me that I would have to see a specialist to get a fuller diagnosis, but he suggested I should stop diving.

'Stop diving? For how long?' I asked.

'Altogether, ideally.'

I walked out with fury in my veins. That stupid moment, those stupid men; they didn't deserve to be able to wreak this havoc and then walk away laughing. They shouldn't have that power. I thought about the year ahead and my anger and despair only grew. There was work to do and a lot of it – interesting and lucrative work. We had just signed a contract to do a TV series about the ocean. This was the time in my life for work, but where did this stupid moment leave me?

As I walked out of the doctor's surgery I could feel again hands gripping me, picking me up and throwing me. I thought about them staring at me with uncertain gaze. It was not sexual, just drunkenness.

'I thought we'd lost you there, Val.'

It had been an exceptional year leading up to that incident and in many ways the culmination of years of work and effort. It was an end but also, I'd hoped, a beginning. The start of a life I'd hoped one day to have, but only in my most optimistic daydreams.

It all started at a meeting at Channel Nine, or perhaps a few weeks earlier than that, when Ron and I were sitting in the kitchen of our house in Mortdale discussing some very interesting information we'd been given.

Barrier Reef, the dramatic series we had helped to shoot in Queensland, had been sold to NBC in the United States, but more interestingly we'd heard that they hadn't bought all the episodes. Instead they'd cherry-picked episodes of the two seasons to create one season for American consumption. The universal characteristic of the episodes? Underwater scenes.

It seemed that more than anything else, NBC wanted underwater adventure, and Ron and I thought we might be in a unique position to give it to them.

After the grand Belgian expedition through the Great Barrier Reef and before *Jaws* we'd filmed a lot of great footage that we owned outright, in 16-millimetre and also 35-millimetre. We knew more about that footage than anyone else, about the locations and animals, and we hoped that one day we might be able to tell a complete story, not just something as derivative and simplistic as a battle between man and animal.

We had long suspected that a more complete marine story, full of complexities, fragilities and idiosyncrasies, would be of interest to people; a story of large animals but also the smallest. We believed that people would be interested in the reality of the underwater world, in Australia and around the world.

We thought perhaps we could shoot a series in Australia and sell it here, but insist on a contractual stipulation that we owned the rights to the series overseas. We could then try to sell the series to NBC and beyond.

I contacted Channel Nine, set up a meeting and sat down to write the stories of this series we were about to propose. I think perhaps here is where I came into my own.

Ron was a technical genius and he'd given us the tools to film underwater but in many ways I was the storyteller. I was the one who sometimes narrated our films when we had shown footage on the sides of barns and inside scout halls; I was the one who pitched *Surf Scene* to Speedo, I was the one who'd had a sense of narrative and drama and adventure imprinted into the wet clay of my mind when I was a girl stuck in a hospital bed.

I wrote out the treatment for a number of episodes of a show we were calling 'Inner Space'. Each episode had its own contained aquatic story, with a beginning, middle and end, and perhaps as well a central mystery or quest, but also we were able to use footage we had already shot that was excellent; in many cases it was far more interesting than the stuff we'd captured for the producers of *Barrier Reef.*

Most of the stories would need extra footage to be shot, both above and below the water, but it would be much less expensive than starting production from scratch. When I finished the treatment, I was very happy with it. It was exciting, it was whole and, most importantly, we thought it would be financially viable.

Ron and I were not completely untested as producers, but making an entire series was quite different from making a short documentary with network help, as Channel Nine had offered previously. We wanted to own this series and knew we weren't going to be offered a huge sum to make it, if they took it at all.

Nine did decide to make us an offer after we pitched the series to them. They also agreed to our terms, which were that we retained wholly international rights and even Australian rights after four years. As expected, however, with those stipulations in place, we were offered a very small production budget: just $9000 to produce twelve half-hour episodes.

We would certainly have to augment that budget ourselves if we were to produce something that was worthy of being picked up by NBC, which for Ron and I remained the goal.

Perhaps a few months earlier we wouldn't have had to dip into our savings to produce the series, but recently we had been given the opportunity of a lifetime. A very small amount of Crown land in Seal Rocks, the near-perfect little New South Wales diving spot fringed with national park that we'd been visiting since the 1950s, was going to be available for sale.

We'd been in Queensland shooting for *Barrier Reef* when we heard, so we immediately posted an open cheque to Mrs Horgan, the long-time proprietor of the only shop in Seal Rocks, along with a plea to purchase the best block she could for us.

She did just that, buying for us a large, elevated, cleared block just off Boat Beach, with views across to the ocean – for $2000. We were ecstatic about the purchase, but it also meant we were even less able to self-fund our new series.

After a short deliberation Ron and I decided that we would mortgage the house in Mortdale. We had great footage, we had built up knowledge in the marine world and also knew how to tell a story. It was time to bet on ourselves. We thought we could make something wonderful and, more than that, we thought we could make something lucrative. After all, as much as we wanted to make our own films, we also wanted to make our own money.

Of course, there would have to be sharks (*Jaws* was still some time away from release but interest in sharks had been piqued already) and we'd film at Dangerous Reef, with Alf Dean and Rodney Fox, and so we knew we would get our big great whites again. But that would only be one of the stories; there would be other episodes and those would be very different.

One of the most interesting episodes of the series ended up being about one of the most sedentary animals to which we've dedicated a documentary – an episode that was unplanned and cut out of whole cloth.

The episode came together while we were on a trip on the Coral Sea, out on the Chesterfield Reefs, perhaps two-thirds of the way to New Caledonia. We knew it was a wonderland out there, teeming with all kinds of marine life, big and small, and there were a number of shots we needed to pick up for episodes we were planning.

As I've already mentioned, we usually split the cost of chartering Wally Muller's new boat, the *Coralita,* when we needed passage on it, and in this instance we were travelling with some professional shell collectors, who had become particularly excited when they heard that we were planning to visit the Chesterfields. We found out later it was a name that had minor fame in Australian shell-collecting circles. Our contacts at the Australian Museum were also excited and, we would discover later, for the same reason: the possibility of finding what was then one of the rarest shells in the world: the Thatcheri.

At the time, the Australian Museum held perhaps the only example of that shell in the world. Chipped and faded, the shell on display looked wholly unimpressive but when one of the scientists told us the story of that specimen's provenance, it seemed far more interesting.

More than 150 years ago a British merchant vessel ran aground on the Chesterfields and one of the surviving crew members, a man whose first name is lost in the mists of time but whose surname was Thatcher, spent his time waiting for rescue by combing the beaches of the coral island looking for unique shells.

One of the shells he found was the shell that I saw at the Australian Museum, a specimen never previously catalogued in Western annals and, as far as I know, hadn't been seen since. The Australian Museum requested that while we were at the Chesterfields, we should try to pick up another Thatcheri shell and, if possible and more importantly for them, a live shell with the animal intact. To that end, they gave us a large black drum with a solution inside that would preserve both animal and shell.

We told them we would try. We were always happy to help out the museum if we could.

It was a two-day passage from the Queensland dock to the first line of Chesterfield breakers, and our first indication we were close to land was when birds began wheeling over the top of us with alarming cries. My skin bristled happily. This was a barely known and barely visited area of the ocean, and I was excited to see what we might discover.

There are eleven small islands in the Chesterfield cluster, and when we saw a small green-pancake spot of land, we loaded into the *Coralita*'s dinghy and headed for it. It is a unique feeling, standing on a speck of land in the middle of a vast ocean, unaffected by plastic, brick or smoke; calming and also pleasantly diminishing.

Ron and I took time to photograph some nesting gannets and then took a walk along a beach fringed with chirping frigate birds and littered with nautilus shells. The sounds on that beach were of purity; roaring waves, calling birds and nothing else – and then that pure mix of sounds was pierced with a wild, strangled yelp.

Ron and I went to investigate and there we found one of the shell collectors (one of the two named Bob) holding a broken and faded shell.

'It's here!' he said, very excitedly. 'It's going to be down there!'

It was a Thatcheri.

The next day Ron and I started diving the reefs, often filming sharks that were seemingly far more excited and aggressive than those on the nearby Great Barrier Reef. While we were doing that, the shell collectors were dredging under the boat, using a dredge that would pull items just under the sand into a net then up to the swim platform.

We were filming some wonderful sequences, but the collectors were having no luck and after a few dives Ron and I realised why. The Thatcheri lived well under the sand and very close to coral bomboras, not on the open sand. We knew that because we picked up a number on our first night dive.

The shell was larger and more beautiful than I had expected, with vivid red banding over a gorgeous cream base. It was elegant and striking to behold. We transferred the shell and animal into the black drum and on our next dive we found far, far more. When we surfaced we had perhaps ten Thatcheri. I immediately renamed the shell Ruby Thatcheri and as we got back to the deck of the *Coralita* we were met with envious eyes.

After I'd cleaned up and was headed towards the saloon to meet Ron, one of the Bobs pulled me into his cabin.

'Val, I'll give you fifty dollars for each of those shells,' he said.

That was very decent money in 1972, and I was considering the sale but thought I should speak to Ron about it before I made any guarantees. I told Bob as much and walked on to the saloon but was pulled aside by the other Bob into the galley.

'What were you talking to Bob about?' he asked.

'He offered me fifty dollars each for the Thatcheri.'

'That robber!' he said in disgust. 'I'll give you a hundred dollars.'

Ron and I met and conversed and agreed to sell most of his shells under the proviso that the animals be transferred into the museum's black drum. The shell collectors couldn't care less about the shells' animal inhabitants and the sale was made. I must add that all the shells we had put into the museum drum vanished after our first night dive. After that, we kept the museum drum in our cabin.

When we got back to land Ron instantly turned his windfall into a helicopter rental, filming out the side of the aircraft as it flew across the Great Barrier Reef. I kept my Thatcheri, selling them at a shell shop that used to exist in The Rocks in Sydney.

'How much do you want for them?' the man in the shop asked.

'Three hundred dollars?'

'Done.'

'Each.'

'Of course.'

I walked away thinking I had pulled a number on this man, but in reality it was quite the reverse.

I later found out that one of the shells from our expedition ended up being sold to John du Pont, heir to one of the richest families in the United States and a keen collector of rare stamps and shells, for US$20,000.

I can imagine the scarcity of the shell would have driven an obsessive like du Pont to a vastly overinflated price, and I never thought each shell would be worth such a huge sum, but mine certainly could have been sold for far more than $300. (In an aside, du Pont's obsessive focus turned to wrestling in the 1990s when he set up a wrestling centre of excellence at his estate. There he murdered Olympic champion Dave Schultz, in a strange incident detailed in the film *Foxcatcher*.)

I spent my shell money on furniture; wonderful, well-made English oak furniture, a rare luxury in a life that was wonderful but largely ascetic.

Both Ron and I got something more important than cash from that expedition though: we had a successful episode of our new series – one dedicated entirely to a marine animal that could hardly be more different from the great white shark.

This is what we wanted our series to be, about the scope and scale of experience that was possible off the coast of Australia. Not just a place of terrifying beasts, but also of interesting and wonderful adventure.

We had travelled to South Australia and made an episode about the great white but I was also thrilled to be able to dedicate an episode to the animal directly under the great white in the food chain. An animal that I can honestly say I would do almost anything for: the Australian sea lion.

I don't think there's anyone who has swum with an Australian sea lion who hasn't fallen deeply and completely in love with that animal. They are playful and kind, curious and loving and interesting beyond belief. In my long life of diving I've befriended many animals, but the Australian sea lion was perhaps the first aquatic animal that I ever realised could be befriended.

For the shoot we found a delightful colony of Australian sea lions at Hopkins Island, a short boat ride from Port Lincoln. There they were using the beach as a haul-out site and were waddling in their hundreds out of the water and onto the rocks, where they would rest or mate or perhaps conduct the former before the latter.

We filmed the animals on land first, and there they provided great heart and comic relief, waddling around like giant wet labrador puppies. When we filmed them under the surface of the water, however, they became something else altogether.

Below the water the Australian sea lion is fast and sleek and graceful. With that mobility the animal does not lose character, it gains it. Underwater they dart around you, playing quizzical games and they also play with each other. One of the greatest pleasures I've ever had diving is to dive with them. If I could only dive once again in my life I think it would be off Hopkins Island, South Australia, with the Australian sea lions, among a variety of sea grasses and plants.

South Australia is a wonderful place to observe the leafy sea dragon too: a sublime animal which can easily be confused for seaweed at a glance, but reveals itself to be majestic and unique, with near-translucent fins that propel the animal in a way that I have never seen another sea creature move.

Swimming with Australian sea lions is just one of the many pleasures one can have diving in South Australia. Queensland and perhaps more recently Western Australia get most of the recognition for being premium diving locations in Australia, but for mine I think South Australia is not only the greatest state for diving in Australia, but offers some of the greatest diving anywhere in the world.

We created three episodes in South Australia for that series, with the third being about cave diving – then a nearly completely unexplored activity.

The idea had come to us years earlier purely because of a sense of curiosity and pioneering spirit. While camping off the road and on our way to port we saw small access points to what seemed to be huge caves and caverns filled with water. We had heard from another diver that these caverns had been dived but only a few times. We'd never personally known of anyone in them, but we saw no reason we couldn't dive them. What would we discover down in the dark depths? There was only one way to find out: we ventured down there ourselves.

Those dives into caves around Mt Gambier remain as some of the eeriest dives I've ever done. One moment you are in a sundrenched field, with sun on your skin and grass under your feet and the next you're slowly working your way down a mass of seemingly endless darkness, sometimes your only link to the world above was a thin sliver of vertical light through crystal-clear water.

While those dives were very cold (especially since I'd started diving without a hood, my blonde hair and pink ribbon becoming part of my aesthetic signature), very dark and very quiet, they were also quite incredible in their own way. Of course on those dives we saw no colourful coral or playful mammals, but we did find blind and near-translucent fish, and bones and fossils of now-extinct animals that had fallen into one of those caverns many thousands of years ago.

These were, again, trips that benefited the Australian Museum greatly.

That particular episode used a great deal of footage that we'd shot in the mid-sixties, especially for a stand-alone documentary that was on Nine in 1967 called *The Cave Divers*. Another episode using mostly recycled footage was dedicated to a whale shark that swam past the coast at Sugarloaf Point in Seal Rocks.

Now interactions with whale sharks are relatively common, but I believe Ron and I were two of the first people to ever film the animal underwater and the images we shot were front-page news the next week in both Sydney's *Daily Mirror* and Melbourne's *Sun* newspapers.

It was a completely unplanned encounter. We were in the tinny filming something or other and the giant fish swam past us, all thirteen or fourteen metres of it. We were straight in the water filming, swimming as fast as we could, trying to keep up. When the shark disappeared we'd rush for the tinny, and race ahead while loading the film. We'd get back in the water, greet the whale shark and then get as much further footage as we could.

While the footage had nowhere near the overall stock and lighting quality of the *Inner Space* episodes, I think the television executives and audiences forgave us because of its uniqueness and the unexpected majesty of the animal being captured on film.

Some of the episodes were planned and also wholly shot for the series, like our search to find a route through Fish Rock Cave, an underwater cavern near South West Rocks in New South Wales, a site known then only to divers. It is a deep and dark underwater passage, with branching chambers leading to more branching chambers. No one knew then whether there was a route all the way through the cave but Ron and I had long suspected there was.

We thought the search for the route might be an interesting episode. With cost being an ongoing constraint, we arranged an above-water crew, shot the top and tail of the show with one ending showing success and the other disappointment, and then spent days mapping the main tunnel through the cave. Our lights' cabling was our tether back to the surface.

It took perhaps five or six attempts to get all the way through, but we did find an exit. Deep in one of the caverns we could see a shimmer of light in a small hole just big enough for a diver to fit through. I swam down. Our light cable was at its limit but the opening I was swimming through became brighter. Then I was in a narrow cave full of fish. When I was close to the exit of the cave, the roar of pounding waves shook the walls. We had managed it. We had found the exit. It was too turbulent to surface but a black coral growing near the entrance showed it must be about nine or ten metres deep. We were able to use our 'success' ending.

I've always loved Fish Rock Cave, in no small part because of the abundance of grey nurse sharks. My perception of this animal changed greatly over the years. As a child and young woman I saw the grey nurse as an adversary, an enemy, simply because I had been told that was what the shark was. By 1972, however, my own experience showed something quite different.

Over hundreds of dives with one of the species of shark most likely to be seen in my home state, I'd barely ever seen a grey nurse that had any interest in me. Not just that, I'd noticed that the grey nurse had teeth completely inconsistent with devouring large mammals. Unlike the great white, bull or tiger shark, which have large, arrowhead-shaped teeth, the grey nurse has long, thin teeth, best used to catch and hold small fish.

It seemed my understanding of the shark had changed, but the public's understanding hadn't. Every time we dived in a spot where we expected to see grey nurse sharks, there were fewer and fewer. This was true of many species, but at that time there was no more obvious symbol of oceanic depletion to me than the disappearing grey nurse, which was being relentlessly hunted by spearfishers and divers for no other purpose than to be able to say they had killed a shark.

It depressed me greatly when I thought of how the sharks were being killed. They were placid animals and would barely have recognised the danger of a macho man with a powerhead.

The *Inner Space* episode about this shark was called 'The Disappearing Grey Nurse'. I suppose it was the very first documentary we made with a strongly conservational bent. Perhaps in 2019 you may not think that that's a radical move, but in 1972 it was something of a quantum leap.

We made thirteen episodes for the series *Inner Space*. Channel Nine enjoyed the episodes, as we knew they would, and scheduled them to be aired. But what we really wanted was international sales, especially to an American network; ideally to NBC.

That we would have to wait on. We'd partnered with an American producer, Don Taffner, who was well known for bringing British comedies to American screens, to attempt a sale. But as he told us, what we were trying to sell was rather unique.

While we waited we kept working, of course; we couldn't afford not to. A week after *Inner Space* aired on Channel Nine we were working in the Coral Sea, on the boat that we'd had to share with those rugby players.

Those bastards, that carelessness. They called it poor luck, but of course they would. It was assault.

When I got back to Sydney from the trip where I had been thrown off the boat, I was in constant pain and having regular dizzy spells. I saw a specialist, who said that he would be able to fix my ear so that I wouldn't have any issues on land, but if I wanted to dive again I'd need an operation that required specific and expensive surgery in Los Angeles.

Of course I decided to have the surgery. I didn't know what my life would be if I couldn't dive, and I certainly didn't know what my marriage would be if I couldn't be Ron's diving partner.

It ended up being a very fortuitous decision, not only because the surgery was a success, but because of the by-product of a side trip I took to the east coast of the United States.

Stan Waterman, the man with the silver tongue, a friend we had made while making *Blue Water, White Death,* had been sending invitations over to stay with him and his wife and daughter in Princeton. As I was already going to Los Angeles, I thought I might see him and his family first.

Stan was, as always, lovely company but also, as always, directing attention and conversation to his favourite subject: Stan Waterman. Each night at his house we would have a slide night, with Stan holding court showing photographs and explaining, in his entertaining but profuse way, the origin of each image.

I had also brought some slides to show Stan, but they were only shown on what was planned to be our last night together when Stan's wife, Suzy, said she would like to see my photographs.

They were quite unique, those images. They had been taken on the Great Barrier Reef and in the Coral Sea, with many taken on the fateful journey where my eardrum had been knocked out. It wasn't the location that made them different, though; it was the subject and composition.

Back then, in the late 1960s and early 1970s, it was nigh on impossible to use flash in macro underwater photography and therefore many marine animals had never really been photographed in their natural environment. The difficulties were many in that endeavour, but the greatest problem was figuring out the lengths of exposure that would be required for shots of different distances.

Using his lathe and technical ability Ron created a device for my Mikonos camera, a series of geared rings attached to prongs that protruded past the lens. The prongs would gauge the distance between the camera and my subject; the camera was totally manual which allowed me to adjust the aperture and so on.

I would get perfectly lit and in-focus images every time, whereas other underwater photographers would get great results only when they had moments of good luck.

Stan was both awestruck and apologetic when he saw the images.

'Why didn't you show us these earlier, Valerie?' he asked, before imploring me to delay my journey west for a day or two so he could arrange a meeting with *National Geographic* magazine, then one of the world's great print publications.

However, I needed to get home so Stan, being the true gentleman he is, took twenty images to *National Geographic* on my behalf. He was going there for his own work but presented my images to the editor and picture editor. They contacted me, asking if I had more images of the same quality and of course I did. They then asked if I could take them to Washington DC to show them.

I was always interested in more work, but first I had to attend to my ragged eardrum.

The surgery and recovery were miserable, but made better by the fact that Stan had arranged for me to convalesce at the nearby Beverly Hills home of Jack McKenny, a legendary diver and underwater photographer in his own right.

I came home with an ear that I could safely dive with again and a deep and powerful yearning for my husband.

I'd been mildly perturbed by the fact that Ron didn't confront the men who caused my injury, and that he showed little sympathy, and in fact even some annoyance, that my ear had been damaged. As the plane broke through the clouds on the descent home to Sydney, however, and I saw my city, my coast, and anticipated seeing my Ron, that annoyance was gone.

Ron was a unique man, in the way that all interesting people are, and his responses to certain events were not always going to be what I would like or expect. Ron's emotions were opaque and would continue to be, but I decided that shouldn't colour my feelings.

I think of the lines from the W.H. Auden poem 'The More Loving One', where the narrator of the poem expresses the desire to be the more loving one if affection cannot be equal between two lovers. Those lines from Auden's poem are not exactly fair. I know my Ron loved me, even though he was not a man with the capacity to express it.

When I saw Ron again my heart soared and I think he was happy to see me too. He was very happy to find out that I was now able to dive without hindrance.

We went straight back to work and I was glad and relieved to find no physical pain or dizziness when I dived, regardless of depth, nor any afterwards. The only discomfort that persisted was trying to get our insurance company to pay for the surgery. The case eventually went to court and the insurance company tried all avenues not to have to pay out.

First they claimed that the surgery I took in Los Angeles was unnecessary, then they claimed that the surgery could have been done in Australia. When both of those claims were proven false, they tried to claim that a woman had no business being on a boat like the *Coralita* with the men we were travelling with. The type of injury I sustained should have been anticipated, they argued.

Their arguments fell on deaf ears and eventually they were forced to pay out the cost of the surgery and the legal proceedings. This was just as well, as Ron and I had financially exposed ourselves quite considerably in shooting *Inner Space*, and while we were working as hard as we ever had, we were somewhat cash poor.

And then everything changed.

Don Taffner had sold an American version of *Inner Space*, with a very fun jazz music soundtrack from Norwegian–

Australian composer Sven Libaek and narration from *Star Trek* actor William Shatner, to NBC; every episode, every story. It had also been sold for a considerable amount. We knew if NBC bought the series we should expect quite a bit more than the AU$9000 that Nine had given us, but we didn't know we'd be offered US$2 million.

This was a life-altering moment. Even after that number had been whittled down by partnership obligations and debts and tax, we had money to spend on a house, something I insisted upon. I insisted on very little in our marriage, but I was adamant that we move from our fibro shack to somewhere with a garden and real walls and living areas that would make me happy. Ron didn't really care where we lived and told me he had no problem with me buying a new house as long as it had space for the Land Rover and boat and a workshop where he could build and edit.

I bought us a mansion. A wonderful dream home in Roseville, a short drive from Manly Beach and Sydney's CBD, with a foyer itself perhaps as large as all the floor space in our old house and a huge garden that I'd soon fill with vegetable plants and orchards.

We also built a house on our Seal Rocks plot – a delightful two-storey fisherman's shack to which I have been regularly travelling ever since.

This was a time of near unbridled happiness; I could scarcely believe the life I was living. I was thirty-seven years of age, but I felt ten years younger. Ron and I had some money, not much but enough. We didn't have to sell fish for petrol any longer, but more than that, we had opportunity. We were becoming known and rather than having to hustle constantly to sell our footage, people were commissioning us.

I vividly remember being in our place at Seal Rocks after having driven up from Roseville and becoming giddy like a schoolgirl. In many ways, I felt like my life was just beginning. I didn't know what adventure would be on offer next, but I knew it would be good.

All those years of struggling to keep film in the cameras was at last paying off. True, we paid thirty percent to our agent and sixty-five percent in taxes but there was enough left over for new dive gear, a new car and a debt-free future. Ron and I were on a roll.

CHAPTER TEN

Fighting for the ocean

Jaws came out in 1975 and it changed film forever. There were queues around the block at every cinema that was showing it, and local media were reporting that as soon people finished watching a screening many were heading to join the end of the queue to watch it again. The movie wasn't just an unexpected hit, it was monumental and transformative; it started an epoch. The age of saturation marketing, wide release, back-to-back showings, and pervasive international release – procedures studios and theatres adhere to when releasing a modern blockbuster – really took off with *Jaws*. It took only a few weeks for the film to become the highest-grossing of all time. When it aired on American television, it captured more than half of all potential viewers. Before long, most of what was commonly 'known' about sharks had been gleaned from *Jaws*.

This became a problem. The general public became seemingly obsessed by *Jaws* and although it was a fictitious story about a fictitious shark many people believed it. Even today when I am shopping or on the beach people come up to me and tell me how *Jaws* changed the way they looked at the ocean. How they were even afraid of having a bath after seeing the film and will never swim in the ocean again. No matter how I explain that *Jaws* is a story about a shark that only existed in the mind of the author Peter Benchley it seems the human race wants to have a demon lurking in the depths waiting to attack. Similar to the way some people believe in witches, ghosts, and the devil living in the centre of the earth. Perhaps humankind needs a demon. It wasn't long ago that there were many different gods both good and bad who controlled our lives. Deities we could blame for misfortune. The biggest difference between the shark in *Jaws* and a dragon slain by St George is the shark in *Jaws* does exist. I have seen possibly hundreds of great white sharks. They are very big, powerful, well armed and amazingly beautiful. However they do not think like the shark in *Jaws*, revenge is not part of their thought process and they would never decide to destroy a large boat. True, they will swim up to a boat and test it with their teeth. I have seen this happen many times but it is mainly just a test. Lacking hands they investigate the unusual with their nose and teeth, something other animals do.

Unfortunately what many people believed about sharks, especially great white sharks, was due to a lack of understanding. *Jaws* changed the way they thought about the marine environment, especially sharks. This beautiful fish became a fiendish monster lurking off the beaches waiting to attack. This of course was not true but *Jaws* was so well made it seemed as though there really was a monster shark lurking beyond the breakers along every beach in the world.

I think perhaps there's never been such a time of carnage for shark populations as there was after *Jaws* came out. Men (and it was pretty much always men) would be greeted with cheers at any beach as they emerged from the water with a shark they had just killed or in Australia cut an already dead shark from the mesh shark nets off some beaches and thrust a spear through it. Regardless of the species, regardless of the size of the dead aninal, the men were treated like heroes.

In Australia of course it was the poor old grey nurse who bore the brunt of the offensive, but every shark was in the firing line, from the great white all the way down to the harmless hammerhead and bottom-dwelling bamboo and tawny sharks.

It seemed an open season had begun on sharks, and a thousand would-be Alf Deans, the South Australian fisherman Ron and I had worked with who claimed to have killed more than a hundred great whites, popped up around the world.

I was quite appalled. In 1975 I understood that people were going to kill sharks, for food or for bait or for scientific purposes, but I just didn't think people would be killing sharks as a pastime. Or even worse, in order to be seen as so-called heroes. One Australian guy claimed for every shark he killed he saved a hundred lives. Total rubbish but it got him on television claiming to be a saviour of swimmers, dolphins and sea lions. The fact that he harpooned dolphins to use for shark bait was never mentioned.

* * *

Ron and I were from working-class families. However, we had friends who could live whatever life they chose mainly because their families were wealthy. They did not have to pay off a mortgage or save to buy a better car.

We were workers, and while we had some financial security after *Inner Space* we were still functionaries, assets on a film crew. We loved our work and loved the ocean, but during those early years when a paying job was on offer we could not afford to turn it down.

After *Jaws* was released and became such an explosive success there was a great deal of work that came our way, some of it from Hollywood – and Hollywood was certainly where the money was. A very successful producer of exploitation and horror films called Dino De Laurentiis contacted Ron and wanted to speak to him about a film he'd greenlit in the wake of the success of *Jaws*.

The film was to be called *Orca* and, like *Jaws*, was to be based on a popular novel. In the novel the revenge-seeking orca hunts a sea captain who killed the animal's pregnant mate and unborn calf but for the film the producers wanted to start with a scene where the orca hunts and kills a great white, hurling the shark into the air, in a sequence it was hoped would establish a story about an orca that was even more vicious than a great white.

An animal that had the intelligence to hunt down the man who was his enemy.

Dino De Laurentiis was confident they could film the orca sequences at SeaWorld in San Diego by using dummies, as well as the living animals but the scene with the great white was another matter. Ron told Dino De Laurentiis that we would be able to get the shots he needed and we started planning another trip to Dangerous Reef in South Australia with Rodney Fox.

When we dropped anchor and started preparing to bait in a shark we found to our dismay we were not wanted. The local abalone divers had dropped several slaughtered bronze whalers around our anchorage. They were lying on the bottom where we had planned to work. Past experience had taught us that the best shark deterrent was a dead shark, preferably several days old. Among divers this was fairly well known.

Rodney became very nervous when he saw the carcasses. He still worked as an abalone diver and he had no doubt that this was the work of the local abalone fishermen, who were a very possessive and territorial bunch and, it seemed, didn't like us working in their area. There were no abalone in the waters around Dangerous Reef but the abalone divers wanted us gone.

Speculation aside, this meant one thing, in the immediate future; we were going to have to find another place to look for a suitable shark.

We decided to keep going west, where we planned to meet Hugh Edwards, a West Australian writer and self-styled shark expert. Ron knew Hugh personally and had worked with him on several successful documentaries.

Ron contacted Hugh who said he knew where we could easily find a great white. He told Ron that if we met him in the town of Albany, on the southern coast of Western Australia, he'd be able to guide us to a sizeable shark. Hugh towed his boat to Albany while we crossed Australia. We met Hugh and his wonderful wife, Marilyn, in a camping area where we rented a self-contained hut. The following day armed with the script, a gun, several spears and two orange floats, we launched Hugh's boat into the bay close to the Albany whaling station. There were about seven sperm whales buoyed off the flensing station waiting their turn to be dragged up the slipway into the work area. We drifted among the buoyed carcasses floating in the bay. We realised we were not the only vessel among the harpooned whales.

Whale catchers had hunted whales out from Albany for decades, towing the harpooned whales into the holding area adjacent to the flensing slipway. White sharks, lured by the smell of whale blood, would follow the vessel towing the day's catch into the bay.

Game fishermen would frequently fish for the great whites that, attracted by the free meal, were easy prey for a man with a hook on a line. There was plenty of bait, just a lump of whale meat was all that was needed and there were several tons of it floating around.

It didn't take long before a sizeable shark was already feeding on one of the whales. Hugh, with considerable skill speared it behind the gills, tethering it to our boat. The shark, feeling the restriction of the spear, spun away – unfortunately entangling the rope on the spear around the game fishermen's boat's propeller. Dragging the weight of both boats slowed the shark but although tethered to our vessel the shark was only slightly wounded. Before it could cause any damage one of the fishermen freed their propeller and the shark started towing our boat away from the kill zone. Realising what was happening Hugh took the opportunity to raise his rifle and fire a number of rounds into the shark. He thought this would kill the animal but the beast kept swimming, towing our boat backwards. Marilyn threw another spear but the shark although seriously wounded continued swimming. It was now towing our boat and two large orange buoys attached to the spears with at least four bullets in its body.

We thought for certain that the shark must die, but it swam on, making a great effort to reach the opening of the bay.

This amazed and devastated me. When I'd watched *Jaws* I'd thought the scene where Quint's boat was dragged by a shark pushed the bounds of believability. Yet here we were in a similar scenario. As our boat was slowly dragged towards the ocean, my heart bled. I could feel this animal's yearning and its desire to get to open water and freedom.

I'd not really felt this about the great white before. It was a long stride in 1975 to consider any large predatory shark as anything but a potential threat. My attitude to the grey nurse and other smaller sharks had long been benign. They were a part of the marine world, easy to accept. Watching this magnificent animal fighting for its life, for freedom against overwhelming odds, was distressing to say the least.

It wasn't an intellectual thing; it was a feeling, an emotion. I felt such yearning, I wanted the animal to win its fight for life even though I knew if we had not harpooned the shark it would now be dead, its jaws removed on the deck of a fishermen's boat. I felt real sadness and I feel it now pulling at the memory of such courage, such an uneven fight to survive. Sharks like most animals all have different personalities and this shark had the heart of a lion. It was with relief I watched Hugh shoot the fatal rounds in the shark, finally putting it out of its misery.

We towed the dead animal to another very isolated beach at a nearby national park, where we'd hired a crane and there we dropped the shark from a great height into the water, which, in reverse, would work as a shot of the shark being tossed into the air by the evil orca.

Except for a few underwater shots of me doubling for Charlotte Rampling, our part in the film was over. I never saw the finished product. It did not do well at the box office and then disappeared into the dustbin of cinematic history. *Orca* lacked the magic of *Jaws*, with none of the tension and class of Spielberg's directing or the brilliance of editing by Verna Fields.

My memory of the making of that film, however, lingered, along with my changed attitude to big and potentially dangerous sharks. I'd had an appreciation of the little sharks, and the placid sharks, that couldn't defend themselves but perhaps I'd not given as much thought to the big and potentially more aggressive sharks until *Orca*.

The truth of the matter was that no shark could defend itself, really. Not against man when man was dedicated to the cause. If someone went out to kill a great white, as we had, one didn't dive in the water and attempt to wrestle the shark. We killed from boats and with guns or spears. There was no reason to feel any animosity towards the great white because only in the rarest instances were we in the animal's hunting profile.

I suspected even the great white only killed humans because it was confused; thinking a surfer or swimmer splashing around on the surface might be an injured seal. Fishermen killed them, for what purpose – for their jaws, which might sit on a mantlepiece for a while before migrating into a box in the garage? For a photograph, with the killer grinning alongside the corpse? Or in our case one shot in one film, which came and went and was possibly forgotten afterwards by the people who saw it?

At the time that we filmed *Orca* almost every person in the world would have commended us for being part of killing a great white and yet I felt empty and disgusted. Throughout 1976 the shark slaughter continued, and on a scale that was becoming an issue for Universal, who were already planning on creating a *Jaws* sequel using extra footage that Ron and I had shot for the original film.

Some experts were suggesting that entire shark species could become extinct because of *Jaws*, so to combat bad press that threatened to derail what otherwise promised to be a lucrative franchise for them, Universal put together a visibility campaign about the reality of sharks. To that end they paid Ron and me to travel to the United States appearing on every talk show in the country and talking to every newspaper and magazine that was interested, explaining that man and shark interactions were never like the way they are depicted in *Jaws*.

The Mike Douglas Show and *The Tonight Show* with Johnny Carson and *Good Morning San Diego* (or whomever) were not, however, in the business of keeping sharks alive – they were in the business of prime time TV entertainment; the business of telling a good, short, snappy story while families in South Dakota gasped at Ron's shark footage as they munched on a pizza or sipped a Coke.

The story people wanted was one that was a bit like the one being told in *Jaws* and every question led to that.

The truth of the matter was that sharks did kill people, and when they were killed they were killed in the most gruesome manner. Being eaten alive has a terrifying ring to it, but sharks rarely eat their victim. They realise they have made a mistake and let go. Ron calls them shark biters not man eaters. That was the truth but people could see in their minds sharks who could work things out and tear boats and people apart vividly and without remorse. The flip side of that truth, however, was that being killed by a shark was a fate suffered by far fewer people than the number who choked to death while drinking orange juice. The first truth was vivid and bloody; it was something that stuck in people's minds, something people would think of when swimming, surfing or diving.

There were certain stories people wanted and, as a budding production entity looking for visibility and more work, we felt almost obliged to play along. Also, we did enjoy playing along. We had good stories. Our friend Rodney *had* been mauled by a great white, Ron and I *had* been bitten by lesser sharks. In each instance we and Rod had been engaged in behaviour that confused or aggrieved the shark, and we'd explain as much, but people heard what they wanted to hear. Perhaps we toured America to educate, but in the outcome of the shows we were there to entertain.

There was one thing I wanted to get across, however, and that was a plea for people not to kill sharks just for the thrill of it. I found that I was quite passionate when I spoke on the subject, truly hoping that something I said would save the life of a poor shark who might otherwise end up on the wrong end of a spear or with its brains blown out by a powerhead.

When I came back from America I was starting to realise that our attitudes to the marine world needed a revolution in thinking.

I've always thought regret is a pointless emotion, as all one can do is do better tomorrow but the thing about emotions is that you can only control them to a certain extent. I do regret that we'd killed sharks, and continue to regret the killing, even as the years go by.

You may have picked up this book assuming that I'm a 'greenie' or a 'do-gooder' and I have been considered such at times in my life, but that's not who I am, and certainly not who I was. I was a fairly standard, perhaps-a-little-right-of-centre suburban girl who developed an appetite for adventure, and found that adventure underwater.

What I didn't expect to find, under the waves, were friends, neighbours, confidantes, local weirdos, misunderstood villains and a whole cast of characters on the reefs and in the currents. As a young girl, I had been led to believe that fish and marine mammals were alive in the same way that a tree may be, but experience was telling me that that was far from being the case.

The great white we killed in Albany had a personality and I'll never know anything about it but that it wanted with every atom of its being to get to the open ocean. It wanted to be alive, free, rightful king of its domain.

It took me a while to understand that within species there was also a great deal of emotional variety. Perhaps all grouper shared characteristics, but some were timid and some bold; some became frustrated and others endlessly patient. Some of the animals had fantastic memories also.

I suppose the idea first came into sharp focus while we were filming the underwater scenes for the *Barrier Reef* series, which had us working in one area for an extended period of time. During half a year we started to learn many of the idiosyncrasies of all the individual species who lived, loved and bred around our work site. We learned that simply because an animal darted away when they saw us, that didn't mean the animal was less than intelligent. In fact, it often meant the opposite.

There were animals with which I developed casual relationships but also some with which I built up lifelong friendships. On the bommies out from Heron Island I met two moray eels, whom I named Harry and Fang, and whom I have been visiting for decades, probably more reliably at one location than any of my human friends.

They remember me; Harry and Fang are rather plain-looking moray eels. They were very shy at first, showing caution, retreating into their holes as I approached but a few handouts of old fish had the eels almost like best friends. Even if I haven't seen them for months or perhaps years, they remember me as an old friend and one small piece of fish has them sliding around me begging for more. I hug them as though one might hug the old family dog but never restrain them.

I became very protective of Harry and Fang, and also of a large family of potato cod that Ron and I discovered north of Cairns on the Ribbon Reefs. We went to great lengths to make sure the location of their home remained a secret for as long as possible. We had realised these magnificent fish lived in family groups selecting a suitable area for their home range. They wouldn't move location, which made them a target of game fishermen who feel proud at catching and killing a big fish even if that fish is harmless and friendly.

I suppose you only know about marine depletion if you are a diver and see it with your own eyes or a fisherman and you see the depletion in your haul. With incentives not to see what you don't want to see, fishermen can come up with the most absurd reasons and justification for more rapacious methods.

One of the excuses they had was that their fish (and they loved to call them 'their fish') were being scared away by divers and swimmers. Another was that they were being eaten by other species, and in the instance of Seal Rocks, by the fun-loving Australian sea lions.

When the sea lions started disappearing from Seal Rocks I simply couldn't countenance it. People killed sharks because of the misguided notion that there was an existential battle between them and us, but a sea lion? A lovely, playful, graceful mammal that loves to play with anyone in the water with them?

They were killing them because they thought they were eating fish they could sell, they were killing them so they could use them as baits, and one guy was collecting the pups so they could be sold to marine parks who would keep them as attractions for as long as they stayed healthy, which was never more than a few months, usually only a few weeks.

This state of affairs was distressing to me and I'd tell the fishermen that, and the reply would be that they weren't doing anything illegal and that I should mind my own business, sometimes with a few expletives peppered in.

It was true that they weren't breaking any Australian laws – almost no Australian marine animals were protected at that time – and I did mind my own business for a while. By this time we owned our small house in the tiny Seal Rocks fishing village. Ron and I did not want a war with our neighbours, but it galled me.

Seal Rocks was changing – not the land side of the waves as all the bush behind the small village was protected as national park, but the ocean side. Entire species were disappearing from the water we dived and snorkelled in regularly. There had been a time in the fifties when Ron and I had to stop our filming underwater at Seal Rocks in order to wait for schools of kingfish to pass that were so large they blocked out the sun. By the mid-seventies those fish were all but gone.

We were learning the behaviour of marine animals, and of the fishermen too. We knew that if a kingfish in a school was injured or trapped, the other fish wouldn't keep going as most species do, but would stop and try to help their wounded comrade. Now it seemed the fishermen did, too, creating traps that would use a captured kingfish as bait.

They were wiping out whole kingfish schools at a time, until there were no more schooling kingfish in the area, just a dozen or so swimming together where once there had been hundreds. Alongside species that were exceptionally easy to catch like the placid boarfish, the kingfish was soon all but gone from the area. I still see them and a newcomer to the waters around Seal Rocks would be delighted to see a kingfish or two but sadly they will never see what Ron and I took for granted forty-five years ago.

The fishermen were only concerned that they would have to start harvesting smaller and smaller breeding aggregations. They blamed everyone but themselves, never thinking about the inevitable time when the fish they relied on to earn a living would be so depleted fishing would no longer be a viable resource. I thought about it often. It wasn't just Seal Rocks that was becoming depleted, but most places we had been diving since the fifties. The Pacific Islands were being seriously depleted by longlining trawlers, mainly from Taiwan. The same was happening in the Indian Ocean and sadly the Coral Sea between Australia and New Caledonia.

Coming from a family of farmers, I had absolutely no ideological issue with fishing but it seemed to me that there was a major element of farming that the fishing industry seemed to be ignoring. To be a successful farmer one must reap *and* sow, but the fishing industry only had interest in the first part of the equation. They simply reaped, putting nothing back but the dead unsaleable so-called rubbish fish.

The conventional wisdom had always been that the marine environment would endlessly replenish itself, but Ron and I knew from personal experience that was no longer the case. We saw permanent damage to this environment being done in the name of sport or business and felt that certain species could disappear altogether from Australian waters, but I didn't say much to that effect. After all, I was simply a school-leaver and surely someone with letters after their name would be better positioned to protect the coastal animals.

Then one day my beloved sea lion was imperilled.

A sport fisherman who had seen Ron and me on television and had enjoyed the *Inner Space* episode about Australian sea lions, sent us a letter saying that he had just come from Montague Island off the south coast of New South Wales, where he had seen commercial fishermen shooting sea lions, presumably because they thought the animals were eating or scaring away their fish.

The fisherman said he'd seen five dead sea lions, floating in the water off Montague Island. I knew five dead was a catastrophe for that community. Sea lions were not numerous anywhere, and if their slaughter was to become a regular occurrence then, very quickly, my favourite marine animal would no longer exist. This had already happened at Seal Rocks and now it was happening at Montague Island. I felt compelled to do something and to my great surprise and pleasure, protecting the Australian sea lion was relatively easy. I did several radio interviews and wrote some letters to some powerful people I'd recently met, and shortly afterwards a motion was tabled by a very intelligent politician in parliament.

With no legitimate reason not to protect the animal that shared similar characteristics to those of a family pet, the motion was passed and quickly came into law.

I was ecstatic, not only because I thought I might once again be able to swim with the local sea lions, but also that I had proof positive that one person could make a difference.

Then the first death threat came.

'We all earn our living in the ocean and one day we'll get you,' the voice said. I still remember every word. He had called the house late at night and there was such venom in his accented voice, it can only have been a Montague Island fisherman. I wondered just how many fish he thought the sea lion could actually eat. After several more similar calls, I realised that the hatred was more about a woman having influence over what men could and couldn't do to wild animals they encountered.

The next animal I tried to get protected was the potato cod, and that was not such an easy endeavour. (The potato cod is actually a grouper but for some unknown reason Australians call them cod.)

As I mentioned, after finding the Cod Hole on the Ribbon Reefs, Ron and I hoped we could keep it from the game fishermen as long as possible. We knew they'd get there eventually. We hoped they'd show restraint when they did; after all, there is very little sport involved when killing a docile and inedible fish that is predictably in only one area on the reef and is also very rare.

All it took to end the restraint was a lean year in game fishing. Operators out of Queensland were bringing in American and German fishermen, guaranteeing giant fish: tuna and marlin. It was a big money-making concern and still is today.

These big-game fishermen had come a long way planning to catch a record marlin but that year the marlin were not to be found. The customers having travelled so far to catch a big fish were understandaby annoyed so the boat operators took their customers to the Cod Hole in Cormorant Pass on number 7 Ribbon Reef where they could very easily catch a giant fish. That each fish, alive and friendly, was now attracting dozens of divers who all paid for the privilege of swimming with a beautiful fish seemed to mean nothing.

They wanted the same fish dead on a line with the proud fisherman next to it.

All reap, no sow.

The battle to get the Cod Hole protected started while we were shooting a documentary called *The Wreck of the Yongala* about a magnificent wreck, and to tell the story of the *Yongala* and why we were making this documentary I first have to tell you about our friends Dick and Pip Smith.

Most Australians would know Dick Smith. An Australian like no other, Dick, and his wife, Pip, are self-made millionaires, having turned a small car radio business into a huge electronics retailing empire.

Dick is a fine pilot and the holder of many world aviation records.

We met at a party for Australians who had been on the Channel Nine show *This Is Your Life* and probably because we shared a love of adventure and the Australian wilderness we became great friends.

We often went flying with Dick and Pip, mostly around Australia. I loved seeing my country from the air.

They would come and dive with us sometimes too. Dick wasn't a passionate diver, but he was passionate about history, especially Australian history. I remember once when on the *Lindblad Explorer* (which I will come to later) we were visiting Pitcairn Island. It was a rather calm day and we decided to try and dive the remains of the *Bounty*. Normally, diving the *Bounty*'s grave due to big seas is impossible but we thought we might be able to do it. There was Ron, Dick, my nephew Mark and me. The wreckage was strewn between boulders and under ledges. All the bits we collected were sent to the Queensland Museum. If you ask Dick does he dive he always says yes, on the *Bounty*.

Dick is a champion for Australian business and Australian history, but also the Australian environment. This became a guiding principle in Dick's personal and professional decision making, and while he is an astute and very successful businessman, he is often driven by something more important than money.

This is possibly why he decided to fund Ron and me when we told him that we were thinking about undertaking an expedition and shooting a documentary in which we would try to find the SS *Yongala*, a passenger ship that, in 1911, sank off the coast of Queensland with all souls on board lost. Not only were the passengers lost but also the location. The disappearance of the *Yongala* became the biggest search for a missing vessel in Australia's history.

Launched in 1903, the *Yongala* was a modern steamship that, for many years, transferred passengers and goods from Western Australia, where a gold rush was underway, and Melbourne and Sydney and later Brisbane. When the gold fever started to wane, the *Yongala* was rerouted, and started to trade between Melbourne and Cairns.

On 14 March 1911, the ship left Melbourne on what would be its ninety-ninth and final journey. On 23 March the ship had entered the Whitsunday Passage and only hours after that a wireless message was sent out to all ports warning of a cyclone that would soon hit north Queensland.

The SS *Yongala* was due to be fitted with wireless communications, but the delay likely cost the lives of all 122 people. Moonshine, a racehorse whose body was later washed up on Cape Bowling Green, was all that was found.

For decades the fate and location of the *Yongala* remained a mystery.

In 1943 an American minesweeper looking for Japanese mines east of Cape Bowling Green fouled on what was believed to be a shoal. The crew marked the obstruction on a chart and moved on. Directly after the war a Royal Australian Navy survey ship steamed to the 'shoal' and, using new echo-sounding technology, mapped what looked like a sunken steamer lying on its side.

None of this particularly interested the military, so there was no follow-up but for the very few who were interested in such matters and had access to such information, they were starting to think the *Yongala* had been found.

The next evidence of the wreck came in the form of a well-worn Chubb strongbox. In the late fifties a local trochus fisherman had seen, through his glass-bottomed boat, what looked like the wreck of a steamer. Employing the help of a local diver, he managed to retrieve some items from the wreck, including a safe from one of the staterooms.

The fisherman hoped when he opened the safe he might find information about which wreck he'd found. All he found was sludge. Later, however, he sent the serial number of the safe to Chubb and they confirmed the safe had been sold to the Adelaide Steamship Company, who had installed the strongbox into the purser's cabin on the *Yongala*.

For more than a decade after that the *Yongala* had been discovered, but not really found. If any divers looking for gold or artefacts had been on the wreck they kept quiet. No one else had been down there, as far as anyone knew. The location of the ship was somewhat known but completely unexplored; no one had seen what the ship looked like now. Ron and I thought it was a mystery of the sea that would make an interesting documentary. With diving becoming increasingly popular and the location of the wreck roughly known, we knew it was only a matter of time until it would be visited and picked clean by wreck hunters. Ron felt – and I agreed – if we could get there first we could mark the location exactly, salvage what the Australian and Maritime museums might be interested in, bring in the local dive operator who might open the wreck up for responsible commercial visits and also film the whole thing for television. We also planned to invite some marine scientists from the James Cook University in Townsville.

Dick Smith thought all that a very worthwhile exploit and decided to fund the whole venture.

We found it exceptionally easy to find the wreck. Our dive vessel, the *Reef Explorer*, had been fitted with side-scanning sonar, making it easy to locate a large obstacle on the sand. The ship stuck out, a huge dark shape on a pale plain … We anchored off the bow. The water was clear but a strong current was running. I was first in the water. It was like entering a frozen moment in time which had been seized by the sea and placed like a monument on a marine desert.

The ship was still largely intact; with the hull and superstructure overgrown by static life. She seemed quite undamaged although now she listed to starboard. Nature in her wisdom had taken a steel, brass and glass man-made vessel, and turned it into a living vibrant reef. Some of the deck had fallen onto the sand, but the main structure was still intact. Sea snakes, hawksbill, loggerhead and green turtles, spotted eagle rays, Queensland grouper, trevally, barracuda, and numerous schools of smaller fish could be seen darting in and out of the wreck. Clouds of small orange altheas swarmed through the super structure. Platax (batfish) hung in a shimmering cloud above the dining room.

Five giant Queensland groupers were living in harmony with a school of red bass under the bow.

As I swam through the corridors an eel peered out of a toilet then disappeared into ancient plumbing and a wobbegong shark lay like a carpet guarding the galley door. It made my heart soar to see that which had been so violently snatched from the world above now reborn as a new home for sea life.

Over a number of dives we retrieved a fine haul of items that are now on display in various museums in Brisbane, including portholes, lamps, fittings, crockery, jewellery, bolts of cloth, bottles of cough medicine, a wonderfully ornate hand basin and the ship's whistle.

We had brought with us a marine archaeologist from the University of Queensland and a dive operator working out of Townsville named Mike Ball. We told them that, after our film, there would likely be great interest in the wreck and that it was their responsibility to make sure its integrity was maintained responsibly.

Before we headed back to the shore Ron set a large brass plaque into underwater cement telling all future divers that this wreck was protected under the Commonwealth *Historic Shipwrecks Act 1976*, which had recently been enacted, and that all creatures and artefacts on the wreck were now protected under 'look but don't touch' laws.

Unfortunately last time I visited the *Yongala* this plaque had been removed along with many of the brass fittings in the staterooms. Also the ceiling of the dining room was missing, pulled off during bad weather by a dive boat that had anchored on the roof.

At the time the plaque wasn't, technically, stating an absolute truth as the Commonwealth Act only extended to wrecks that were older than the *Yongala*, but when the film came out there was enough political pressure to have the Joh Bjelke-Petersen government in Queensland enact a state law to cover the *Yongala*.

We were still salvaging the *Yongala* when Peter Brisco, a game fisherman more responsible than his friends, sailed his vessel to where we were diving to tell us that game fishermen were fishing at the Cod Hole, which was two days' travel away. Peter told us that he had seen three of the big fish, slaughtered for the pleasure of a fisherman, floating in the pass and he had found the sight very upsetting. Peter was also a diver and had spent time with the fish so he had an affinity for the big friendly fellows.

He felt strongly about them being slaughtered in the name of sport.

When we finished filming the wreck we turned the *Reef Explorer* north heading for the Cod Hole. To my dismay I found that the thirty-two fish Ron and I had counted when we first discovered the sight in 1971 was down to twenty-three.

Another season of game fishing and the reef might be depleted of big fish completely.

I started petitioning immediately that the Cod Hole become a total fishing exclusion zone. Just the Cod Hole, nothing else. Just one square kilometre out of over 2000 kilometres. All the migratory fish could still be caught out of the exclusion zone, in the vast expanse of the rest of the Great Barrier Reef, but this exclusion zone meant these wonderful potato cod and the reef that was their home would be protected.

After the success I'd had in protecting the Australian sea lion, I thought it would be relatively easy to protect such a small area of such a huge reef. I contacted every government and private body, large and small, that I thought might be able to help, from the Queensland government, Queensland National Parks and Cairns Council to the Great Barrier Reef Marine Park Authority (GBRMPA) and Cairns Professional Game Fishing Association.

All said that, in principle, they agreed with my argument that this small area should be protected. None acted. I could tell that there were people within each organisation who wanted to help, but there were powerful men in the fishing industry that effectively tied their hands.

Unlike the unaffiliated commercial fishermen who were forced to stop slaughtering Australian sea lions, these game fishermen were mostly wealthy men who loved to catch and kill large fish for sport. They had friends in business and government. It wasn't that these men necessarily wanted to fish the Cod Hole, but they saw the exclusion zone as a slippery slope. Again, I also think they really didn't want to be told by a woman what they could pull out of the water and kill. The old idea that a woman's place was in the home, preferably stuck in the kitchen, still held true less than forty years ago.

The months dragged on and there was no action but I refused to give up. I contacted all of our media friends and gave radio, print and television interviews explaining what I wanted and why.

On Mike Willesee's evening television show I argued that the game fishermen who were killing these potato cod were stealing a national resource, and also stealing from the future. I claimed that, if maintained and protected properly, the Cod Hole could be a desirable destination for divers from across the world for generations to come.

I brought footage onto the show that Ron had shot of me interacting with the giant fish, feeding them and having them playing around me. That was what made the impact, I think. It's always the imagery that makes the impact. It's one thing to be a talking head on television asking people to protect a family of fish, it's another thing showing footage that people can disappear into; imagining themselves where I was, or perhaps their children or children's children enjoying a pristine coral reef with a rare animal like the potato cod.

I ended the Willesee segment imploring viewers to write their own letters; to their local member of the state government of Queensland. The public profile of the issue was raised, but it seemed the effect had only been to raise the ire of the game fishermen.

Ron and I on our way back from Antarctica had a wonderful *Lindblad Explorer* stop at the Cod Hole. We put down the Zodiacs and had about ninety people in the water snorkelling and diving. The fish were swimming around the visitors, posing for pictures. Everyone was having a marvellous time.

Quite suddenly a game fishing boat came roaring through the snorkellers. The operator and three other men yelled abuse at me, promising me they were going to kill every one of the potato cod.

I was frantic. It had been eight months since the *Yongala* expedition and I feared if the area wasn't protected soon, it would be too late. I'd been writing endless letters and, in a moment of desperation, I decided to call Parliament House in Canberra. No one in Queensland was willing to be helpful. Not National Parks, the Queensland minister for the environment or GBRMPA, who in my opinion should have been totally on my side.

I asked to be put through to the federal minister for the environment and of course I wasn't put through. I did, however, eventually end up speaking to his secretary. She remarked that I seemed upset so I told her my story. She knew who I was and had even heard about my campaign to protect the fish and their home.

'Don't make another phone call, Mrs Taylor; I will find you a champion,' said the woman.

She did, too. That night at about 8 p.m. the phone rang. A man told me he was a member of parliament and he would be my hero. He asked me not to use his name as he had nothing to do with the environment, tourism or fisheries portfolios, but simply believed in what I was trying to do. He tabled my request and I did the *Good Morning Australia* show that day, screening me hand-feeding the big friendly fish and asking the general public to write to the government on behalf of the special grouper. The director of the Great Barrier Reef Marine Park Authority came to our home in Roseville. He was concerned that I had created such a stir. He promised me if I could get my one square kilometre it would give him the toehold to make the biggest marine park in the world. He promised to get the protection of the Cod Hole passed into law – and did just that shortly afterwards.

My champion is possibly still alive so I respect his wishes for anonymity but if he's reading this, I say to him thank you greatly. I can't say the Cod Hole is thriving, but there are enough giant fish at the location for it to still be a vaunted and oft-visited dive site almost fifty years after Ron and I came across it.

As mentioned earlier, only Australians call grouper cod. The true name of the fish is *Epinephelus tukula* (potato grouper).

The *Yongala* is even more popular and visited by thousands of divers each year, coming from around the world to what many dive operators describe as the 'Townsville *Titanic*'. With the site being reasonably close to Townsville, and far more accessible and with much greater sea life than that found around the *Titanic*, personally I don't care much for the moniker, but I do like the fact that the site is enjoyed by so many people, and also brings income to many dive operators in the area.

Later, when we sold our film about the *Yongala* we tried to repay Dick and Pip but they refused. They said their reward would be that the *Yongala* was protected and bringing employment and money to the region. They got both.

Our film *The Wreck of the Yongala* has now become a lasting historical document of a ship that vanished with complete loss of life.

The Smiths have two daughters. They were darling little girls who I was extremely fond of.

There was a good-sized pool in their garden. I decided to teach the girls to dive. By today's standards they were too young but I'd had my nine-year-old nephew Jono down ten metres posing with grey nurse sharks and he loved it. Hayley and Jenny were maybe too young but they, like their parents, had a keen sense of adventure so I took dive equipment to their house and taught the girls the basics. Both enjoyed the experience but Hayley fell in love with diving, as people do sometimes, and has become a lifelong enthusiast. Later I helped Hayley get a job working as a lecturer on eco-vessels and to this day she's a close friend whom I dive with whenever we both have the time. We've travelled across the world together, I consider her family and I'm not sure I have many memories more treasured than those I have of sitting on the back of a boat drinking a gin and tonic with Hayley, our stories bouncing back and forth from many days of glorious diving.

After the protection of the Cod Hole there were a number of successful environmental initiatives I either instigated or was involved in, often in concert with films Ron and I made. Along with Dick Dennison we produced a documentary about oil exploration around Ningaloo Reef off the north-west coast of Western Australia and helped ban drilling near that little wonderland. We also managed to stop mining concessions that had been established in the 1970s and 1980s without any government or public oversight infringing on the parts of the Coral Sea that are Australian territory.

Ron and I made no friends in the mining industry in that period, but who needs friends in the mining industry? We made few friends in commercial fishing circles either, and that made life a little more complicated as there were quite a few fishermen who lived at Seal Rocks, where we spent a great deal of our time.

Perhaps the conservation effort I'm best known for is the one I've had the hardest time with, and that's the conservation of the shark.

Unlike the Australian sea lion and the potato cod, the shark was not an animal that could be embraced and loved, or at least the perception was that it couldn't be. Many also couldn't understand the importance of the shark in marine ecosystems. Just a few years on from 'the only good shark is a dead shark' mindset, it was hard to explain that sharks living on reefs were essential for the health of a reef, and that small changes in the balance at the top of the food chain wreaked monumental changes at the bottom of it.

Experience had taught Ron and myself that an abundance of sharks meant an abundance of other marine life. Nature had designed a web of life around different marine ecosystems each with its own well-balanced life forms. There was always a diverse complexity of static and free swimming individuals and nearly always the main predator was the shark. Actually very few of the over three hundred shark species are true predators, as we know them. Most lead static lives sitting around on the bottom or drifting mouth open through clouds of plankton.

It was also hard to explain such concepts, though. It was hard to explain how imperilled sharks had become. It took some time for people to realise that it was often the largest animals that were most at risk of extinction and to come to terms with the idea that a large, strong fish with razor-sharp teeth can be far more imperilled than smaller and less-impressive animals.

Sharks grow slowly, mature late and most of them produce relatively few offspring – so relatively few deaths due to perils such as longline fishing and drift-netting can punch a hole in a species population that takes an age to repair, not to mention how overfishing affects an animal that requires a large volume of fresh food to survive.

Another idea that was hard to explain was that there is nothing macho about killing a shark.

After the release of *Jaws*, I read in the paper that a Queensland fisherman had gone out and slaughtered eight tiger sharks, claiming to have saved hundreds of lives. In New South Wales I saw, with my own eyes, men coming out of the water with dead grey nurse sharks, slaughtered by a power-head, to the delight of the families on the beach.

They posed like heroes for photographs. Sometimes the sharks were dead in the nets when they found them – such is the power of a macho man claiming 'Look how brave I am, I have just killed this terrible man-eating animal', while holding up a harmless grey nurse or hammerhead.

The poor grey nurse was sometimes killed and left to rot on the bottom. Sometimes it was carved into fish fillet–sized pieces and sold to fish and chip shops. Either way it was a tragedy. There are few more placid animals than a grey nurse shark which, before being killed, would not have understood that the killer was a threat, nor would they have any intent towards the killer other than to swim by them. In most instances, these men might as well be killing a domestic dog or cat. And yes, it was almost always men.

I started writing letters suggesting that the grey nurse

shark should be protected in Australian waters, explaining that the animal was not only perfectly benign, but in many ways quite lovely. It seemed this idea was a bridge too far. My letters were ignored, or so I thought, and the grey nurse was still in the sights of every macho man with a powerhead, a snorkel or a tank.

I went on a number of talk shows to publicise the plight of the grey nurse, and quite often the producers would bring on a commercial fisherman to debate my points, as it seemed they were always against any species protections. In one instance, on I think Mike Willesee's *A Current Affair*, I remember a fisherman explaining that he'd seen hundreds of grey nurse sharks and that they couldn't possibly be endangered.

I asked the man where he'd seen these 'hundreds' of grey nurse sharks and his reply was 'Bass Point'.

'When?' I asked.

'June.'

'And you were diving?'

'Snorkelling.'

'You know you're a liar?' I asked. It just came out.

The man started spluttering with anger and poor Mike Willesee tried to move on.

'Why would you call me a liar?' the fisherman demanded, refusing to allow the conversation change.

'You'd have to be a pretty good snorkeller to get to ninety feet,' I said. 'I've seen the grey nurse at Bass Point and that's the only depth you'll find them at.' Also in June they have all migrated north to warmer water. I felt like yelling, 'liar, liar, pants on fire', but I was on TV so not a good idea.

When it came to sharks, however, it didn't seem to matter how many televised interviews I did well in, many people still reacted to sharks with revulsion and fear.

After *Jaws* was released Ron and I became friends with Peter Benchley and his wife, Wendy, and joined them on a number of international diving trips. During one (which one I can't quite remember) Peter told us that if he'd known how people would react to his book and the ensuing film, he never would have written the damn thing.

'I fear the fight to save sharks from massacre will be one that we'll be fighting our entire lives,' he said. And now it seems he was right.

There were minor successes along the way. For instance, the grey nurse was eventually protected, becoming the first shark in the world to have this status, and I was gratified to find that, when New South Wales Fisheries published a small book about the protection, they published sections of my letters that I'd sent them over the decades. The protection was a great start, but only a start. The species to this day is one of the most threatened in the world, with an estimated fewer than 1500 grey nurse sharks left in the waters of eastern Australia.

Perhaps now most people understand that the bulk of shark species are completely benign and that even the species that can kill are highly unlikely to do so, but more sharks are being killed than ever before, and in a far more brutal manner.

It's estimated that 100 million sharks are currently being killed every year, with the great bulk being hauled onto a boat, de-finned with a knife and then dumped back into the ocean, panicked, disoriented and condemned to a slow and horrible death. I've seen videos of the finning and it makes my heart sink.

The killings are for one purpose only, the supply of shark fin soup; a Chinese delicacy that dates back to the Ming dynasty and which is said to represent health (although all health claims have been debunked), virility (so too all claims of sexual potency) and power.

The way these fins are being obtained and the scale of the harvest is a major issue for those who understand the importance of, and who care about, shark conservation. Some species of shark are being hunted close to extinction and the rise of the Chinese middle class could mean that the scale of the problem could become far more extreme, destroying not only shark species that have lived on this planet without alteration for tens of millions of years, but shark tourism, which is sustainable and is now about to surpass the shark fin trade in some areas as an important money-making industry. One shark alive will attract thousands of divers paying for the great pleasure of swimming with a shark year after year. Dead it will give one pot of tasteless liquid (shark fin soup is flavoured with chicken stock).

Thankfully steps have been implemented though. Shark fin soup is no longer served at official Chinese banquets and most luxury hotels in large Chinese cities have stopped serving the soup. Many countries around the world, including Australia, have signed into law limits on shark fin harvesting and transport, but sadly it still goes on. Even in Australia.

The reality is, however, that laws need enforcement to mean anything and to ensure enforcement, visibility and vigilance are key. For instance, the Costa Rican government voluntarily became a signatory to a pact of American countries which banned the sale, trade and harvest of shark fins in 1999. A few years after that, however, Ron and I were diving off the Cocos Island in Costa Rica, one of the best places in the world to swim with hammerhead sharks, and we saw a boat that I was convinced was hunting hammerheads – then and now very much a threatened species.

I told Ron and the men on our boat what I thought and they said it was a matter for the Costa Rican government. I felt I couldn't just sit around knowing that it was likely some of the sharks we'd been swimming with that day had been hauled out, de-finned and horribly and slowly killed.

That night when the anchored finning vessel had no lights showing I had the crew man on the *Mystic* (the dive boat we were on) row me across to the sleeping, dark, finning vessel in a dory. The only camera I had was my underwater Mikonos and a huge Farallon flash designed by Bob Hollis.

I quietly and surreptitiously took photos of the fins – hundreds slung in the rigging and more laid out on the deck. I took my shots and was creeping down from the cabin roof when I tripped on a loose rope, dropping the huge flash. In a second I found myself surrounded by little men in baggy bloomers all staring in amazement at this woman in a pink wetsuit standing on their deck. I bowed, hands clasped together saying, 'Australie, Australie scientist' then climbed with great speed into the dory. The crew man rowed away as though his life depended on it. When things had calmed down and the fishing boat's lights were out I rowed back and left a flagon of red label scotch on their deck. It would be a nice surprise, a sort of 'I am sorry for what I am about to do'. I know it wasn't much but it was something.

I sent Costa Rican National Parks the images of the hundreds of drying shark fins on the deck of the boat. The photo was front page in the local newspapers. Years later I met the head of Costa Rican National Parks. He had come to Vanuatu while we were there and thanked me for sending the letter and finning photos to him. He said that my photos had been used to raise the money needed to install a ranger station on Cocos to police the activities of illegal fishermen. A friend, Mike McDowell, bought the rangers a motor for their dinghy so they could move faster. Before that they'd had to row after the illegal fishing boats. Today Cocos is a much-visited dive destination. The hammerheads still drift in huge schools around the offshore rocks, whitetip reef sharks by the dozen cruise around the rocky reefs during the day and hunt for sleeping fish at night, manta rays drift past, beautiful, majestic, a delight to the diver. The water is always clear, the island with its rainforest and waterfalls is like no other. It pleases me to feel I played a part in protecting this lonely paradise into the future for there is no doubt that the integrity of Cocos both above and below water was on the brink of falling into the destructive path of greedy so-called progress and becoming just a memory in the minds of the few who had seen it as nature had first made it.

CHAPTER ELEVEN

A woman in chain mail

I've had quite a few sharks bite me over the years, with two of those bites requiring medical treatment. Ron was only ever bitten once; by a wobbegong in Seal Rocks in 1980 while he and I were making every effort to have the shark bite me.

The lead-up to that moment started on a morning in 1967 as we were preparing to shoot on the Great Barrier Reef for the Belgian scientific expedition. There are many shipwrecks along the Great Barrier Reef. Most of them have been stripped of all saleable non-ferrous metals but just south of Lizard Island we came across several divers working on a fairly deep wreck. The divers were all wearing chain mail butcher's boning gloves to protect their hands against injuries from the metal they were cutting through. Ron swam over for a good look at the gloves. When we surfaced we drove our tinny over to the work barge and asked about the gloves. I asked Ron what he was thinking. He told me he was wondering if a suit of metal mesh might be able to protect a human against shark attack.

Chain mail is not a new concept. Medieval fighters wore it as protection against arrows, swords and spears. It went out of fashion after the invention of the crossbow.

Over the next twelve years Ron brought up the idea from time to time, but when in the company of men with PhDs and landlocked offices he was usually told the idea was a bad one. They would argue that the bite power of a shark's jaws would crush the wearer's bones, regardless of whether the teeth pierced the skin or not.

Ron and I were not so sure. We spent a lot of time with feeding sharks, and while many species had power in their jaws, they didn't seem to have the intense pressure most expected. Our experience was that sharks tore their prey apart, using torque from their bodies; they didn't bite cleanly through an object using jaw pressure. Although the idea was brought up several times we were too busy working on different filming projects to do much about it.

Still, experts were experts.

The idea of the shark suit came to the surface again and stayed there when, on the deck of the *Lindblad Explorer*, Ron was speaking once more about it, this time with a young American diver named Jeremiah Sullivan. He was intelligent, energetic, respectful, good looking and we liked him a lot.

Jeremiah was a good diver. He agreed with Ron and me about the bite power of sharks and thought that the right suit using the right material would give excellent protection against attack. Ron had asked about the boning gloves all those years ago and, all these years later, he remembered the company who had made them – Whiting & Davis in Massachusetts, in the United States. We had since learned that the company had a number of products utilising the mesh used for the boning gloves.

Knowing that, we didn't think a request for a whole suit from the material would be a completely strange one, but we also knew it would be an expensive piece of gear. The hundreds of links in each seam would need to be hand welded. At the time, a mesh glove cost about eighty dollars. A whole suit would cost thousands.

The weeks dragged while Jeremiah attempted to get funding, and Ron became doggedly convinced that the suit would work. Eventually we decided we would just pay for the suit ourselves, sending Ron's measurements to Whiting & Davis along with a large deposit.

We saw this outlay as an investment. We would make a film about the suit, and the testing of it, and we would sell that film, like we had the *Inner Space* series. First Ron planned to have a suit made for himself. He would test the suit and if it provided the type of protection Ron thought it would, we would have a second suit made to fit me. A blonde girl being bitten by sharks is far more marketable than a man in the same situation. In the iconic *Jaws* movie poster, it didn't feature a middle-aged man with a shark heading his way.

When the first suit arrived, Ron had a real struggle getting into it. We had sent the company Ron's wetsuit measurements, without factoring in the tensile difference between neoprene and mailite (as the company called their mesh).

Although Ron could get into the suit, he had no chance of diving in it. It was perfect for me, though a bit baggy. My first tests were in a swimming pool. I found the suit surprisingly comfortable. Previously I had been concerned about the extra weight. It wasn't an issue at all. In fact, the suit without the gloves ended up weighing six kilograms, which was roughly the amount of extra weight I would require when wearing my thick wetsuit to be neutrally buoyant underwater.

Ron and I decided we would skip the pre-camera tests and go straight into finding sharks, with me as the test subject. We first tested the suit off Moore Reef in the Coral Sea. We employed Wally Muller and his launch the *Coralita* for the trip, and when we were ready to dive we trailed a long line of dead, dismembered and bleeding fish. The sharks came quickly, a school of grey reef sharks big enough to bite me. I was in the suit and slipped into the water in a flash; amid a feeding frenzy of blood and flesh I waited to be bitten.

I waited and waited, but the sharks all rudely refused to attack. Sometimes they would bump me then turn away as if I had hit them.

We tried again and again, at different sites in the Coral Sea, with different sharks but they all refused to bite me, no matter how close I got to them while they were feeding. Following one unsuccessful dive after another, Ron and I sat silently in the saloon of the *Coralita* until Ron said what I'd been thinking.

'Valerie, I think you may have to force yourself into the mouth of a shark.'

I needed no persuasion. At Holmes Reef, about seventy kilometres from Cairns, we attracted a number of whitetip and silver tip reef sharks. As I fed the sharks by hand, I tried to force my arm into their open jaws, but even that didn't work. They all baulked, jolting their heads away and then swimming off.

It was frustrating and we were a long way from having the film we had imagined. By then we had ordered another suit, which Ron had redesigned and had Whiting & Davis make specifically for me. This suit would look better and provide greater safety, provided that I ever managed to get one of the sharks to latch onto the damn thing.

Jeremiah Sullivan came to Australia to see if he could help, and we drove from Sydney to Seal Rocks for another try. We had always planned to try the suit out there at some point, regardless of the success in the Coral Sea, because in Seal Rocks we knew we could find grey nurse and wobbegong sharks, both species with long, thin teeth. We wanted to know if those teeth would go through the links in the mesh.

After our Coral Sea failures, we thought it unlikely that a lovely, placid grey nurse would bite me, but we knew the wobbegong to be quite an irascible character, and thought the species might bite if excited and provoked. We anchored off Seal Rock, a lump of granite about fourteen kilometres off the coast and well known for its shark population.

Wobbegongs, unless annoyed, are a placid bottom-dwelling shark. They have bitten a few divers, generally when the diver has reached into a cave for crayfish and not noticed the shark lying on the bottom. There was a nice mature wobbegong lying between two rocks. I did everything I could to get that shark's teeth on my arm, even rubbing fish flesh all over it. The shark flatly refused. I cornered it and fed it and led the fish to my fish-covered arm, which I offered over and over, but the animal just wouldn't bite. He did not like the mesh and would have nothing to do with me. However, he was becoming very annoyed.

Suddenly the animal darted forward while opening its jaws, striking not to eat but to show displeasure. The shark didn't bite me, despite me being covered in fish flesh and wearing a brand-new chain mail suit, nor did it bite Jeremiah, who was wearing Ron's old suit. It bit Ron, who was filming and wasn't wearing a mesh suit at all.

I could practically hear the cursing, even though we were all ten metres underwater. The shark had attached itself to Ron's elbow and wouldn't let go until he dragged the huge fish towards the surface.

Once the shark released Ron's arm I could see blood oozing from a line of holes in his wetsuit. Ron's elbow had a few lacerations that required stitches, and he was quite annoyed with himself, but at least now we were confident that we could get a wobbegong to bite. Now all we needed was for the shark to bite the right person.

It took time, patience and further care that the cameraman wasn't within striking distance of an agitated shark. We got some good bites in the day that followed; some on Jeremiah's arm and some on mine. In each instance, the teeth did not pierce the skin, nor did they come close to crushing human bones.

Soon we had all the footage we needed and considered the tests a success. It was time to try the suit out against larger and more dangerous sharks.

That American summer Ron and I were invited to travel to the United States for a shark-tagging competition to be undertaken off San Diego, and we thought this the perfect opportunity to test the suit further. The competition, arranged by a local research centre, was similar to one we had been involved in a year earlier; we were to tag as many oceanic blue sharks as we could in a certain time period, with the whole thing filmed by CBS as a 'special spectacular'. The main reason for the competition was a scientific one. All the tags were numbered and displayed a phone number. It was hoped that the tags from any sharks caught by commercial fishermen would be returned to the scientist who was conducting this research.

The tagging happened around a cage inside of which cameramen filmed. The oceanic blue shark was known to attack seemingly without serious provocation, and I'm sure the American network was hoping for some bites, but there were none. All those competing were professionals who had previously worked with blue sharks without incident.

Ron and I came first in the competition, winning by one tag; the American team came a close second. Afterwards our attention turned from trying not to be bitten to the opposite.

We were confident that if we amended our behaviour we could provoke the blue into attacking. Oceanic blue sharks, like the oceanic whitetip sharks we dived with in South Africa, had a reputation as an opportunistic attacker, and we just needed to exploit that behaviour. To that end, Jeremiah worked with us again, and another marine biologist specialising in shark behaviour named Fay Wolfson also joined us.

Usually when working with the blue shark we would use fish mince, which would give the sharks the smell and taste of fish but wouldn't excite them into a feeding frenzy. Large pieces of fish – well, any meat they could chew on – would have the sharks competing with each other. On this trip we decided instead to use whole fish, a real meal that would create a sense of competition and excitement in the animals.

It worked. It took little time for the blue sharks to start trying to bite me. It was a very strange feeling, seeing a large shark, its black eye staring into mine as its teeth chewed into the mesh. Only when the impact of the shark's teeth jolted my arm, violent and powerful and with a grinding, industrial sound, did my evolutionary instinct for survival kick in and I thought, What if the shark decides to drag me down? The ocean floor was several kilometres below.

There was a moment after I felt the first bite when the first shark and I locked eyes. The nictitating membrane of its jet-black eye flicked back and forth. The metal seemed to confuse it but the fillet I had stuffed under the mesh on my sleeve to entice the shark into biting oozed fish aroma into its mouth. For a moment it seemed to wonder – while I wondered too – whether I was food. The shark knew there was the taste of fresh mackerel and I knew he could not get it.

Luckily for me, the suit worked wonderfully. I teased the predators into several attacks but after the first bite I felt all-powerful. I enjoyed watching the sharks watching me as they clamped onto my arm time and time again. Afterwards there weren't even any marks on my arm where the shark had bitten. Ron shot some incredible footage, with the blues chewing on me regularly. The whole process also meant Ron and I managed to learn a great deal about sharks when they attack. Once they had chosen to investigate, no manner of splashing and activity could dissuade them from trying to test the disturbance and, as I said earlier, lacking hands, sharks generally check out the unusual with their teeth.

This was all very useful information, perhaps especially for those caught in a shipwreck, because the blue shark, like the oceanic whitetip, had a history of devouring survivors who ended up unexpectedly afloat in the middle of the ocean. I noticed one interesting pattern. Every shark that bit me hooked in his smaller bottom teeth before dropping down the top teeth.

The next day we moved to Scripps Trench, an area famous for the shortfin mako shark, not only the fastest shark in the world, but one of the fastest animals. Makos look like small great whites and can swim at about seventy-five kilometres per hour. They do not have the triangular saw-edged teeth of many dangerous sharks but they make up for it in speed and lack of fear. Ron wanted to see if the suit would hold up to an attack at such an incredible pace. After the experiences I'd had only twenty-four hours before, I was very confident the suit would hold up, but Jeremiah, who was also suited up, was less so.

He needn't have worried – not about the mako sharks anyway, because there were none to be found. The blue sharks at the trench were a little more difficult to deal with.

The day before, our blues had obediently attacked the arm in which we held fish, and we thought that behaviour would continue, so I just wore the tunic and hood of the suit. The pants made me a bit overweighted and I could not relax while in the water but had to keep flippering. Of course, a shark then attacked from the bottom and behind me. I had disrespected the first rule of shark safety: always be most concerned about the shark you can't see.

The blue didn't attack with hungry intent, instead it was just seeing what I was all about. Three of the shark's bottom teeth penetrated my wetsuit and buttocks. I had a few small puncture wounds, a little blood but the greatest damage was to my confidence. I couldn't stop thinking about what these sharks would do if they attacked my legs with the lust they had attacked my arms.

On the next dive the sharks attacked with even greater action than before. One of the sharks even bit my hooded head, the excitement of which was mitigated when I readjusted my mask and saw that Jeremiah was coming to help instead of taking photos.

Ron had always said that if I was having trouble with a shark he would keep the camera rolling, and that he would expect the same from me. It seemed Jeremiah worked to a different code, and that had cost him a dynamite photo. Regardless, it was an incredible day. Another idea that had previously existed only in Ron's head was out in the world, fully formed and now tested and proven. We had amazing footage, too, ready to be put into our documentary.

The mesh suit had proven all Ron's expectations as a success. Today it is used by divers who work with sharks all over the world, some wearing the full suit and others a mesh glove that covers only the arm.

An opportunity for a third blue shark expedition came from Hollywood and, as you have already read, Ron and I were not ones to shy away from an opportunity.

The offer had come from Alan Landsburg, a prolific American producer of scripted and unscripted movies, who was working on a series called *Those Amazing Animals*, a spin-off of *That's Incredible*, to be hosted by Burgess Meredith, Priscilla Presley and Jim Stafford. Alan was interested in an episode on the blue shark, and Ron and I told him we would have no problem providing him with footage.

We went out with an above-water film crew a week after our documentary filming finished. Unlike that trip, which we funded ourselves, this Landsburg production involved a considerable budget. This extended to a well-known dive boat called the *Sand Dollar* and also a fully professional crew, which included our friends Howard Hall, a wonderful filmmaker, and Marty Snyderman, who was to be one of our shark wranglers. We also had on board Fred Fischer, an expert diver brought in to be the dive buddy of actor Chris Atkins. Chris had expressed an interest in diving with sharks and Alan Landsburg was pleased at the idea of having a well-known young actor included in the cast. I had taught Chris to dive in Fiji while working on the feature film *The Blue Lagoon*.

He had been a fast learner but his experience with sharks did not go beyond Coral Sea whitetips and grey reef sharks. Chris was looking for something a little more adventurous.

Chris had been especially excited about the prospect of diving with blue sharks. However, sadly, at the last minute, he'd been dragged to Salt Lake City to promote a film. But we still had an extra professional diver in Fred Fischer, which is always a help.

Normally the sharks are at their peak of activity during the early afternoon, but it looked so good Howard had suggested we have lunch before midday, and start the underwater filming earlier than usual. I was having lunch when Howard called out, 'Sharks off the stern!' Ron and I dashed out and started suiting up. There was a contract next to my plate but there were sharks; no time to bother with a contract. I was not wearing the mesh suit, although I had it with me. Landsburg wanted me to look vulnerable. We could see a dozen or more sharks behind the boat cutting to and fro in the chum line.

It was an overwhelming scene. There were two makos off in the distance and numerous blue sharks. They filled the clear ocean water with their sleek dark-blue bodies. More blues arrived and by noon there were more sharks than we could count swimming around the boat. On several occasions we noticed one shark biting another shark simply because he was in the way, and they paid constant attention to the small bait cage, chewing uselessly on the wire as they blundered about seeking entry. Underwater visibility was superb, over thirty-five metres, and the water, though very cold, was a touch warmer than usual. Conditions were pretty near as perfect as a diver could hope for in the open ocean.

We had been teasing the sharks with whole mackerel tied on a cord. The mako sharks in particular were keen performers, lunging at the fish with surprising ferocity. During this time, I tried to count the sharks, but upon reaching a count of twenty-three I gave up.

The cameras were reloaded and it was decided that Howard would film Ron and me as we entered the water. As always, we divers were joking among ourselves. 'Looks like I might film my first genuine shark attack today,' said Howard. 'As long as it attacks you and not me, I don't mind,' was my answer.

Once Howard, Marty and Fred had submerged, we threw a few nice mackerel chunks off the swim platform, concentrating the sharks into the area where we would enter the water. I went first, followed by Ron. We had no safety divers, preferring to rely on each other rather than a third person, a system that always worked well. It was exceptionally clear. The scene was stunningly beautiful. Down and out as far as we could see, sleek shapes, blue against blue, cruised lazily around. There must have been in excess of forty blues ranging in size from 1.5 metres to 2.5 metres. The makos fortunately were no longer around. Howard, Marty and Fred could be seen about fourteen metres down. Marty and Fred were busy with their short bang sticks beating away sharks.

Back to back they were protecting Howard and themselves with more than usual vigour. The sharks seemed unusually persistent, but more curious than aggressive. Howard was filming us. As their exhaust bubbles shimmered in ever-increasing spheres towards the surface, a shark attracted by their movement snapped uselessly at the silver shapes. Seconds later, I was too occupied with my own snapping sharks to continue observing the bubble biter. Ron indicated for me to feed the fish I was carrying to one of the sharks circling my head, but for a few minutes I was too busy fending them off to concentrate on feeding them. My new six-millimetre-thick orange wetsuit contrasted brilliantly against the ocean. I looked up and saw Ron beckoning me towards the surface. He was not using underwater lighting and wanted to make full use of the sun's light by working about six metres down.

Sharks constantly approached, but I hit them away with my fist. They seemed faster and more aggressive than usual, but I wasn't worried; in fact I was pleased. Conditions were so good, the action fast. Everything was better than normal. I thought, Wow! Alan Landsburg is going to get a super piece of film.

As I neared Ron, two good sharks came towards me and I decided to feed one. I was concentrating on getting the composition right, using the mackerel as a lure to lead the shark towards Ron's camera lens, when at the last moment the shark lost interest. I must have teased him too long without reward for he swam away in a bored fashion. I offered my fish to the second shark, holding it near his mouth.

Everything seemed normal. Howard with his plume of bubbles, Ron, the sharks – even the one on my leg didn't look at that moment to be particularly out of place. Then I reacted.

Instantly I began to hit the shark. I grabbed his nose and tried to push him off my leg. There was no horror or fear, just annoyance that the shark was so persistent. On the fourth hit, he reluctantly withdrew his jaw. I saw the gum followed by white saw teeth retract through the thick orange neoprene. Green blood gushed out, clouding the water. I knew the wound was deep. The shark dashed away. I grabbed my leg, holding it tightly, trying to stop the bleeding.

My middle finger sank from sight, swallowed in the wound on my leg. I tried to pull the torn neoprene over the bleeding gash.

Suddenly Howard was there, and Ron. I surfaced and called to the above-water camera crew. 'Start filming. I've been bitten and I think it's deep.' I found myself being escorted back to the *Sand Dollar*, thirty metres away. Someone was helping me – Ron or Howard, I think, but I can't remember too well.

There was some difficulty getting me from the water as the boat was rolling and my leg was not working properly. I can remember demanding to be allowed to climb the ladder by myself, realising I couldn't, then calling for assistance. Everyone was trying to help. Never have I seen so many worried-looking males. I stood while my air tank and weight belt were removed. Blood that had been invisible on my wetsuit spread in a bright pool on the deck.

They lay me down. Ron held my leg up. I lifted up the torn piece of wetsuit and felt sick at what was there. All that steak-looking stuff couldn't be my leg, I thought. Ron tried to roll the suit leg back to see the extent of the bite and stopped, horrified. He tried to cut the suit away with my leg knife, but it was too blunt to penetrate the nylon lining. Someone handed him a sharper knife. My lovely new wetsuit was cut up, destroyed, ruined, and after only ten minutes of wear. 'You have really done it now,' said Ron. 'It's a bloody mess.'

My leg looked horrible, but there was no pain. Howard immediately offered to stitch it up, but I wanted a plastic surgeon, not a diver. I heard one of the crew saying helpfully, 'Don't worry, she is an Australian and they're bloody tough.'

Weeks later, I asked Howard why he wanted to stitch the wound. 'It looked so awful hanging open, I just thought it should be sewn together quickly,' Howard answered. It was a typical Howard Hall thought. Let's get the thing fixed.

Howard came with a roll of cotton wool, which he wrapped around my leg, sticking it in place with gaffer tape. Ron just sat holding my leg and muttering, 'What a bloody mess.' Meanwhile, our skipper, Bill Johnson, was on the radio calling the coast guard. I had Howard pour a bucket of fresh water over my hair. I would have liked fresh water poured over all of me, but that would have been impossible. Marty, wanting to help, gave me an orange to eat. The men carried me to a raised section of the deck as the waves were beginning to break over me.

There was still no pain, just numbness. I was more worried about going to hospital all salty and with no nightie than about my leg. Then I made a mistake. I decided to move my leg. A terrible cramp knotted my calf and I could hardly keep from screaming. It took several minutes of total concentration to force my leg to relax. Ron was trying to pack a travel bag for me. He seemed dazed and couldn't do it properly. I kept calling instructions as to where my clean underclothes, lipstick, and so on, could be found.

It's funny looking back on what I wanted. Firstly, my face cream, brush and comb, then laxative (the thought of a bed pan makes me instantly constipated), make-up, underclothes. My favourite red leather purse containing over $500, my few bits of jewellery. I kept on to Ron until he had everything together.

The coast guard was already in the air when Bill radioed, and was expected within minutes. All moveable objects were cleared from the decks, lest they blow away when the helicopter arrived. It's difficult and dangerous to pluck someone from the rocking deck of a boat. One slight mistake could lead to disaster. The helicopter (it was a big twin-bladed job) arrived. It looked most spectacular. I lay there, now helpless because of the cramp and the pain it had triggered. The *Sand Dollar*'s crew was around me. All wore life preservers in case I fell into the sea. A metal stretcher dropped on a cable from the helicopter. It swung a little before making contact. I was amazed at the precision with which everything happened.

It was not pleasant as I swayed away from the *Sand Dollar* and all those friendly men. I felt vulnerable and lonely. The great orange helicopter whirled above me like an awesome insect that had trapped me with its web and was sucking me into its body. Even the coast guard men looked alien in their flying suits and helmets, like smaller insects within the larger one. There was an instant of real fear when I thought I would not survive, then I was inside the insect's belly and efficient hands were releasing the straps that held my stretcher to the winch. The wind was freezing; I was still wet from the sea. Seconds later Ron swung through the door, carefully curled up in a wire basket.

By now my teeth were chattering. The helicopter lifted, the door was shut and I was on my way. In fifteen minutes I had been transferred from a vicious primeval world whose inhabitants had not changed in 300 million years to the epitome of technical efficiency and human consideration.

There was no lining in the rescue vessel, or perhaps I should say it was lined with cables, wires, lights, lifting devices and first aid equipment. A young man with nice brown eyes took my pulse and tested to see if my toes worked. He peered into my eyes with a bright light. 'No shock,' I mouthed at him through the noise. 'I want a plastic surgeon please.' This performance was repeated every few minutes, both by him and me. The metal stretcher was cold. It dug uncomfortably into my back and buttocks; however, the attention I received was professional and reassuring.

As we flew the pain increased. It became difficult to lie still. Although I was covered with a blanket, I was still very cold and could not make the helmeted young man leaning so attentively over me understand that I was freezing from the underneath, not the top. There was nothing for it but to concentrate on relaxing my leg and on not going into shock even though I was so cold. This kept my mind busy until we landed twenty minutes later at the coast guard heliport.

At the hospital, Michelle Biner was waiting with smiles, tears and sympathy. How nice it was to see her. Michelle is a fine diver, excellent photographer and qualified nurse. Howard had contacted her using the *Sand Dollar*'s radio asking her to try and get me the best plastic surgeon possible. Fortunately Michelle is friendly with one of the finest plastic surgeons in California. Realising speed was essential, she left her job and went to find him. Dr Merton Suzuki was donning his jogging shoes when Michelle arrived at his home. He agreed to come immediately.

The University Hospital's resident plastic surgeon came down. He was not in the least upset when asked if another doctor could sew me up – in fact, he seemed relieved as he had another appointment within half an hour. The emergency room was becoming crowded with friends and other interested personnel. It looked more like a party than anything else. Dr Suzuki arrived and went straight to work cleaning the wound. (He wasn't very impressed with the cotton wool stuck to everything.) The shark had made a very neat cut though my thick wetsuit. My retaliation to its attack had without doubt saved my leg from further damage and possible permanent mutilation.

Meanwhile, Ron had arrived with a distressing piece of news. My bag, with all its contents, had been stolen from the waiting room.

People were wonderful. SeaWorld rang and offered help. Ray Keyes, their top ichthyologist, came to the hospital and offered not only help, but also his jacket as all my clothing had been stolen and I had nothing to wear. Columbia Pictures rang and offered help. Chris Atkins came rushing to the hospital full of concern and held my hand. Alan

Landsburg offered help. In fact everyone did help, just by offering.

All I could think was: if one ever has to be bitten by a shark, do it in the USA. From the *Sand Dollar*'s crew to the coast guard, to the ambulance, to the hospital and Dr Suzuki and my many fine friends, the care and attention was overwhelming. With all that help no wonder I recovered quickly. In four days I was walking with crutches, in nine days without them, and in three weeks I was back in the water.

I don't know whether I am tough or not, but what happened to me was an accident. The shark did not attack me in the true sense of the word. It bit me, and there is a world of difference between an attack and a bite. Sharks in general merely bite people. If they attacked, no one would ever survive, for they are king of their environment and we, out-of-place intruders, helpless against their agility, speed and razor-sharp teeth. I was fortunate. My shark was only a little larger than me. If it had been a four-metre great white, this story would have had a very different ending.

The type of shark that bit me is an inhabitant of the open ocean throughout temperate zones. They are a deep-water shark, not found in shallow water close to beaches or human habitation. I sought out the shark in the initial stages, not him me.

Working with sharks is part of my business as an underwater filmmaker. Just as a racing car driver or a jockey must expect that some day they could have an accident, so too did I. I bear no malice towards the shark and I hope that other people reading my story understand this.

I will continue working with marine animals for as long as I am able to dive. It was Ron's and my living, our pleasure; in fact our special way of life and I will keep doing it until the day I die.

As I had not signed the contract with Alan Landsburg, while recuperating I made several demands, the most important being that after four years the footage of the bite would become the property of Ron Taylor Film Productions. Alan Landsburg very reluctantly agreed to everything we wanted, with one caveat; we must go back to the dive site where I'd been bitten and finish the shoot. I had no problem with that.

The rest of that shoot went off without a hitch. I was very happy to get back in the water, and very happy to see the blues again, and while I couldn't tell which was the naughty girl who'd had a nibble at my leg, I would have been happy to see her, too.

We all make mistakes and we all have regrettable moments of distress and weakness. Thanks to my wonderful plastic surgeon, no lasting harm was done. We had shot some dynamite footage for *Those Amazing Animals*, and a useful beat in our story about the creation of a shark-proof suit.

The bite made Ron and me more determined to prove its worth. The suit demonstrably worked against oceanic blue sharks, but more tests would be required to consider the suit an absolute success.

Ron and I decided to go back out to the Coral Sea. This time we were going to test the suit quite differently. Rather than just being in the water with fish carcasses, I was going to dress in the mesh, putting fish in the spots where we wanted the suit pressure tested. We would soon discover this is a very effective method of getting a shark to bite.

If anything, this method was perhaps a little too successful. We attracted some five- and six-foot (1.5- and 1.8-metre) whalers and a large whitetip. Quite quickly they were in a frenzy, attacking the bait fish hanging ten metres below the surface. I was constantly bumped. It felt like I was being beaten by a gang of strong men, taking blows from head to toe as the sharks tried to get to the fish, and yet I could tell that no teeth were penetrating the suit. Then one of the sharks hit my face.

I felt pain and my mask filled with water. I tried to breathe but my regulator had been knocked out. With fuzzy vision and no air, I tried to push the sharks away, searching for Ron in the haze, but sharks surrounded me. I tried to feel for my regulator, but it was nowhere to be found. In this moment, I was far closer to death than when the blue had nibbled me.

Ron was filming and hadn't noticed me struggling in the frenzy of sharks. My lungs were burning and my vision started to darken. I am not prone to panic, but I could feel my fingers twitching without telling them to do so. I managed to push the sharks off and did a free ascent to the surface where Alex Muller, our surface assistant, was waiting to help me.

Supported by Alex, I climbed into the tinny, panting and bleeding. There had been many bites, but only three had penetrated my skin, just under my chin on the edge of the suit. They weren't serious wounds, but we had some seriously good footage.

Weeks later, when we got back to Sydney, an X-ray revealed that the tip of a shark tooth remained in one of the wounds in my chin, a few centimetres away from a nerve. An operation was offered, but I declined. For nearly forty years, that tip from a shark's tooth remained in my chin. I rather liked always having a little bit of shark with me, but the tooth has now disappeared.

Even though I had been injured, both Ron and I were happy with how the suit was holding up. There was pressure when bitten, but not a pressure that would damage a limb, and as far as the threat of puncture wounds went, we hadn't seen any noticeable damage on either suit or diver.

Looking at the footage Ron had captured, I knew we almost had a wonderful documentary; we just wanted to do one more test. We wanted to try the suit against the great white.

There was no shark more powerful, no shark with larger teeth or greater bite pressure. If the suit held up against an attack from a great white, then it could be universally deployed. We were confident that the suit would protect against any species of attacking shark. Our theory that a shark's power was not in bite pressure but in the ability to tear flesh using torque had proven true in all our tests so far. We were confident even the bite pressure of the great white wouldn't crush the bones of whomever was wearing the suit.

Ron and I had many discussions about what we would do and we decided in this instance, caution would prevail over boldness. We would use a dummy in our first great white tests and observe the reaction from the shark. We were both worried the shark would simply carry me or anyone else in the suit away.

The first great white we attracted was perhaps four and a half metres, typical of the area, but far more excitable than most we'd worked with previously. It patrolled and prowled for a short time before attacking the baits, tearing a few free then disappearing below.

Having attached a steel trace between the boat and dummy, we hurled the dummy off the end of the boat. We didn't rub flesh on the suit or stuff it with fish. We wanted to see if an unprovoked great white shark would attack a human-shaped dummy floating in the water.

A couple of quiet minutes passed, then in a gush of spray the shark exploded from the water a few metres away from the dummy before disappearing again.

As the last of the spray landed on the deck and quiet returned, Ron and I shared a confused look. The shark hadn't touched the dummy at all, and this was quite out of character for a great white; it had just leaped out of the water like a mako then disappeared.

Those moments of confusion were shattered when the water in front of us exploded again. This time the shark took the head of the dummy in its great jaws and violently tried to remove it. Having no success, the shark dived sharply, dragging the dummy to the extent of the steel cable. A minute passed, and the dummy resurfaced, the tethering cable still intact.

We were keen to see what damage had been sustained, but also to figure out why the shark had exhibited such strange behaviour. We pulled the dummy up onto the deck and could see the suit had held up wonderfully. There seemed to be no big puncture wounds, which is not to say a human would necessarily survive an attack like the one the dummy had experienced. Before the dummy disappeared below, the shark had shaken it like a dog with a cloth doll in its mouth. The violence was extreme. I thought about the small puncture wound I had suffered on my chin, and the size of a great white's tooth. I decided I was not going to test the suit against a great white.

As far as the aberrant behaviour we had seen in the animal, we never figured that out. Ron wondered whether an electrical charge between the boat's motor and the suit had agitated the shark, but we didn't know, and we wouldn't be doing any further tests.

It would be extreme folly to test the suit with one of us in it, because there was potential to hurt not only the human subject but also the shark. If I was ever attacked by a great white shark I would rather be wearing a mesh suit than not. Had someone been in the suit during the attack we witnessed, they might have survived; without it they most certainly would have died.

Regardless, I still saw the suit as an undoubted success. Ron and I sold our film documenting the suit across the world, and we also produced a picture book called *The Great Shark Suit Experiment*, which was published a number of times and in many territories. That success benefited not just us; after the release of the film we started seeing mesh suits, or parts of mesh suits, across the world when people engaged

After witnessing salvage divers wearing chain mail butcher's boning gloves to protect their hands, Ron wondered if a suit of metal mesh might protect a human against shark bites. Here we are testing the prototype. It was a strange feeling watching a shark biting onto my meshed arm. Luckily for me the suit worked wonderfully.

Jaws started as just another job. We had no idea of the success it would become.

Top: Me and Roy Scheider on the set. *Middle*: The cage Carl Rizzo was supposed to be submerged in.

Bottom: Steven Spielberg, Roy Scheider, Richard Zanuck, me and Ron.

Top: A photo of me with one of the 'Bruces', the name given to the animatronic sharks used for some scenes in *Jaws*. *Below left*: Ron was an innovator and very clever in creating underwater housings for both still and movie cameras. He really was a genius. *Below right*: The open jaws of a real great white shark. This shot was taken at Dangerous Reef, off Port Lincoln, South Australia when we were gathering footage for *Jaws*.

Above: On the set of *Blue Lagoon.* Left to right, Brooke Shields, Ron, and Christopher Atkins.

Right: My very handsome husband.

Top: Filmmaking is not all glamorous. This is Peter Gimbel, me, Ron and Stan Waterman on the deck of *Terrier VIII*, an ex-whaling vessel.

Left: Working with bull sharks in Fiji.

Below: The lights that dazzled everything were hard to handle but were essential for capturing night-time footage of the sharks feeding.

Above: Me patting a great white – sharks on land worried me much more than any I encountered in the ocean.

Below: Meeting local tribespeople in Asmat, Indonesia – that's Mick Jagger in the blue shorts. Francesco Boglione, a good friend, is on the far right.

Left: Arthritis may make it difficult, but I still paint and draw most days and I am still diving as much as I can.

Below: Me with my darling nephews, Mark (*left*) and Jono.

in dives where they were likely to encounter aggressive or feeding sharks.

After that success we dallied in another shark protection suit, far less expensive and less cumbersome, but also, we found, far less shark-proof.

A notable American marine scientist had been on a media blitz saying, with great certainty, that all sharks were terrified of banded sea snakes and therefore also terrified of banded black-and-white wetsuits. Features were published in *National Geographic* and even *Time* with his banded suit that supposedly repelled sharks, and he was filmed swimming towards a pack of feeding sharks, shedding an overcoat to reveal his banded wetsuit and giving a satisfied look to camera as the sharks all scattered.

I wasn't so sure. The film was shot around Lord Howe Island, where there were no banded sea snakes and as far as we knew there never had been. It seemed to me, by the behaviour of the sharks, that they were scattering because of the frantic motion of the overcoat being shed, not because of the banded suit.

But if it worked, great! We made our own banded suit to investigate the theories of this Great Man and it seemed to Ron and me that the sharks simply couldn't see me when I was wearing a banded black-and-white wetsuit. This was concluded after a number of tests where I, in a banded wetsuit, was placed between a pile of fish and the sharks. They kept pushing into me as if I wasn't there.

Undertaking these tests was the only time I ever drew my diving knife on a shark. One shark, confused by this unspecified mass between him and his food, tried to chew his way to the bait. I tried to push him aside, but I was wedged in and thought for a moment the only way to deter the animal might be inflicting pain, but thankfully I wriggled out without having to use my knife.

Afterwards we spoke to our friend Dr Eugenie Clark, a truly wise shark behaviourist, and she wasn't surprised with our results. She had been doing behavioural tests with sharks. The sharks in her tank had learned to push a yellow button for food. When she banded the buttons black and white the sharks went crazy trying to find them.

I suppose those adventures with shark-proof suits were, alongside the exhilarating oceanic whitetip dive we did while shooting *Blue Water, White Death*, the most dangerous shark dives we did, but these incidents made me comfortable around potentially dangerous sharks.

Sharks bear us no ill will, and have no interest in killing or eating humans. Usually they would bite us out of curiosity to learn what we were and when they did, they usually seemed to regret it, suit or not.

* * *

When travelling around the world I knew the greatest danger was not in the water but out.

Ron and I once spent months working in the Arabian Gulf shooting the underwater segments for a Gulf state TV series. It was a wonderful and fascinating experience, and we met some truly sublime individuals but unfortunately those lovely men with whom I spent happy dives, banquets and weeks will have to give way in these pages to a group of men whose names I don't know and hope are now dead.

It happened in the Empty Quarter, the huge sandy dead space that passes as a border between Yemen and Saudi Arabia.

We had been shooting nearby and the dhow we were working from had lost power and was being pushed towards a reef. As a precaution we took the film and cameras ashore by tender. We had to make a few trips, and I ended up waiting with some of the equipment on an empty sandy shore so the tender could go back for more.

I hadn't been alone on the beach long before a group of men appeared, first as specks on empty dunes, then I could see they were men wearing local dress, a gang of perhaps eight or perhaps a dozen. I tried to greet them but they were not there for greetings. They circled me, not dissimilar to the way certain sharks might regard a shipwrecked sailor.

These men had no interest in the equipment. I was a female alone and wet sitting on a camera box surrounded by sand.

I tried to keep the men in my line of sight, but it was impossible. If three or four men were in front of me, just as many would be behind. They pinched first, darting towards me and grabbing at my hair or my clothes, pulling hard then retreating.

They became more brazen, their pinching more personal.

I just needed a weapon, something hard and heavy. I picked up my very large Farallon flash and prepared to bash out the leader's brains. I was not the girl I had been, stuck in a phone booth out the front of East Sydney Tech. I was a woman who had fight in her – and I was ready to fight. I could kill if I had to kill. If the worst for me was coming, then so be it, but I was ready to fight to my last.

It didn't come to that. An old man emerged from the haze out of which the aggressors had first appeared. He stood next to me, and the young men, mumbling to each other, drifted away. The old man just stood there. He stayed with me until we could see the tender, with Ron on board, approaching through the surf.

This man then left without a word. I gave him no thanks as thanks were not what he wanted.

I told Ron what had happened but made no mention of what I knew they were planning and what I was planning to do in return; it was enough just to know the strength I had to draw on, if perhaps I ever found myself in a truly desperate situation. I did ask Abbas, one of the crew we'd worked with, where the men had come from but he had no answer. They were not Bedouin but village men and that is all I knew.

CHAPTER TWELVE

The little red ship

I first started to paint when I was four or five years old. I don't remember exactly when I began, but it was certainly before I went to kindergarten. My mother was the instigator, of course, one day coming back from the butcher with meat and white butcher's paper. I also recall her steeping jars of water with beetroot or crepe-paper hats to create the colours for my paints.

I don't remember my first paintings either, but I do remember the first painting that my mother deemed of a high enough quality to put up on the wall. I suppose it could be considered a still life: violets I had seen outside, painted with beetroot water, the details scored by my pencil.

When I showed my mum, she reached down and looked at me, beaming with pride.

I felt very proud to be able to make my mother so pleased.

As Mum put that painting on the wall, it occurred to me that with a little bit of effort and creativity, one can literally turn a few items that are close to useless into something of value. Valuable items were in short supply in my early life, but it seemed they could be created through the meagre sacrifice of effort. It was Mum's idea to squeeze dye from the crepe paper. To me this seemed some kind of magic. I suppose I still feel that way today.

Work, to me, is magic, and a magic I will always respect. Work is the wondrous alternator that turns butcher's paper into art, a house into a home and poverty into wealth.

I consider art – writing and filmmaking – work. It's not an esoteric pursuit for me, not some investigation into the soul; art is moving something from a state of disorder to a state of order through the medium of time well spent, and that *is* magic, but so is gardening or cooking a nice meal.

I never have and never will allow myself periods of vacillation and sloth.

Perhaps it was the period I grew up in; perhaps it was the family I grew up in; perhaps it was just in me, but one thing I know is that it was something that Ron respected.

Ron also had a compulsion for useful activity, and I loved him for that. Though our work ethics were very similar, our capabilities and the scope of our plans were quite different. In the simplest terms, Ron excelled in the professional and the technical and I excelled in the domestic and the artistic. I thought about our work in immediate terms and he on a much longer time frame.

Thinking now, it's probably true to say that Ron loved on a scale of years and decades, too, and I in moments and minutes.

Sometimes, when I would see Ron turn his chin just so, or watch him come out of the water with the sun on his face, I would be lost in a moment. I would have an overwhelming desire to demonstrate my love with touch and a gentle word, but I learned quickly that macro love is felt very differently. To say 'I love you' or to burrow under a partner's arm is at odds with seeing love in the span of decades, not in moments.

I understood that of Ron and loved that of him, because I loved him whole cloth. Even though I understood why Ron was how he was, it was hard for me sometimes to want affection and not find it. I would never complain, not then and not now, because there was simply nothing to complain about. Ron and I lived the most wonderful life and I owe a great deal to his unique nature.

Those moments he would put his arm around me would be heaven to me and would become a meal that would sustain me for the months of scarcity. The scale of his love was part of the fabric of his being. I would never have changed anything, because that would change everything – and I loved everything. I loved my life. Besides, I was never sitting still long enough to think about what another life might look like, with a different man.

Like I said, we were workers, Ron and I, seizing every opportunity and wringing them all out like wet dishtowels. That left little time for gazing at one's shoes.

Once Ron and I turned a *National Geographic* cover into ten years of adventure on the ship of my dreams and with a band of fellow adventures I don't only call friends, but family too.

Ron and I always had quite regular film and television work, but the very nature of the business meant there would be long gaps between jobs. Whenever Ron and I had a fallow period, and when I was finished with gardening and cooking and housework, I would paint pictures for sale or as gifts, or sell photographs – perhaps from our archive, perhaps new, petitioning commissioning editors or picture desks, or I would write stories for the popular periodicals of the day.

I think stories are the very best kind of magic and I would say that I had a knack for them. When something unusual happened to me I knew whether or not it was a story, and which parts of my experience made up the elements of the story and which parts did not; the two are the essentials of storytelling.

I once saw a cat who had appeared on a deserted beach on Heron Island and in that cat, an animal strictly forbidden on the island, I instantly saw a story. The cat was unafraid of me and wet but happy. He dug a hole in the sand, did his business and filled in the hole. The questions to be answered in a story appeared in my head: 'Where did the cat come from?' 'Whose is it?' 'Why is it so happy swimming?' I followed the cat back into the water. It swam across the reef channel. I followed, and found the answer to each question.

The cat had come from a yacht moored in the Heron channel nearby, and hence he returned, shimmying up the anchor chain and into his owner's arms. The owner, a young man named Bill Stewart, told me the cat's name was 007 because he was perhaps the most adventurous tabby in the world. And why was the cat so happy swimming? He was well practised, having swum in the ocean since he was a kitten.

That was a story.

I put all that information together, with some pictures I'd taken, and sent it off to Australian Consolidated Press and on 21 October 1970, it was the cover story of *Australian Women's Weekly*, then the biggest magazine in the country, in a time when magazines were king.

'He's just an old (swimming) sea cat!' shouted the cover line.

This was just one of many covers I had in the 1960s and 1970s for *Australian Women's Weekly* or *Australian Outdoor* magazine or *Skin Diver* magazine, or for the newspapers or magazine supplements. Many covers and stories were born of a strange occurrence, like finding a cat on the beach or hearing an old-timer talk about a giant anchor off the coast of Norfolk Island, or adopting a crayfish as a pet, but some were commissioned, as is the momentum of media. When an editor was planning their spring issue, or if they wanted a wildlife story, or if they just wanted a blonde wearing a red swimsuit with pink ribbons in her hair, they would see if 'that underwater girl' or 'that shark girl' and 'that girl on the TV' could suggest something. I always could suggest something.

I saw stories in my mind; Ron saw devices – and it was using a combination of the two that got me onto the cover of *National Geographic*. As I have written, it all started after an impromptu photographic show-and-tell at Stan Waterman's house while I was in the United States fixing my eardrum.

After the meeting Stan arranged at *National Geographic*, the magazine sent a letter to us explaining that some of their staff, including Bates Littlehales, one of their famed staff photographers, would like to accompany us when next we travelled to the Great Barrier Reef. They wanted more images using the photographic macro focus device that Ron had invented. They wanted more photos of marine animals that lived on the reef. They also wanted to know a little more about Ron and me.

When the magazine hit the newsstands, the miniature animals were inside the pages and an image was on the cover of me holding the camera and device that made the macro photography possible; something that had once only existed in Ron's mind. Now here it was on the cover of a magazine that was available all around the world: in Australia, Europe, South Africa – and in the United States, where a copy ended up in the hands of adventurer and businessman Lars-Eric Lindblad.

Born in Sweden but with his businesses based in America, Lars-Eric was also someone who saw an idea in his head and worked tirelessly to make it a reality. His idea was a completely new type of tourism and something that was, in many ways, at odds with then-current concepts of leisure. In the 1960s, when Lars-Eric started operating, holidays were primarily taken at places built for the purpose of leisure, but the Swedish–American saw another market, a market he knew would start small, but perhaps, over time, would grow.

His idea was that tourists would like to see what previously only scientists had seen; a world unknown to most, a world of ice and snow, a world of remote tribes and baffling ritual, and a world of marine majesty and untouched reefs. Lars-Eric's tours would not be built around modifying a foreign location so it would have the familiarity of home, but instead engage in the uniqueness and difference of that foreign location, and make every effort to leave that location exactly the way it had been when Lars-Eric and his guests arrived.

To that end, Lars-Eric had custom-built a 2400-tonne ice-hardened ship called the MS *Lindblad Explorer*, which could get to almost anywhere in the world, from the frozen north and south of the globe to the equatorial tropics. It would be a self-contained home base for his guests, bypassing the need for restaurants and roads, hotels and hosts.

Many remember Lars-Eric, quite rightly, as the father of responsible ecotourism.

In the letter he wrote to Ron and me in the early 1970s, he explained that he had read the *National Geographic* piece about us and very much hoped we would join him on his next adventure. We would be paid for our time, and all of our expenses would be covered, and in return he asked that we teach his guests how to dive and snorkel, and also give some lectures on the ship.

His letter ended by saying that he had already paid for a number of advertisements that offered adventurers the opportunity to 'travel with the girl on the cover of *National Geographic*' – so he was very keen for us to join him. Enclosed in the letter were two first-class tickets from Sydney to Bali, from where the ship would depart.

It was an offer too good to refuse. Ron and I cleared our schedule, locked our house and ventured out into that big, wonderful world.

When we arrived we found Bali to be the green, blue and yellow paradise that people still imagine it to be but isn't anymore. We were then only a few years removed from the violent anti-Communist purges that saw tens of thousands of Balinese pulled from the streets and slaughtered, so tourism was an uncertain proposition, but at the secluded surf hideaway of Kuta Beach, we saw that ground had been broken at sites where resorts would be built.

At that time, however, there were no hotels, so we stayed at a homestay in Benoa Harbour. While we waited for Lindblad the man and *Lindblad* the ship, we toured an island that was free of cars and largely free of modern buildings. We saw men wearing traditional dress, women baring their breasts as they had since time immemorial, and everywhere we went we saw streams full of fish. To me, Bali looked like heaven. I was enraptured by the place and wanted to stay there, until I went to the dock and saw the red-and-white ship of Lars-Eric's visions.

That ship was one of those things in life that you fall in love with the moment you see it. It was big enough to comfortably traverse an ocean and small enough to feel like home, and when we boarded and met the other staff we could tell instantly we were meeting people we would know and love for years to come. There was Dr Lawrence Blair, a former actor and model and now a world-renowned anthropologist; his brother Liam, a photographer; Sir Peter Scott, famed ornithologist, painter and only son of Antarctic explorer Robert Scott; and his equally capable and knowledgeable wife, Lady Philippa Scott; Dr Rodney Salm, an expert on coral management and ecotourism; and then, of course, Lars-Eric Lindblad himself.

A man who was undeniably Swedish in his looks and American in his manner, the bespectacled Lars-Eric had a ready smile and incisive eyes, and in every conversation revealed himself to be an adventurer at heart. Lars-Eric explained that as a young man he had sought out the most intrepid commercially available experiences the world had to offer and found them all rather bland. Instead of accepting reality, he remoulded it, telling Ron and me over many long happy hours in the ship's saloon about his ground-breaking expeditions to Antarctica and the Arctic, the Falkland and Sandwich islands and the Galapagos.

Now we were helping him explore another tourist frontier: Indonesia, then a country barely thought of outside of the context of the Cold War.

After meeting the staff, we met the clients, and we were ecstatic to find they were cut from the same adventurous cloth as the staff. Most were American (few Australians then could afford passage), most were friendly, most were intelligent and intrepid and all were looking for adventure. There was no tier of experience on the ship, and no first and third class. Once you were on the ship, you had passed a threshold and nothing else mattered. We were all in it together.

In my mind many of our *Lindblad* expeditions bleed into each other, but that first journey was certainly its own thing. From Bali we hopped to the Gili Islands, which I thought offered wonderful diving, until we ventured further east into the Flores Sea to a site I still consider one of the best dive sites in the world.

Most days when the ship was at anchor, Ron and I would greet the morning sun and take a Zodiac out before breakfast to locate a nice spot for guests to dive or snorkel during the day. One morning, near the island of Komodo a few hundred kilometres east of Lombok, we found a spot that could barely be believed. As soon as we entered the water we were in the company of more fish than I had ever seen. Not just that – there was a reef, too, a technicolour dream of coral that only my national pride keeps me from saying makes the Great Barrier Reef look rather drab.

That day we took the guests on a dive they will never forget.

It was only a few days earlier that I had taught Lady Philippa Scott to dive, and I can still see now the wonder on her face as she went underwater with me. I can also see her husband, Sir Peter Scott, underwater and drawing the fish using his waterproof pencils.

As a diver you spend most of your life trying to find the perfect dive, and only a lucky few ever find it. The discoveries didn't end when we went ashore, either. In the way that there were pre-dive preparations, there were pre-landing preparations also. This entailed a forward party, usually including Lawrence Blair, who spoke a nearly unfathomable number of languages, going ashore with gifts and entreaties to the chiefs of whichever village we might encounter, and a promise that we would take nothing, upset nothing and leave no rubbish. Once the path was cleared of impediments, we would all come ashore, and in the case of Komodo Island, of course Lawrence Blair had arranged for us to meet the island's famous dragons.

As we came ashore two villager men were already leading goats over the high hills to an area clear of bush and trees. When we were all on land, the villagers slaughtered the goats and tied the animals to the ground. Slowly but surely from the surrounding bush came these beasts; low slung, scaled, foreboding and huge. I was amazed as I watched them tear their quarry apart. I went over and stroked one, picking ticks off it. He seemed to enjoy it, so I continued until Lawrence told me about what a bite from one of the beasts might mean.

It was a journey of discovery for all of us, staff and customers alike, because on every Lindblad trip the itinerary was usually altered almost as soon as it was created, for some more exciting experience that was made possible or necessary because of weather, current or local discovery.

We dived untouched reefs across the world, discovering sites that would become famous in SCUBA circles but at that stage had likely never been visited. In the 1970s the slaughter of sharks and the overfishing of reefs was happening in many places in the world but not all, and there were unbounded treasures off untrammelled coasts.

There were also adventures to be had on the coasts. In Indonesia and in Papua New Guinea we met tribal people who had never seen the likes of us, eagerly showing off their customs, dance, food and children. In the Papuan area of the Asmat the men, wearing grass skirts and with fearsome face paint, explained their not-so-distant history of head hunting and cannibalism to assuage evil spirits and ancient revenges. Some of the men even suggested that the practice was not only a feature of the past.

In the mountains of Sulawesi we met the Toraja people, an ethnic group who worship animist gods and build their houses attentive to spiritual divisions as they see them. The pillars of their houses support the floor and act as a scratching post for their animals represented in the underworld. Above that, a living area represents the world of men and then, above that, their saddle roofs reached towards the sky like stairs that the Toraja believe will be made available to a recently deceased villager if they are to be invited into the realm of gods. These sail-roofed houses and ghostly funeral figures remain in my mind today as vivid as any memory.

Just as vivid are my memories of Fiji. Perhaps the Fijian customs were not as exotic as those we found in New Guinea, but my heart was stolen during my first kava ceremony, and a part of it will forever remain with those sweet-voiced, strong-limbed people.

In Fiji we invited villagers onto the ship and showed them footage of the ship's adventures. The Swedes were always keen to show the locals their Antarctic trips; perhaps because it reminded them of home, or perhaps because of the pride they took in their role in first bringing tourists to the seventh continent. The men and women of the Pacific seemed vaguely interested in the icy deserts of Antarctica, but it seemed to me they were more enthusiastic when we showed our underwater films, some shot just a few hundred metres away from their villages. As I watched them watch, I wondered what dive industry might one day exist in places such as Fiji.

When Ron and I returned from that first trip we were floating on a cloud and very much hoping that we would get the opportunity to do it all again. That, however, was not to say life in Australia was any less desirable than life on the boat, just different.

We had our house to get back to. I had a garden that was overgrowing and under-watered and Ron, a voracious reader, who as far as I know never read a piece of fiction in his life, had a pile of technical periodicals and scientific volumes that needed attending to.

Need was the word, too.

Like me, Ron was not traditionally well educated, but he had undoubtedly picked up a PhD many times over in the amount of study he undertook on photography, engineering and material fabrication. In fact, Ron was so dedicated to his study and self-improvement that the cadence of life in Sydney was built around it, with dinner needing to be served promptly at six in the evening so Ron could take a scheduled break from his study and his building work, which he would do nearly all day and then after dinner in the evening.

This strict regimen didn't change much when my nephews came to live with us, either – the first of whom was Mark, eldest son of my brother Greg.

Greg had made money young and, before even the age of forty-five, had retired and moved to a beautiful farm south of Sydney. There he and his wife Jessie raised wonderful children: first Mark, and then two more boys, Greg and Jono, and one girl, Monique. We loved those kids, and still do and found them exceptional and interesting children, but as they got older they started to crave life outside the bounds of the farm.

When just a teenager, Mark discovered surfing and with it the company of fellow surfers. As was often the case, those surfers included some rougher boys and men, and my brother became increasingly concerned that Mark might follow in the steps of those surfers whose lives were tainted by drugs and alcohol. This became a point of contention between my brother and his son, and when Mark walked out of school one day and refused to go back, Greg sent him off to us in the hope Mark might gain a practical education.

We were more than happy to have him with us. I loved having company in the house, and Ron fed off Mark's enthusiasm for ships, diving and cameras.

As I said, our house's regimen did not change when Mark arrived, and after dinner Ron would not be available for either Mark or me. At other times Ron was an excellent and patient tutor, explaining to Mark the finer points of diving and underwater photography. While living with us Mark discovered that his interests coincided with Ron's, and in Mark we found a fertile and willing mind.

Ron was a man of few passions, but Mark was one of them, and sometimes I would think that perhaps Ron wished that

Mark was his son. He was a quick study, and that's why, when invited on his own second trip on the *Lindblad Explorer*, Ron told Lars-Eric Lindblad we wouldn't be able to join the expedition unless we could bring Mark with us.

Mark was sixteen then and Lars-Eric told us that the boy was too young to be on the ship, let alone part of the crew; he had only ever hired people over the age of twenty-one. I petitioned hard for the boy, telling Lars-Eric that not only would Mark be a hard worker, but one who initially would work for free, with Lars-Eric only needing to supply Mark's food and board.

Lars-Eric relented and, as I knew he would, Mark did as he was told, and worked just as hard for Lars-Eric as he had for Ron. When I saw how natural Mark was on the bridge, I pushed him to get as many working hours as he could up there, which would help count towards getting his professional skipper's ticket. Mark quickly became a diligent, intuitive and wholly excellent sailor; a marvellous exemplar of the power of having a goal.

There was only ever one bump on the otherwise smooth sailing of Mark on the *Lindblad Explorer*, and that happened when, one night, Mark decided to exercise his unfettered access to the bar.

Even though he was just a teenager, I had no problem that Mark had a drink after his shift. In fact I'd told him that he could have two beers a night if he was so inclined – if it was good enough for the British Navy it was good enough for us. But he knew that Ron and I wouldn't abide drunkenness.

For my part, I knew that my brother had put Mark in our care to get him away from the boys who were tempting him with drink and drugs, and for Ron's part – well, Ron abhorred alcohol altogether. A man who prioritised control over perhaps anything else in this world, Ron to my knowledge never let alcohol pass his lips.

It was the ship's steward who came to me to tell me that Mark was passed out on the floor in the lounge. It was early in the morning, so I rushed to the lounge in an attempt to get there before any of the staff or guests. When I arrived, Mark was gone. Eventually I found him in his cabin. I did not mince my words and I gave him a few very hard smacks. When I had finished, I knew he would never drink heavily on the ship again. I never had a problem with Mark at all after that.

I think after that moment he was no longer a ward or a study, but an equal member of the dynamic *Lindblad* family. The retention of staff on the *Lindblad* was incredible, but there was some turnover. The new staff were inevitably just as intrepid and interesting as the people they had replaced, which is not to say they were ever like the people they had replaced. There were people on the *Lindblad* who, I think, were unlike anyone else on earth, and this seems like the perfect time to introduce our friend Mike McDowell, someone who came on the *Lindblad* for the first time on the fifth or sixth trip Ron and I took.

We were warned about Mike before stepping foot on the deck. There was, we were told, another Australian on board, a man who was younger and perhaps not quite as refined as Ron and me. What you might call a 'rough type'. He was the new Zodiac driver, unlikely to last.

As soon as we met Mike, however, we liked him immensely. A scientist who had spent many years working on Macquarie Island – a tiny, frigid, windswept outcrop halfway between New Zealand and Antarctica – Mike perhaps hadn't spent much time thinking about which was the right fork to use for salad, but he had an intelligence and warmth that practically radiated from his skin along with a nearly unparalleled nose for adventure.

There were many ways in which Mike differed from Lars-Eric Lindblad, but in many more ways they shared a similar spirit.

The complete story of Mike McDowell deserves its own volume, but by way of introduction to a man who will feature later, it's enough to say that Mike worked his way up the Lindblad ladder, eventually becoming cruise director and from there built a ground-breaking company that had the distinction of selling the first commercial tours to the wreck sites of the *Titanic* and *Bismarck*, and sent the first tourist to space, arranging with the Russian government to lease an empty seat on the *Soyuz* spacecraft to the international space station.

Mike was especially useful in a pinch, and there were a few pinches while we were on the *Lindblad*.

This was a time before Google and Trip Advisor, and even before *Lonely Planet* and other guidebooks to remote locations, and I think we were far happier because of it, but it did mean that every trip required patience, gall and an acceptance of a certain level of risk. After all, there is often danger when you are having a true adventure.

I found Indonesia and the Pacific quite placid and safe, but Central America and the Caribbean, where we found a heady mix of young men, weapons and scarcity, was a place I kept my head on a swivel.

Often were the times when bored men in unironed uniforms with dented weapons suggested that we might be interested in giving them a gift: sometimes money, sometimes whiskey, and sometimes a watch or two. This casual larceny, without a gun pointed or a direct threat levelled, was usually just a threat, but there were times we were subject to a traditional robbery.

I remember one instance when, while we were in a Zodiac looking for Guatemalan crocodiles, a man on the shore pointed an AK-47 at us. I looked at him with my telephoto lens and saw he was furiously motioning for us to come to him. We considered making a run for it, but we decided against it, figuring that the man potentially only had to puncture the boat to put us in great crocodilian peril.

When we got to the shore we found he was part of a larger ragtag military attachment. We spoke no Spanish and they no English but we quickly established that this was a kidnapping and that we had to pay a ransom to continue on our way. With neither money nor valuables we would have to go to the ship to pay. They got their boat and followed us towards the *Lindblad*.

We took off at a slow pace and called the ship, telling them to up-anchor and start moving slowly. As we got closer we told them to pick the pace up and when the time was ripe, we opened up our huge outboards and powered ahead. When all were on board, the *Lindblad*, a ship with surprising pick-up, sped away.

We were targets of opportunity, or perhaps not even that; just a way to enliven the monotony of conscripted life.

I loved all of it. Ron and I were truly happy on that ship, which ended up being our home three months of the year for more than a decade. We were busy and contented. Ron always brought his latest camera and housing, and every day was an opportunity to test his equipment and to film a new reef, or a new animal. For me, every two weeks I was introduced to a new group of wonderful and fascinating people, from writers and actors to millionaires and royalty, not to mention the wonderful permanent staff. On that ship life changed for me and for Ron and it certainly changed for my nephew Mark.

Each time when we returned to Sydney after a trip on the *Lindblad* I would sit with Mark and ask what else he might be able to do to progress in his fledgling career as a mariner and dive instructor. I paid for him to do courses in maintaining and repairing diving regulators and compressors and, with those capabilities and the deck time and skipper's tickets Mark was garnering, he started to put together a solid marine resume. Mark not only became more capable as the months and years went on, he also became an integral part of our movie work.

* * *

After *Jaws* and *Inner Space* Ron and I had become quite a desirable commodity, not for our personalities and profiles, but for our capabilities. We established ourselves as the pre-eminent underwater filmmakers in Australia, not only for nature documentaries and films like *Jaws* and *Orca* that required the wrangling of wild marine animals, but for any underwater sequences, and each year brought better and more interesting work.

The thing that really set us ahead of the pack was, once again, Ron's unique ability to build underwater camera housings for the latest 35-millimetre and cinematic cameras and operate them expertly, ensuring continuity between first- and second-unit shots.

In the late 1970s Ron and I worked on three films in quick succession with Australian documentarian-cum-narrative-filmmaker Peter Weir, two of which helped propel Weir and the star of both films, Mel Gibson, across the Pacific and into a position of Hollywood access and power. Those two films were *The Year of Living Dangerously*, a movie about a foreign correspondent sent to Indonesia who is caught up in a coup attempt, and *Gallipoli*, likely the best film this country has ever produced about the madness of war.

The scene we were hired to shoot for *Gallipoli* entailed Gibson and his fellow soldiers being interrupted while bathing in Suvla Bay when shrapnel starts landing. While principal photography was to take place in South Australia with some scenes timed on location in the Middle East, our scene was to be shot in New South Wales, just a few hours south of Sydney, which meant we could take Mark.

We drove our tinny down, and I took my camera so I could get some stills of wobbegong sharks that a nature magazine had requested.

The first I knew this was to be a nude scene was when, as I was sitting on the beach with a woman named Joan Long who had long been part of the Australian film industry, a fit, young, naked man ran past me while Ron was setting up. Then another, and another and then Mel Gibson in his glorious nakedness (and glorious it was).

They were trying to stay warm before plunging into the icy waves for their scene. The reason the soldiers were diving below the surface was because, in the narrative of the film, they were trying to escape a barrage of artillery and in the scene shrapnel was required to rain down on them, and Mark had been enlisted to sprinkle the prop shrapnel into the water.

'Is Mark a board rider?' Joan asked as we sat on the beach. I told her he was and a rather good one.

'Do you think he might be interested in being in front of the camera?'

I thought he might. Joan was producing a film version of Kathy Lette's coming-of-age book *Puberty Blues*, which included scenes showing the two main female characters trying to ingratiate themselves into a group of surfers, one of whom, Joan thought, might include Mark.

When I asked him he was horrified by the idea. I told him it would be an opportunity to make some good money. 'My mates would make fun of me,' he said.

Perhaps, perhaps. I didn't press the issue. After all, it quickly became apparent to me that Mark's desire was not to be on the screen, but in the ocean.

In 1979 we were asked to work on a film adaptation of Henry De Vere Stacpool's novel *The Blue Lagoon*, which detailed the romantic awakening of two teenagers marooned together on a desert island. When we agreed, I knew nothing about the sexual nature of the story except that when my mother read the book, she did so locked in her wardrobe.

When Ron and I arrived on Turtle Island in Fiji, we were greeted by a hive of activity the likes of which we had never seen. Now Turtle Island is covered with a luxury resort, but then it was as remote a location as one could imagine. Whatever was needed for filming would have to be brought in. To that end, a tent city had been built, and a small cruise ship, also called the *Blue Lagoon*, had been moored just off the coast of the island.

Ron and I were to work primarily with the film's stars, Christopher Atkins, then eighteen, and Brooke Shields, a fashion model and socialite who was just fourteen years old. They were delightful co-workers and, despite their age, learning quickly the free-diving techniques I had picked up while spearfishing and that they would require for the long underwater takes the director had in mind.

On that shoot any problems arose not from the actors, but their mothers, or more specifically Brooke's mother, Teri. I often sympathised with Teri, because young women and girls on film sets were at risk of being exploited by overbearing and lecherous men and needed a strong and wise hand, but Teri seemed to want to tread a perilous line between sexualising and protecting Brooke, and a line that seemed to move depending on Teri's spirits.

Thankfully Ron and I were not the ones deciding what

was the appropriate amount of flesh this child should bare, but often Teri slowed us down somewhat.

We got through it all, blocking the shots that were needed while the actors were wearing masks and then doing it naked-faced, after they had applied the breath-holding techniques and followed the line of white shells we had laid on the ocean floor, the route the camera required.

Chris and Brooke were such joys to work with. I spent many of my days off with them also, teaching them to dive using SCUBA.

It was a wonderful shoot, all things considered, and on location Ron and I received an honour that is exceedingly rare in the Hollywood milieu. A sheet had been strung between two palms for showing rushes and Ron's underwater footage was shown. It was screened without sound, colour correction or editing but the crew, usually tired, often jaded and not naturally inclined to false approvals, rose to their feet and applauded.

I have never seen that happen before or since.

In 1984 my nephew Mark came with us to the Cook Islands where we were shooting a New Zealand film called *The Silent One*. The script retold the myth of a deaf–mute Polynesian boy who befriends a magical turtle and has a run-in with a rather large tiger shark. The animals we would not only have to film, but source.

Ron and I arrived on Aitutaki Atoll in the Cook Islands before Mark so we could observe the construction of the reef that would serve as our main location and create the mesh barriers that would enclose the animals we needed for the story.

We trusted Mark to bring over the large turtle that would star in the film. After he arrived, we petitioned the local fishermen for a shark, which we knew they caught when fishing. One fisherman told us he had a large shark, and when we went to him we found a handsome and captive ten-foot (three-metre) tiger shark.

While we worked, Mark was in charge of keeping the turtle and the shark happy, healthy and fed, and he had enough sense to know that keeping the shark fed was directly related to keeping the turtle healthy. They were strange set-fellows, those two animals, but they became friends to all of us. The shark, which in other circumstances would have been feared, quickly became as placid as a house cat. We all swam alongside it without fear or trepidation, and to that end, in many ways I credit Mark.

* * *

For most of the 1980s Ron and I did a stint on the *Lindblad* each year, until the ship was sold to a German corporation. The Germans tried to maintain the magic – and most of the staff, including Ron and me, came back for a trip under their ownership – but the excitement was gone. The Germans were in it for the money, not for the adventure. None of us came back for a second trip with them, not Sir Peter and Lady Philippa, nor Dr Lawrence Blair nor Mike, nor Ron and me, nor Mark, who was then an in-demand seaman on dive boats around the Pacific.

A few years later the *Lindblad* hit an iceberg and sank, in somewhat mysterious circumstances.

Ron and I did similar trips on other ships, the operators of which were trying to recreate the spell that the *Lindblad* managed to cast. Sometimes we would take my other nephews, Mark's brothers Greg and Jono, on those trips, as both of them lived with us for a spell, as Mark had. Those two boys were quick studies like their older brother and soon learned about diving and underwater photography.

When I look around my house in Seal Rocks or my Sydney place in Fairlight I see artefacts of those wonderful years in which Ron and I filled our calendar with *Lindblad* trips and movie work, and in between those dates I could be found painting and writing and taking photographs. I see a painting that Sir Peter Scott painted for me, and in the living room hutch some Ming china bought on a deserted beach alongside salvaged bottles and fossils. I see piles of magazines I have been in or have written for, and I see books I have written for and paintings that have been reproduced, and framed photographs used in this magazine or that, and in a filing cabinet there are notes from *Lindblad* guests and actors and producers and directors. But my proudest legacy is not any of those things – it is our time with the boys, the nephews we loved like sons and who are now men. Wonderful, wonderful men.

My nephew Jono is a professional camera operator now, specialising in underwater filming after becoming an expert under Ron. My nephew Greg has a dive operation now in Flores, taking people out to the reefs and drifts that Ron and

I 'discovered' in the 1970s. And Mark – well, Mark has his own boat, not the *Lindblad* but very much a vision come true in its own way.

The boat, called the *Seven Seas*, is a forty-foot (twelve-metre), traditionally built Buginese schooner specially built for snorkelling and diving. It too traverses Komodo and Labuan Bajo and Papua and all the spots Ron and I dived on the first *Lindblad* trip. And, like the *Lindblad*, that vessel is as much a family home as it is a boat.

My old body doesn't allow me to dive as much as I used to, but when I do it's usually with Mark in the Flores Sea, with the *Seven Seas* nearby and my gin and tonic waiting for me. When I'm diving those familiar reefs and in those warm waters I feel weightless and ageless, and it occurs to me now that perhaps there are small places in my existence where I don't feel the need to be working and can just be, well … happy.

CHAPTER THIRTEEN

Memento mori

In ancient Rome, when generals returned to the city victorious after some conquest or another, the senate sometimes granted them a celebration called a 'triumph'. This honour allowed the general to bring his legions and his treasure and gold and slaves into the city, and march down a triumphal passage while the populace covered him in adulation and praise.

On that day, the general had the run of the city and was considered more god than man, but had to adhere to one tradition, one that lasted throughout the age of the republic and much of imperial rule too: he was to have a trusted slave behind him throughout, whispering two words: '*Memento mori ... memento mori ... memento mori.*'

Remember you are mortal ... remember you are mortal ... remember you are mortal.

Someone told me about this little nugget of ancient history recently when they came to visit my place at Seal Rocks and met Mr Tojo, whose skull I have in my cabinet there. They wanted to know if Mr Tojo was my *memento mori*, and although I hadn't thought about it in that way before, perhaps he is.

I suppose I should explain Mr Tojo, lest people think he was the remains of one of my enemies. And I know that some readers may find this story disturbing. I can't undo the things that have been done, good or bad in my life, and the story of Mr Tojo is of another time and another place.

In 1979, Ron and I were asked to help film several underwater scenes for a British feature.

One scene called for the star of the film to find the remains of his friend who had been lost when the ship he was on sank.

Our job was to film the star diving down and finding his friend's remains. The location chosen was one of the wartime wrecks lying in the depths of Rabaul's harbour. In World War II, the aftermath of an Allied bombing campaign against the captured Papua New Guinean port of Rabaul left at least sixty-five Japanese ships sunk in the harbour like deep-water tombs. The Japanese had defended the port from the water and the land. Many Japanese combatants died in the jungles surrounding the bay and many more on the vessels as they sank.

The story attached to the shoot I don't remember, and I'm actually not sure we were ever told. For us it was a job that allowed us to travel, film and dive, so of course we said yes.

Ron and I arrived in Rabaul via Port Moresby and almost instantly we were presented with difficulties. The man who we were supposed to be filming was not an experienced diver. The wreck with the skeletons lay in about 140 feet (forty-three metres) of water. We knew that the shallowest wrecks had no human remains on the bridges of the ships and yet retrieving remains was critical to the scene we had been employed to shoot.

What to do?

We explained to the producers that we weren't comfortable taking the inexperienced diver to any of the deep wrecks. Wreck diving can be treacherous, especially when navigating old and unknown rusty, decaying ships.

We also explained that while Ron and I would be able to dive the deep wrecks, we would have a very short down time if we did, due to the decompression requirements and Boyle's Law, meaning each breath at depth takes a toll on the tank equivalent to two breaths in shallow water. Very few people, if any, had dived the deep wrecks and although we knew there were human remains there, Ron refused to work with an inexperienced diver at depth. It was simply too dangerous.

Along with the British film crew we were staying at a Travelodge in Rabaul and there I had become friendly with the local man who had been bringing me my gin and tonics. Ron and the film crew were discussing the problem at another table. I was at the bar chatting to the bartender. I asked him if there were still remains of Japanese soldiers in the bush around the port. The war had ended nearly thirty-five years earlier, but Rabaul is quite an underdeveloped place and, while there was no infantry battle in Rabaul to end the occupation, the bombing was relentless and scores of Japanese soldiers died from this as well as from disease or malnutrition.

The waiter said he wasn't sure but he thought there were many. I asked if he knew someone who might know for sure.

He said there were still a lot of skeletons near where he lived. I told him if he could get a complete skeleton by 6 a.m. when the dive boat was picking us up, I would pay him fifty kina, the equivalent of twenty Australian dollars.

When I arrived at the dock in the morning the man gave me a hessian sack containing bones and I gave him the money.

Off we went to a shallow wreck we were familiar with. It was lying in eleven metres of water. The perfect location, no chance of the bends, good light and an easy dive.

The bones were placed; the hero swam left then right searching for his friend, then found the bones laid out on the bridge. The whole shoot was over in half an hour.

The next day the sun was shining, which made for even better shooting. Ron did a few more takes then climbed out and started packing. I asked, 'What about Mr Tojo?'

It didn't seem right to leave him there. And I couldn't leave him back in the jungle. There was no way I could find out who the bones belonged to, no way to somehow trace him back to his family. And I didn't feel right just handing him back in the hessian bag to the fellow behind the bar. I dropped back on snorkel into the water with the sack, swam down and collected the bones.

Ron and I flew from Rabaul to Moresby and then from Moresby to Sydney and, alongside our camera and dive gear, was a hessian sack, tied at the top. I picked up the sack from baggage claim like the rest of our items and when it came time to write our customs declarations, the contents of the sack were duly and truthfully described, like the rest of our items.

Camera casing.

Motion camera.

Lights.

One Japanese soldier.

All of Mr Tojo from the neck down is still in that sack, but his head keeps me company in my cabinet, from where he stares out at trees, kookaburras and dinner parties. He is rubbed with olive oil regularly and, when the light shines just right, his silver fillings shine.

It doesn't seem a bad life for a skull.

A number of times over the years my nephew Mark has told me I should take Mr Tojo to the Japanese embassy, but I've baulked at the idea. Mr Tojo and I have lived together for a long time now, close on to forty years. I have told Mark that he can take Mr Tojo to the embassy when I die, but until then, he stays with me. His companions have probably rotted away. All the wrecks were buried when the local volcano erupted. There is no doubt that my Japanese skeleton will be delivered to the embassy and I hope returned to the country of his birth. That would be a perfect ending to this story.

I don't know why I'm so adamant about keeping Mr Tojo, but I am. Perhaps it's a reminder of a successful adventure Ron and I had. Perhaps it's something else. Perhaps it is, as my friend suggested, a reminder of my own mortality. I've been charmed in my life, luxuriated on yachts and in palaces, but if, perhaps, there were moments in my life when I might have started to think I'm anything but mortal, stark reality has always been a beat away.

I discovered that I had cancer on 13 April 1987. It was a quite advanced case, the cancer left to grow and metastasise for several years. My GP and a great specialist kept telling me I had mastitis. They were wrong. The four X-rays all showed cancer, but who was I to know? One day I felt so bad I walked to Roseville shopping centre, into the first doctors' rooms I saw and sat down. The receptionist told me to come back after making an appointment. I said, 'I am not leaving until I see the doctor.' So I waited until finally I was sent in to see Dr Dowe. He examined me and said, 'In my opinion you have a malignant tumour.'

I remember when I was told: it was a windy and rainy autumn day. I felt sick and very angry.

I felt competing emotions in that moment as I can imagine one always would when being told something like this. As the physician spoke, explaining that time was not on my side, and that treatment, including surgery, would be required immediately, one emotion started to wash the others out, like a stage-light shining too brightly.

As I was given my diagnosis I had been flushed with panic and despair and confusion and also hope and love and, certainly, fear, but soon, and above all, I couldn't help but feel an overwhelming amount of rage against the great specialist and my GP who kept sending me to him.

Soon all I felt was anger, or at least that's all I remember. *Those bastards. THAT bastard. That bloody BASTARD.*

I had found that lump in my breast a long time before: first the size of a pea, then a grape. Perhaps six or seven months before my diagnosis I went to my general practitioner and asked him to check it. After his examination he assured me the lump was benign.

'It's likely mastitis, Mrs Taylor, nothing to worry about.'

That lump changed shape and size, and I went back to him. He reassured me again, but said I could see a specialist friend of his if I liked and if I must.

When I saw this specialist, a breast-health expert and surgeon, he was dismissive and disparaging, not in his words but his manner. I actually took solace in that. He told me, after his examination of the X-rays, that I would die of old age before I would die of cancer.

I wrote in my diary after that meeting that I thought he considered me hysterical, something I didn't want to be, but one would rather be hysterical than cancerous.

I trusted this man with a large office and letters behind his name, and then went about my business. Well, as best I could anyway. Even after seeing this specialist, alarms rang in my head every time I felt the lump in my breast.

I did manage to quieten those alarms, though, I think only because I was so busy, filling my head with offers and itineraries and sights and deals.

The first place I visited after my general practitioner gave me the all clear was Italy, where Ron and I had become minor celebrities since working with Italian director Bruno

Vailati on the film *Uomini e Squali* (Of Sharks and Men). Ron and I had appeared on Italian television a number of times, responding to very lucrative offers.

The problem with those offers, however, was that they rarely resulted in money in our bank account.

We would always leave Italy with iron-clad guarantees that money would be sent as soon as humanly possible. We would wait and wait for the money, but none would arrive. We would write and sometimes even call, but our letters were 'lost' and on the phone it was always impossible to find an English speaker when it was time to talk about money, even if we had been put on to one previously.

Sometimes the money would eventually turn up, but often it was far less than we had agreed upon. It was usually enough, however, to make us accept the next offer to visit Italy, for I truly loved Italy and especially the Mediterranean coast.

By 1986 we had new Italian rules. If someone wanted to invite us to Italy they had to guarantee first-class tickets, and pay for the hotel of our choosing. If Ron and I were going together, they also had to pay for a trip to Capri. Then, even if the money never arrived, we had enjoyed ourselves enough that it didn't matter so much.

In 1986 I had a lovely time in Rome, which was enjoying the first warmth of a European spring, and from there I went to Sweden on my own, where a publisher wanted to talk about me doing a coffee table book on the marine world.

After that business was concluded I had the pleasure of meeting up with some friends of Lars-Eric Lindblad and, under blue skies and over herring and wine, we talked boats. I don't remember exactly what was spoken about except that someone told me about the *Sea Cloud*, which they described as perhaps the most perfect vessel ever created by man. I was told this was the first privately owned mega-yacht, but unlike the modern monstrosities that looked like miniature hotels, this was a square-rigged barque sailing ship.

'The ship of your dreams,' someone had said.

On my flight home I drifted in and out of consciousness, thinking about that ship. I had always loved square-rigged sailing ships but had had no occasion to sail on one since, as a little girl, I sailed on the *Pamir*, the German ship seized by the New Zealand Navy in Wellington Harbour.

I thought about Ron, too, and how anxious I was to get back to him. Ron had become increasingly reliant on me at home, and I was wondering how he had coped while I was away. I hoped he was eating and changing his clothes.

I also thought about the lump in my breast.

It didn't feel like nothing, or a blocked milk gland, as mastitis is. It felt unhealthy and dangerous and I was sure it was changing shape and changing size. I had been told not to worry about it, but when I touched it, it set off alarms in my head.

I arrived home and visited the doctor again, and again I was told it was nothing to worry about.

Once again I was off travelling, once again with those words ringing in my ears.

You'll die of old age before you'll die of cancer, Mrs Taylor.

I recited those words to myself as Ron and I boarded the *Bali Explorer*, one of the live-aboard dive boats that have plied the tourist beachhead that the *Lindblad* opened up.

On the *Bali Explorer*, Ron and I took up a similar role we had taken on the *Lindblad*: as guides and lecturers. My diaries tell me that it was a wonderful trip but they also speak about my unexpected fatigue, and the latter is the thing I remember. I wasn't someone who felt fatigue. I was now a little over fifty, but I was fit and full of purpose. I attacked every day with vigour and if some days I started the day without drive, that changed by the time breakfast was finished.

On the *Bali Explorer* I was slowing down and feeling an ache in my bones and my muscles. I was waking tired and staying tired. I forced myself to do everything that was expected of me, but I didn't do it all easily, which was not the person I normally am.

You'll die of old age before you'll die of cancer, Mrs Taylor.

After that trip I was to travel to Europe on my own again and, feeling the way that I was, I would have happily cancelled, or at least waited to travel with company – a friend who was interested in heading to Germany and Amsterdam also, perhaps – but this was an important trip, with an unmoveable date.

I had a date with royalty.

My first stop was Frankfurt, Germany, for the *Buchmesse* or book fair, an event that has been run in one way or another in the German city ever since Johannes Gutenberg pioneered his moveable type printer. I had contributed to a number of books that had been published in a number of markets and my role at the fair was to convince publishers in markets where my books hadn't been published to do so.

It was a whirlwind of European names and small talk and books, books, books. As much as I love reading and books, it was all exhausting. It was a relief to return home but after about three weeks I found myself flying first class to Holland.

I had been invited to attend an event at the Dutch palace and, not just that, the event was partially in my honour. I was to be awarded the Order of the Golden Ark for Marine Conservation, an accolade that had been introduced into the Dutch honours system by Prince Bernhard, the consort of Queen Juliana of the Netherlands and also a keen diver and conservationist.

At the palace, a grand building of high ceilings, huge paintings and exquisite furniture, I was pleased to find that David McTaggart, the wonderfully eccentric Canadian oddball who had founded Greenpeace, was also being honoured.

Being dropped into a royal world can make one feel quite overwhelmed and drift into the company of other commoners, and in David McTaggart I found the perfect ally. David was a man who cared deeply about the environment (that was why he was there, for the press and prestige this award would bring to his organisation and cause), but he was also a man who loved to smoke and drink red wine, and while I was with him he dedicated his time to both.

On the day of the awards ceremony I wore a dress of blue silk, which I found was quite at odds with the drab dress of most in attendance. As soon as I walked through the gates of the palace I stayed close to David, who was as unawed by his surroundings as a lovely labrador might be, only wanting to sniff around for a waiter serving wine, or a place with an ashtray.

I was introduced to the Prince and the Queen, and they could not have been more welcoming, disarming and human. They were so well versed on my conservation efforts, it seemed they knew better what I had been doing than I did. I hadn't felt that I had been on a campaign, which suggests planning, organisation and coordination, but the way they told it, it seemed I had been.

In my life I had seen situations that bothered me enough that I would write a letter, or go to a rally, or speak to a reporter, or go on television, or contact a politician. The slow but swelling realisation that those animals I considered friends were disappearing from existence was one that sparked activity from me, always.

I say slow realisation because that's what it was in the 1960s, 1970s and 1980s. For thousands of years previously there was practically no thought of marine conservation. Some people didn't want raw sewage or industrial pollution spewing into their favourite swimming spot, and others didn't like the image of whales being killed with exploding harpoons, but aside from that, the ocean was both garbage can and breadbasket. One could take whatever one could from it, and could dump whatever one liked into it, and one never had to think about it afterwards.

I started my life underwater with that attitude, but that attitude changed as I went to Seal Rocks and found there were fewer and fewer (and then eventually no) sea lions. It changed when I went to the Great Barrier Reef and saw thinning populations of large fish. It changed as I met individual marine animals and became friendly with them and feared their death from a spear or in a net. They were not family pets but animals that I knew and trusted.

My conservation efforts were personal. I wasn't a scientist, nor did I consider myself a public figure, even though I became one. I was just someone who became increasingly upset about what I was seeing under the waves and felt I had to do something about it. To most people the marine world is an alien environment far from their everyday life. It is not a spectacular wilderness where forest-covered mountains reach to the clouds or sunny beaches kiss the waves as they wash across the sand.

It was incredible to see it all laid out in front of me – the individual marine species protections and the exclusion zones I had championed – and by royalty, no less. I'm not someone to stop and take stock in life, but after Prince Bernhard spoke, I asked him, 'Why me?' He said that an aide had drawn his attention to a story in the *Reader's Digest* about my fight for the potato cod. He had his aide check the Australian archives and discovered all the other animals for which I had campaigned for protection. I was quite flushed and, I must say, proud.

I floated home, and straight back to work. Ron and I flew to Uluru, then known as Ayers Rock, to be in a short documentary celebrating the Australian bicentenary with a huge cast of notable Australians including Delvene Delaney, Jenny Kee and Thomas Keneally.

Afterwards I went home for some much-needed rest. I was still fatigued.

I spent the next small while with my mother in Seal Rocks. She was getting very old very quickly. I resolved to appreciate every moment I had with her, and we enjoyed slow days and slow walks, cups of tea and sunsets over beaches that were empty of anything and anyone except a fishing boat or two.

It was autumn then, a time when the sun hitting your skin wasn't taken for granted. The nights were cold, the days short, there was quiet and stillness and space in my mind. In that space the idea that things were very wrong went from the back of my mind to the front.

I didn't have mastitis. I just didn't. I was tired all the time and the lump was changing shape. I knew something more extreme than a blocked milk duct was happening to my breast.

It was after that time in Seal Rocks that I went to see Dr Dowe at Roseville. He pulled out a flyer and gave it to me. He said it was from a woman who had just finished medical school and was specialising in breast cancer. I made an appointment with her for the next day.

It was only moments into the examination that the specialist told me that the lump in my breast was undoubtedly cancer and that I must have that breast removed and probably the other one too. The doctor told me she would normally do the surgery herself but she was travelling overseas the next day. She was instantly on the phone looking for someone to perform the operation quickly.

It's no hyperbolic statement to say that this doctor saved my life and also that the earlier specialist's ineptitude almost ended it.

I went home in a daze, feeling so many emotions I could barely discern when one started and another ended but, like I've said already, one overwhelmed all of the others: anger.

I told Ron about the diagnosis and surgery, but his response was muted. He didn't feel my emotions, nor, I could tell, did he really understand them.

When I went into that surgery a few days after the diagnosis, most of the emotions dissipated and by the time I went under only the strongest one remained. Afterwards, I recovered in a sunny room filled with flowers and friends, but I kept thinking about that dismissive GP and his friend, the equally dismissive specialist.

If I had been treated sooner, perhaps I would still have my breast. As I was taken from one appointment to another in the hospital, for scans and tests to see if the surgery had been enough, or if the cancer was still polluting, multiplying, I wondered if the time wasted might be the difference between life or death.

I asked the doctors and specialists about the diagnosis lag, and while professional courtesy kept them from accusing another doctor of gross malpractice, I could tell in the space between their words that that's what they felt.

I knew I would be best to forget my anger and concentrate on my health and my recovery, but I just couldn't. I would lie in bed thinking about this man, this specialist who saw women all day every day but sent me away; this man who was still seeing other scared women all day every day and possibly telling them not to worry, to ignore what their body was telling them. I have to admit my anger turned into cool, murderous intent.

I assumed when I got out of hospital those thoughts would go away, but they didn't. I became fearful of those thoughts; I knew they were counterproductive and potentially degenerative and sapping in a time I would need all of my strength.

The surgery was to be just the start of my treatment, not the end of it; a pre-emptive strike against what might be a very resilient foe.

I instantly liked my oncologist. He was calm and straightforward and told me what he knew and what he didn't know. He knew I must immediately start a six-month round of chemotherapy but he didn't know whether, at the end of that treatment, I would be cancer-free. He said I would be in a better state than if I didn't have the chemotherapy. He also told me that good outcomes were linked to the patient's capacity to fight and stay positive.

I knew staying positive was essential, I knew it in my core, in the way I had known that something was wrong with my breast ... yet visions of what I wanted to do to that incompetent man would not leave my mind.

When I got home, I did manage to find some equanimity. My seventeen-year-old nephew Mark came to live with us for a spell to help out. He would do some of the groundwork, and name my slides which left time for me to sit in the garden in the sun and appreciate the small moments in life; a friend, a book, the light at the beginning and the end of each day.

People rallied around me, visiting, bringing gifts. My brother Greg brought me spring water, telling me that if this was all I drank, my health would improve. Jenny Kee brought me matching dresses and scarves for when my hair fell out. Others brought books or wine and flowers; many beautiful flowers.

Every day I wore a beautiful dress and put on make-up, and I had euphoric moments, happy moments. Images of destroying my former doctor never completely left my mind, though, especially when the treatment started to really affect me.

Chemotherapy is, of course, horrible. I could feel the drugs coursing through my veins, to the tips of my toes and the ends of my fingers, killing cells good and bad. I would come home from hospital in an awful mood, weak and sick.

Ron had become withdrawn, and while he was still excellent company with friends and family, he wanted to spend more and more time alone with his thoughts when at home. Those thoughts he wouldn't share, even with me.

When I was away I would notice things: that he had worn the same clothes for days, or that the only food he had prepared was toast. It wasn't that Ron couldn't wash his own clothes or cook his own meals, but he simply wouldn't. It didn't seem important. He was very much a creature of habit, and I had become an extension, a part of him; the part that cooked and cleaned. I was concerned as to how he might cope if I did succumb to the disease.

Oh, the misery that that uncaring, incompetent specialist had wrought!

As I became increasingly sick, my obsession with the specialist grew and I feared the only release in my mind would be enacting those terrible acts I had dreamed of. Then I thought perhaps bringing legal action against the specialist would still my murderous mind. I set up a meeting with my GP before I saw my barrister.

I entered the doctor's room and instinctively asked how he was. He said things were terrible on account of his mother having cancer.

'Now, what can I do for you, Mrs Taylor?' he asked, seemingly unaware of my mastectomy and chemo, even though it was as obvious to anyone as the nose on my face.

'I wanted to read your letter to the specialist.'

'I see. And why exactly?'

I told him I just wanted to. We danced around for a little while until I blurted out that I had cancer.

'How do you know?' he asked.

He was questioning, once again, whether I actually had cancer, or why I would dare to see another medical practitioner. These men, these bloody men.

I forced myself to be calm. I told him I didn't blame him, but I wanted to know why the specialist had been so inept. In pushing my anger away, sadness and tears were coming and I hated myself for that.

Of course, my doctor defended his specialist friend.

'He is a great man,' he said. 'One of the best. I'm sure he did everything by the book.'

I cried. I didn't want to think about the life I wasn't living, that I could be living, but with my breast removed and that poison going through my veins, I couldn't help it.

'You should have come and told me how you felt,' he said. 'I am sorry, I am truly sorry … you understand that I am guided by the specialists I use. All doctors are.'

He was now consoling me. As I left the surgery the doctor told me he hoped I would come to see him again.

Afterwards, I met with my barrister and told him everything I knew. He told me that while I might have a good case, a suit like this could drag on for years and would be very taxing.

'Mrs Taylor, is this how you'd like to spend the next few years of your life?'

The question he was really asking was: 'Is this how you'd like to spend the *last* few years of your life?'

It wasn't, I suppose, but I just couldn't get that rage out of me.

I told my dear friend, Joan, how I was feeling and she gave me wonderful counsel. My obsession with my specialist was not about me; it was about him and about the other women he treated. Perhaps it was admirable that I wanted to act against him (if not in the most admirable way) but I must concentrate on my recovery and my health right now, and be concerned with a luxury like justice later, when fully fit. It was time to be selfish.

Joan was right, but the only problem was that I couldn't concentrate on anything else. These negative, draining thoughts were always there, either in the periphery or front of my mind. When Joan suggested I see a counsellor, I agreed, and she found someone for me.

There was no point in lying to the counsellor. I told him exactly how I felt. He said he understood my thoughts; they were valid and not unexpected given my circumstance. He also said that such thoughts would do me no good; that at the best of times such negativity could only bring on bad mental and physical health, but in the situation I was in, it could be fatal.

The words echoed, mirroring what my oncologist had said. 'Stay positive, stay in the fight.' It was something I already knew, but, like an addict, I simply couldn't do what was good for me. He said that I might try to redirect that vengeful energy into a more useful avenue.

'Tell me, Valerie, is there something you have always wanted to do with your life but haven't?'

Looking back, I had been lucky enough to have experiences that most people would only dream about. I had travelled all over the world, from royal palaces to breathtaking reefs. I was very much living the life I wanted to live … and yet something did immediately come to mind.

The *Pamir*, that square-rigged sailing ship of my youth. It had been fifty years since I'd heard the snap of a sail and the creak of a timber hull, but I had not forgotten the sounds or the smell. The *Pamir* smelled like adventure, like another way of life.

I had been on whalers and research vessels, luxury liners and fishing boats, but never a ship like the *Pamir*. I hadn't because I had no reason to; when you lead a life that feels like a holiday, you make no time to take a holiday.

'I'd like to sail on a barque,' I told him. 'A ship called *Sea Cloud*. It's the most perfect ship ever created by man.'

He told me that a sea journey was a far healthier obsession, and suggested I book passage as soon as I could. It was worth a try.

A super-yacht with class and history, the *Sea Cloud* was commissioned by a Wall Street businessman in the early twentieth century, and enjoyed by him and his family for decades before being converted into a floating US embassy in Moscow before World War II, then into an anti-submarine guard ship during the war.

After the war the ship became private property once again, suffering a few decades of retirement, disrepair and neglect before being raised and restored once more to a glorious state, ready to give passage to those with the means and discernment.

It was a very expensive passage. I thought we could afford it but wasn't sure. I was in charge of the house, but Ron was in charge of the pocket book.

When I got home I told Ron exactly what I wanted to do. I asked if he would pay for it and he said he would, even when I told him that he would have to pay for two tickets – after all, I would need to take a doctor to administer my chemotherapy injections.

Ron agreed, and it wasn't spoken about afterwards; not even when I told Ron he would have to pay for three passages, the doctor thinking it would be inappropriate for him to travel with a woman on a trip like this without his wife.

I had spent most of my adult life with a trip on a boat circled on the calendar, but this was something completely different for me; I would be taking a journey purely for the enjoyment of travelling.

As I crossed off the days a new feeling was stoked: curiosity. I had been on so very many ships, but nothing like the *Sea Cloud*. Not since the *Pamir*, anyway. Memories of that short journey across the harbour had been held tightly and lovingly over the decades in my heart, but had fantasy seeped into them? The speed managed with only timber, cloth and wind, the feeling of symphony when the crew tacks or jibes, the magic that washes over you when on the deck; could these memories be real? Surely they were the fantasies of a naïve girl hung on the bones of far lesser experience.

I'll see, I thought as I prepared to fly to the Philippines, where I would greet the ship. Soon, I'll see.

The ship was everything I had seen in my dreams – and more. Over three decks the ship boasted perfect public areas of teak and brass, cabins of marble and gold leaf and, aside from some modern navigational augmentations, functional seagoing appointments as they had been more than a hundred years ago.

When I got on board the captain, who knew of me, greeted me personally and warmly. He asked if I had any questions about our passage, and I had only one.

'Is Mark Heighes on board?'

My nephew had been a darling since I became sick, living with us and ferrying me around for one appointment or another, but some weeks earlier work had called him. There were a number of ships that could use his expertise, but Mark knew only about his first commission. He'd told me he might end up on the *Sea Cloud* but, in that time of analogue communication, he hadn't been able to tell me where he was when I left Sydney.

'Mark is aboard,' the captain replied.

I was delighted.

'His mother said he is to fulfil any duty on the ship except those that take him atop the main mast,' I said to the captain, only half-joking. The *Sea Cloud* was one of the tallest ships of its kind in the world, and Mark's mother had been worried about her son working at such perilous heights.

The captain pointed and I followed his finger, up, up, up, many feet in the air to where, at the top of the main mast, Mark was rigging a sail. He could barely be seen, but even at that distance I could tell he was doing what he was doing with confidence.

It made me smile, seeing him up there. He looked like a man up there, not the boy we'd taken on his first trip on the *Lindblad.*

We sailed down from the Philippines south, through Indonesia to Bai, travelling waters I was very familiar with but, even so, it was a trip that was unique and wholly wonderful.

However, it was not always an easy one. North of Indonesia we tried to navigate between two hurricanes but didn't wholly succeed and had to ride out 140-kilometre-per-hour winds and huge waves, which the wonderful ship rode like a seal. I was very ill sometimes, with painful ulcers in my mouth and pains in the arm that had been affected by the cancer, but none of that mattered. I was living a dream. My childhood memories were my reality on the *Sea Cloud*, enhanced with delicious food and wonderful company.

The second evening I dined with the captain.

'Did you know we have SCUBA equipment?' he asked. 'It's used for cleaning the hull. Now, normally I would never offer it to a guest …'

It's incredible to me how one experience can be enjoyed in myriad ways. When I had dived Komodo from the *Lindblad* and for the first time, I dived with a thrilling sense of discovery, and on every trip since I returned to part of that joy, looking for new discovery; a new animal, a new reef. Diving from the *Sea Cloud* I felt something altogether different.

It was a quiet happiness I felt on those dives, not striving, not yearning but just being. I didn't feel anguished or nervous or angry, I was simply content. I had not felt that way for a long time.

That dive was only the second most memorable experience on that trip, however. The memory I have, which will never fade, is not below the water, nor even above the water but on land.

One day my chemotherapy was to be administered in a hospital, and although there was a very fine little hospital on board, when the opportunity presented itself we would go to the local hospital, I think so my doctor could see these small hospitals for himself. The *Sea Cloud* tied up to a jetty in the town of Ternate in Maluku. While the guests were enjoying a land tour, my doctor and I took a small bus to the local hospital. It was the poorest hospital I have ever seen, with dozens of patients lying on cots in open, cement-floored wards with only sarongs for sheets.

There was only one doctor, a young Balinese man who spoke little English. He took us into a sparse treatment room and with his several nurses watched as my doctor administered the chemo. After it had been completed, the syringes, tubes and saline packs were thrown in the rubbish bin. As we were leaving, my doctor saw the young Indonesian nurse rummaging through the bin. He rushed over and tried to stop the nurse.

'No, you can't. Infection,' he said. 'It's not safe. You can't.'

Soon they were almost wrestling, with the Indonesian doctor swearing that the needles would be sterilised before use.

'Please, please,' the doctor said, now practically begging. 'We don't have. We don't have.'

Eventually the young Indonesian doctor agreed to give up the disposable equipment that had been used for my chemotherapy treatment when we promised we would bring back clean needles and more.

We gathered up everything we could on the *Sea Cloud*: from the stores of materials we had brought for my treatment and also from the surplus of the ship's medical supplies as we were close to our final destination of Bali, where the ship would resupply.

The Indonesian doctor broke down crying when he saw what we'd brought, with his hands pressed hard together in a symbol of prayer. He thanked us for every package, every bandage, and every need that we fulfilled. He was so grateful he could hardly bring himself to touch the boxes. He prayed over a box of needles.

Tears came to me also, I sobbed for quite some time. The humanity of the moment was overwhelming, this gentle man who was breaking down just so he could have the opportunity to help other people in his community. To me this man was the embodiment of the Hippocratic oath, and also the embodiment of goodness. I thought to myself, this journey of mine has not been in vain.

I remembered this moment and this man as I went through the rest of my treatment. It was calming to hark back to someone who didn't work for the benefit of himself, but others.

That whole trip was a moveable feast, ready to nourish me with its memory whenever I needed it. And there were so many moments I carried with me and carry still, from my first glimpse of the ship in Manila, to my last memory, which was of Mark paddling away from the ship on his surfboard.

Mark and I had been on the deck of the *Sea Cloud* together as we approached Benoa Harbour and he'd spotted a very surfable break. All of his obligations were fulfilled and he was now on leave, so he asked if I could take his bag with me to the hotel.

Of course I could. Mark took his shirt off, put some money in a waterproof pouch, which he stuffed in his shorts, and then threw his board and himself over the side of the ship.

I can see him now, paddling towards that break. Although I was never a board rider, I understood exactly what Mark was feeling in that moment. My love for Mark was stoked through my understanding of him. That showed me my love for Ron was altogether different.

I had been married to Ron for nearly twenty-five years and there were parts of him that I understood and parts that were never available to me. He was neither caring nor kind to me when I was ill, but I still couldn't wait to see him as we touched down in Sydney. We didn't have a tearful or heartfelt reunion, but it felt truly wonderful to be back in my house with my husband.

That first round of chemotherapy was a complete success. When I was scanned after the last injections I was found to be cancer-free and would require no further treatment.

I celebrated with friends: a new life, or at least a renewal of my old life. It's a powerful, gratifying thing to realise that what you really want is what you already have. Perhaps life wasn't perfect, but only children and fantasists believe in perfection.

When I told Ron I was in full remission he seemed unmoved until he spoke. 'That's good. I was getting sick of eating baked beans.'

It was only later, many years later in the 1990s, that I discovered Ron had suffered a nervous breakdown that likely went on for years and likely coincided with the years I was ill. The breakdown had required psychiatric help, something Ron would have been loath to ask for.

Ron spoke of this illness to me only once, and we never spoke about it again. By the time he told me, his mood was different and we were in a different stage of life. There was no point in labouring over his pains, nor mine.

There were more important concerns then for us. After all, life is finite and Ron and I would always rather spend our time looking forward than back. I'm not perfect, and nor was Ron, but he was perfect for me.

Only gods are perfect and we are not gods.

Memento mori, memento mori.

CHAPTER FOURTEEN

The sharks that saved a reef

I am often asked about the places I have been to and the people I have met. I am blessed to have seen so much of the world before it started to suffer the effects of modern intervention: Fiji, Indonesia, Germany, Sweden, Africa, South Africa, Antarctica, the Caribbean, South America, Papua New Guinea, all the states adjacent to the Arabian Gulf, India, Sri Lanka, Jordan, most of Europe, most of the Pacific Islands and most of Asia. In each of those places I have learned something new and met interesting people. I am not overly impressed by fame and status. It is intelligence, humour and kindness that make an impact on me. And people can be surprising. I was not expecting Prince Charles to have such a wonderful sense of humour, though the fact he was friends with Spike Milligan should have been a clue.

On my way to a private cruise trip in Indonesia I was in a remote airport when a gorgeous tall blonde with a drawling Texan accent started to talk to the guy next to me in the luggage area and comment on their four missing bags that couldn't be found. The very slender Englishman with her said, 'Don't worry, darling. We still have the other fourteen.' I liked him immediately. I don't follow pop culture and so didn't really know much about Mick Jagger and Jerry Hall, but they were both lovely company. I would end up teaching Mick how to dive while we were off the coast of Papua. He was a fast learner and we did several dives together. Mick asked me what was the most dangerous thing he was likely to encounter and I said it was the coral; just don't get scratched. Coral poisoning can happen very fast if not treated immediately. Once it takes hold, only massive amounts of antibiotics will help. The tropical ocean is a soup of tiny microbes. Our blood is about the same salinity and temperature as northern tropical water. The microbes will enter any opening in your skin, find a nice warm home and flourish. I have seen Ron bed-ridden for two weeks; our companion John Harding nearly lost a leg. And other people, usually fishermen, sometimes die.

I noticed Mick ignore a couple of reef sharks and a good-sized grouper but he stayed well away from the coral. I have enjoyed Mick's company in England and when he came to Australia (I received concert tickets and an invitation to dinner) and I am delighted to have had his company for those weeks we spent exploring the remote parts of Papua. Mick is what Australians call a good guy.

One interesting event. We were riding in Zodiacs around the high islands off the Papuan coast. The islands look like mushrooms. No one can live on them. The high cliffs of these islands are pitted with caves. It looked virtually impossible to scale these cliffs but Mick and I were wearing good sneakers. We found a spot where part of the rim had collapsed and, with some difficulty, we climbed up to one of the caves. It was astounding. Human remains were scattered against the walls but it was the wall paintings that blew my mind away. I believe they were Aboriginal. I had seen similar artwork in caves along the Kimberley coast in north-western Australia. I may be wrong but I think Mick and I found something no one else had seen for thousands of years. I took a few photos. I would have loved to explore more of the caves that were accessible but we only had a short time available. I still think often of what we discovered.

I was often asked if I know (and now am asked if I knew) Jacques Cousteau, the famed French underwater filmmaker and adventurer. The answer is, no. I met him but we never shared a meal or a drink, nor did I ever dive with him.

That's not true of his eldest son, however, Jean-Michel Cousteau, who entertained a career on land in architecture, and then very much became a chip off the old block.

When we first met Jean-Michel he was in his early thirties and had just finished a stint working with his father's production company. Together they had worked on a number of films but Jean-Michel wanted to get out of the very large shadow his father cast, and do something that was his and his alone.

Jean-Michel first contacted us late in 1972, after the *Inner Space* series had finally given Ron and me international visibility. There was a business opportunity he wanted to talk to us about, one that was folded into a dive trip he promised would be special. The opportunity and the diving was at a place called Wuvulu, a tiny island a couple of hundred kilometres north of New Guinea in the Bismarck Sea.

Like all of what would later become Papua New Guinea, Wuvulu was then an Australian colony, and the colonial administration was very sympathetic to Australian businesses. To that end, Jean-Michel Cousteau had partnered with an Australian lawyer to gain control over half the island. His plan was to build a settlement for like-minded people who loved nature both on land and underwater. The island could support a unique dive resort with an ahead-of-its-time eco-friendly bent and, most important of all, bring work to the local villagers.

Unlike at other resorts, guests at Wuvulu would not be invited to stay for a few nights or weeks, but forever. There would not be a hotel on the island, but instead 180 acre-sized blocks would be sold, with those purchasing the blocks also taking on the financial responsibility for the upkeep of the island, which would include windmill-generated power, a processed septic system and a total ban on petrol-powered land vehicles or marine outboards.

Actor and conservationist William Holden and author James Michener, whose book *Tales of the South Pacific* had won him the Pulitzer Prize and Presidential Medal of Freedom, were already involved, as well as other less notable but even more moneyed residents.

The way Jean-Michel described it, the value of the island was that it was unencumbered by industry and would stay that way in perpetuity. He also explained that he wanted to gift us one of the blocks on the island, in return for Ron helping to promote the island.

Well, it was a nice enough place, with palm trees and blue water, but it wasn't anything exceptional; nothing that couldn't be found on most tropical islands.

Then we dived the surrounding coral reef.

The coral reefs surrounding Wuvulu were like those of the northern end of the Barrier Reef, but it was as though that coral had been dressed with more coral, in colours and shapes I had never seen. That was true also of the fish, large and small, and turtles and sharks and eels. Other than at Komodo, it was the greatest amount of marine biodiversity we had ever seen in one place.

Jean-Michel tried to explain what had created this explosion of life and colour, or at least as it was understood in the early 1970s. He spoke about the overlap of the Pacific and Indian oceans, and the unique currents, and the volcanic soils, and the exceptional conditions of the last Ice Age. Ron and I were very much on a journey of scientific discovery, and while we didn't then completely understand why that reef was special, we knew that it was. We already knew there was no anchorage. The island and its beautiful lagoon sat atop an ancient volcano. Having no anchorage meant the island was not popular with visitors arriving by boat. An airport was yet to be built by the new owners and, best of all, the locals were all Seventh-Day Adventists, who do not eat any marine animals unless they have scales. This meant turtles, crabs and all fish with skin were never hunted. The island was a paradise of wildlife.

Over the next few decades we started to understand that, while Wuvulu was indeed special, it wasn't exclusively so. We saw similar marine wilderness areas in Raja Ampat and Komodo in Indonesia. The Solomon Islands, and parts of the Philippines and Malaysia also had unique marine life but in these places the impact of man the hunter had long before affected their diversity.

These reefs each had their own individual habitat (in fact, sometimes two reefs only a few kilometres apart would have markedly different microhabitats and species profiles), but all the reefs shared two things: a huge abundance of varied coral, and a massive amount of sea life.

We now know those reefs are all in what is called the Coral Triangle.

Extending from the northern tip of the Philippines, west just past Bali, and east to the Solomon Islands, the Coral Triangle covers a little over one-and-a-half percent of the world's surface but hosts a third of the world's coral reefs, and with three-quarters of the different types of coral found in the triangle. With that coral comes life – massive biodiversity.

More than half of Indo-Pacific reef fish species live within the triangle.

Conjecture still rages as to what makes the Coral Triangle what it is, but it is now acknowledged that it is an area as unique and fascinating as the Amazon or the Galapagos. For Ron and me, the Coral Triangle was far more interesting than the Amazon or the Galapagos; the Coral Triangle, or at least the underwater parts of it, was almost completely unexplored when we started diving there.

After that first visit, we left Wuvulu with plans to build a house on the island, and a great desire to explore the exceptional reefs there and beyond. We never had the chance to fulfil that first part of the plan, however, because in 1975 Papua New Guinea gained independence, and any Australian business claim in Papua New Guinea was dissolved or renegotiated. The second part of the plan was another matter. Our interest in the Coral Triangle never diminished.

The first trip we took on the *Lindblad* was through the Coral Triangle, and we took many more on that wonderful ship. Once the wonder of the reefs in Indonesian, Malaysian and New Guinean waters was understood, the viability of a business like the *Lindblad* was established. Eco-travel imitators emerged but the *Lindblad*, with her dive shop, snorkelling school, love for unusual locations and staff of experts in birds, plants, animals and the marine world, was unique.

She offered adventure, excitement and knowledge. Her lecturers gave me an education far more interesting and useful than I could have received anywhere else.

Throughout the 1970s and 1980s Ron and I dived in the Coral Triangle more than any other place in the world, and it is likely we saw more of the Coral Triangle than any other people. Ron certainly filmed more in the Coral Triangle than anyone else; every time we went down to a new reef, he would take a camera. Usually the footage was not for any specific film (although sometimes Ron would sell half-hour films of the trip, mostly underwater footage, to the guests. He would edit a half-hour story in his Sydney editing suite and post copies to them. Later, when video became popular it was easier but originally it was rolls of 16-millimetre film.) The original footage went into our archive.

'You never know,' Ron would say, and when diving in the Coral Triangle, that was certainly true.

For instance once when we were working in Komodo from the *Lindblad*, our diving took us into a very cold current, desperately frigid compared to the rest of the area. There Ron videoed some fish he had not seen before. When showing the footage later that evening Dr Jack Randall, one of the hosts on the *Lindblad* and also one of the world's leading authorities on coral fish, asked Ron where he had shot this footage. Ron said the footage was from a dive we had done that day off Komodo, but Dr Randall felt it was very strange because the fish in the film were cold-water fish that couldn't possibly exist in a tropical zone.

Eventually it was discovered that those fish species had come to the Coral Triangle during the last Ice Age and there, in the coldest currents, had existed since then. Jack explained how as the ice grew and the oceans froze the marine animals were pushed into warmer waters. Possibly because of the incredible volcanic activity the ocean in the Coral Triangle never froze. As the ice receded and the ocean grew warmer, animals who had survived the Ice Age spread out in every direction to repopulate what was formerly a frozen wasteland. This took millions of years and is still happening today.

We were always fascinated by the Coral Triangle, and that fascination only grew as we saw more of it. Ron always resolved that one day he would make a film about that place.

One day, one day.

In the early 1990s we discovered that Jean-Michel Cousteau's eco-tourism aspirations didn't die in Wuvulu, but instead had just migrated over the years to a more traditional form. In 1993 he invited us as guests to a new dive resort – essentially a luxury hotel with a state-of-the-art dive shop attached – at Savusavu on Vanua Levu, the second-largest island in the Fiji islands.

Built on a former coconut plantation, the resort – first known as the Cousteau Fiji Islands Resort and then later as the Jean-Michel Cousteau Resort Fiji – was visited by some of the best people in the world to dive with, from Howard Hall, Stan Waterman, Phil Nuytten and Peter Benchley to Eugenie Clark and Sylvia Earle.

It was lovely to spend time with a who's who of diving and underwater photography, most of whom we had worked with at some time or other, and the resort was (and still is) a world-class luxury property, but, to be honest, it just wasn't really my scene.

The diving at the resort was undoubtedly wonderful for the general public, but it wasn't anything we hadn't done already, so when an offer came to see something we hadn't seen before, Ron and I jumped at the chance.

The offer came from a man named Mike Neumann, a tall Swiss ex-banker we had first met on the *Lindblad*. We met many people on the *Lindblad*, but Mike stuck out, perhaps because of his quiet but powerful presence. He was intelligent, but most of the people on those trips were; confident and capable. The average person does not generally have an adventure as a holiday. Mike was very tall without it defining him; moneyed, but weren't they all. I suppose he was younger than almost everyone else – still in his early twenties – but that wasn't the reason he became a lifelong friend.

I think it was because his personality existed roughly at the mid-point between Ron's and mine. He was (and is) masculine, capable and incredibly focused like Ron, but also a searcher, and had a capacity to have fun for fun's sake.

Mike Neumann was the diver who taught me how to drink champagne underwater. He was also the man who told us about the village where the local men would take tourists out to see sharks they attracted to the boat by feeding the fish offal. After a wonderful week with old and new friends we left the resort and went to Beqa Lagoon.

We had been working with sharks for years but had found the bull shark difficult to attract. It is one of the most fascinating species of shark. Getting its name from its squat and muscular stature, the bull shark only grows to about two, sometimes three, times the size of a human adult, but it can swim very quickly, has incredible attacking power and is responsible for several attacks off Australian beaches.

It's a shark that can survive in both salt and fresh water. It mates in the ocean but when time to give birth approaches the pregnant female swims up a river into fresh water to pup. It is believed this behaviour is to protect her young from the jaws of the male bull sharks who would have no hesitation in devouring a small tender juvenile of their own species or any other species. The bull shark has a presence not as intimidating as the great white but almost. It is one of the most dangerous sharks that inhabit coastal waters. I have never seen one in the open ocean. Ron had never been able to film a bull shark and he was very interested in seeing this Beqa shark feed.

In 1993 it was a rare shark to see, but Mike was true to his word. Near Beqa Island just south of Pacific Harbour on Fiji's main island of Viti Levu, we saw some off in the distance. We kept still, hoping we were unthreatening as we tried to will them towards us. We had whitetips, black tips, grey reef, silver tips and one tiger shark but the bulls hung back. We could see them down about ninety feet (27.5 metres) near the dropoff but no matter how carefully we approached, they would slip over the edge into deeper water. They were likely scared or at least concerned about this strange intrusion and wouldn't come any closer. On that trip anyway.

We kept going back to Fiji. Each time we went we would dive with the Beqa divers, and each time the sharks came a little closer. I would take down fish and hand-feed the smaller sharks that milled around but the bulls remained nervous. They would take a fish head but not when we were close.

Mike had retired young, giving up his banking career when not even forty. He had been a young star within Deutsche Bank, making good money first for other people and then for himself. He told us when we first met him in his early twenties that he thought there might be more to life than just padding out bank accounts.

Afterwards he bought a boat so he could sail and dive all around the world and figure out what he wanted to do with the rest of his life. Ron and I travelled around New Guinea with Mike on his lovely vessel, diving far-flung reefs and exploring new dive sites. It was a fabulous trip. The other guests were all diving friends. There was no pressure to do anything but enjoy ourselves.

Mike was not someone who would be happy idle, but he didn't know what to do next. He knew how to make money out of money, that's what he'd been good at, but having done that he also felt he wanted to do something associated with nature, particularly the ocean. He told Ron and me that he wanted to do something good, something useful – he just didn't know what that might be.

After a few false starts, Mike eventually set up his own dive business in Fiji. Mike's dive shop was always going to be unlike any other. He would never be happy just buying some tanks and a boat and taking people to see whatever it was they could see; he conceived of a dive business with a purpose and with scope.

Commercial overfishing had been as much of an issue in Fiji as it had been all around the Pacific and around the world, and as an intrepid diver Mike knew all too well the sinking feeling of arriving at an empty reef. Instead of retreating to safe but busy locations, or venturing to ever more remote reefs, Mike could see the potential of Shark Reef. The local men had already created the beginnings of a shark dive just by feeding the sharks and attracting them to the same area of reef.

He figured this could be good for everyone; good for the marine animals and divers, but also good for the locals, because a number of economic studies suggested that in places like Fiji far more money could be gleaned from dive tourism than from irresponsible fishing. Mike knew that a reef where unusual and exciting marine animals were easily encountered was always a big attraction to divers. Like us, he also knew most divers loved to interact with the more dangerous species, animals that were not easily found around the usual dive locations.

It had long been suspected that sharks are essential to both reef health and recovery. There was scientific conjecture as to why a healthy shark population almost always meant a healthy spread of other marine life, from the smallest polyps to the largest fish.

Mike concluded that the sharks would be essential to the recovery of the reef and also essential to the business, because he believed that people would travel from around the world to swim with bull sharks. Ron and I wholeheartedly agreed. Diving in Fiji is a lovely diversion, but the possibility of getting nose to nose with a bull shark – that's worth travelling for. Because we had spent over forty years working with sharks we knew more about their individual behaviour than most people. It's humbling being in the water with an apex predator; also exhilarating and, if you manage to capture good movie footage and photographs, extremely rewarding.

Mike's financial career had been built around project management, and he knew this project would need to build slowly and with local integration, something Jean-Michel and his partners on the Wuvulu project had had in mind. Mike took the time to establish relationships with certain sections of the Fijian government, including the department of fisheries. 'Let's protect one reef with a total fishing ban,' Mike suggested, 'and we'll see what we can do with it.' He also built a relationship with the traditional Fijian owners of a reef only a short boat ride from Pacific Harbour, an essential part of the business.

The second relationship would be more essential than even Mike suspected.

When the reef was protected from fishing, the first sharks to come were the small sharks: grey reef, black tip, whitetip, nurse sharks. Sharks that could easily be encountered in many parts of the world. What was needed to bring the tourists was the big sharks, the highly publicised sharks like the bull shark and the tiger shark. To bring those bulls in close to the reef, someone was going to have to build a personal relationship with fish that could, if they wanted to, tear the flesh from your bones.

This is where two men, named Rusi and Manasa, came in. These village men became not only capable dive masters, but also protectors and almost co-workers of dozens and dozens of large and small sharks. Mike was the organiser. He created a shark dive like no other in the world. More importantly, he convinced the government to ban all fishing on and around Shark Reef.

Several local men learned to bring the sharks in closer by hand-feeding them, and went on to develop a personal relationship with each animal, naming them and knowing well their moods and tendencies.

As Manasa explained to me once, he had no fear of the sharks because one of his culture's traditional gods, Dakuwaqa, who is an ally and a friend, *is* a shark.

'Dakuwaqa would never hurt me,' Manasa told me.

Whenever we went back to Fiji it was a pleasure to see this reef and the bull sharks, once only shadows in the distance, eventually appear often at arm's length in front of the lens. It's something that is a total adrenaline hit and usually results in a very good image.

I did speak to Manasa and Rusi about their own personal safety. I told them while it was true that the bull sharks would not see these men as prey when underwater, that didn't mean the sharks couldn't accidentally bite them. I implored them to wear protection when feeding.

Rusi agreed that to have a chain mail sleeve up to the shoulder while feeding would certainly be prudent.

I was happy to hear later that chain mail became standard practice, especially when the sharks became more numerous.

As more and more sharks came, Fiji became a favourite destination for Ron and me, especially after the millennial turn, when diving many of what we called hot spots due to lack of protection had become downright depressing.

For so much of my life it was a sense of discovery that spurred me on and excited me. I would feel a surge when I was on a boat taking me to a dive site I had never been to before, and often no one had ever visited. The excitement grew as I put on my gear. The sense of adventure peaked as I stepped off the boat into the water from one world into another. I didn't know what I would find, but I knew there was a good chance that it would be incredible. The deterioration of reefs and the life they support has been terrifyingly fast.

Seeing a once vibrant life-filled reef that had been fished to obliteration was depressing on so many levels. Sometimes there was more plastic than coral. Dynamite fishing has turned thousands of reefs into dead rubble. Lucipara, an uninhabited series of islands and reefs in the Banda Sea, was once a paradise of fish, colour and sharks. Last time I was there we didn't stay. Dynamite fishing had turned the vibrant living marine wilderness into a dead pile of rubble, but that disappointment was fleeting; an insignificance compared to what the death of the reef might mean on a larger scale.

Some of the fish that had been on this reef might never be seen again. Nature had created a magnificent balanced marine environment but, for the easy taking of a few fish, dynamite had destroyed all the inhabitants both big and small. A reef system is a web of life. Each animal, static or moving, plays a part. Together they make a whole, a small but perfect world.

The biggest problem marine life has is that it's free for the taking. No one has to clear the land, grow a crop, breed an animal. No one ensures that fish will be there the next year.

The fishermen just take and take and take.

So goes the reef, goes the world.

It wasn't something I wanted to think about when the sun was shining and the water was warm, but it was something I couldn't help but think about when looking at a destroyed reef. It is like looking at a wasteland that was once a jungle where birds flew and animals roamed.

This is why Ron and I loved visiting Mike Neumann and the incredible Fijian Shark Reef. It was, and is, a wonderful success story, in and out of the water. When the sharks came back, so too did the fish and the corals. The divers came; dozens of them, from around the world, filling restaurants and hotel rooms. The attraction was the sharks, especially the big bulls.

Each time we visited there were more sharks, more fish, more divers, and more employment for the local men and women. It was a place that seemed to be reversing what we were seeing almost everywhere else. I felt personally thrilled and gratified.

Ron had always wanted to make a film about Mike and this reef. He had been collecting footage from the days of the empty reef and the scared sharks, and I suppose you could say from even before that, on the *Lindblad* when we first met Mike.

Due to the controlled feeding Ron had footage of the sharks interacting with the divers. He also had interviews with Rusi and Manasa, and I even had a title for the film: *The Sharks that Saved a Reef.*

What we didn't have yet, was a suitable ending, but we figured one day we would work something out and be able to complete that documentary.

We felt the same way about the Coral Triangle. We had decades of footage; a lifetime on location. Now all we needed was a finish; just a moment of inspiration.

The Sharks that Saved a Reef and *The Coral Triangle*: the culmination of decades of work, of fascinating trips and adventure.

One day, one day, one day.

Then, in 2009, Ron was diagnosed with advanced myeloid leukaemia. He was told that his chances of survival were slim, but neither of us believed that diagnosis. As far as he was concerned, there was always an out, always a solution to every problem. Ron just thought he had to figure out what that was; the right chemicals, with the right food and the right mindset. From my perspective, the diagnosis made no sense at all. I didn't believe that Ron would just get sick and then die.

He was never sick, always strong as a bull. He always ate healthy food, never drank alcohol and never smoked – it just wasn't right that he would give over to this illness. I was the one who got sick, I was the one who liked sweet things and gin and tonics and late nights. I survived cancer. Surely Ron wouldn't get cancer and then just die.

It felt like I was the one getting old, not Ron. Ron was still a man in the way he had always been. He was the same person, and people acted around him in the way they always had. I suppose people didn't want Ron to be attractive forever, but perhaps they did of me. Women are judged differently as they age. It felt, over the years, that increasingly people's expectations of me were unmet, and that's why it seemed so incongruous to me that Ron would be the one to die.

It was a trying time. It was very difficult emotionally, of course, but also the days filled up with a whole raft of obligations and tasks around Ron's treatment and medications and food and mobility and everything else. Not to mention all the chores that still had to be done.

I was very appreciative that we had given up our mansion in Roseville by 2009. The upkeep of that place, with rooms neither of us would go into for months and gardens that constantly needed tending, would have killed me if I had to do all that and look after Ron.

We had moved to Fairlight, to a gorgeous multi-level apartment with views across the harbour to the Heads, a place that was found for us by my lovely friend Jayne Jenkins.

I don't know what I would have done without Jayne when Ron got sick. She and her husband, Colin, kept me sane, and broke me out of the routine of Ron's cancer. Ron felt his cancer and the controlled damage of his treatment heavily. If Ron had ever been sick before I certainly didn't know about it, but during his cancer he was very ill, very affected. He wasn't one to moan and try to gain sympathy, but I could feel his pain.

Even though I never could consider this illness would kill Ron, he told me once quite soon after his treatment started, in a very matter-of-fact way, that he wished he was already dead. Ron wanted nothing of me in that moment, and certainly was not being hyperbolic, it was just an expression of fact.

After that statement my confidence in his recovery was dented.

One night in 2011, Jayne and Colin got me out of the house for the premiere of a new Australian–American film called *Sanctum*, co-produced by James Cameron of *Titanic*, *Avatar* and *The Abyss* fame. At the party after the screening I was chatting with Andrew Wight (the other producer) when James came over and asked to be introduced. He asked where Ron was and I said he was nearby but staying away from the crowds as he was not well. James asked to meet Ron. He told us about his upbringing on the outskirts of Ontario, Canada, and how his family moved to Los Angeles when he was a teenager. Leaving all your friends and a life you know is hard. I knew because I had experienced the same restlessness when we moved from New Zealand. He said he was walking along the street and on a whim went into a theatre and watched a film called *Blue Water, White Death*.

James told me that *Blue Water, White Death* had influenced him as much as anything else he ever saw. He told me that as soon as he finished seeing the film for the first time, he went straight back in for a second screening. The film, he said, fostered not only a love of cinema, but also of oceanic adventure. He told us he then knew what he wanted to do with his life.

I left that party wondering what adventures Ron and I might have had if we'd met James Cameron when we were younger and stronger.

Around the same time of that movie premiere, I started having a recurring dream that eventually became a nightmare. In the dream I heard the sound of water. Was it the ocean?

I listened for waves, but there were none; this was running water. Was it the sound of a river? It wasn't that either. In the dream I was suddenly at Seal Rocks, or my place in Fairlight, or in Roseville or, some days, even Mortdale. The sound of water was a running tap. I rushed around and it wasn't one running tap, but many. I tried to turn them off but I couldn't, my hands were too weak. All of the plugs were in and the basins were filling. I tried to pull the plugs but my hands couldn't manage that either. My hands were so weak: polio, arthritis, age. I cursed myself. I called for Ron, but he didn't come. I yelled and screamed but he didn't reply because he wasn't there. The sinks filled and water poured on the floor. The room filled quickly. The water rose, the air disappeared. Nothing could be done … It was only a dream.

An expedition to finalise the Coral Triangle story was arranged, but as we were preparing to fly, Ron had to check in to hospital for treatment. I travelled to Indonesia without Ron, but, our nephews Mark and Jono were with me, Jono as the underwater cameraman and Mark now as captain of the *Seven Seas*.

Mark's wonderful dive boat was the home base for the shoot, and I found it was so incredibly gratifying to see Jono, who had become an underwater cinematographer in his own right, pick up excellent shots in wonderful conditions.

It was not a trip, shoot nor film that I remember fondly, though. Dick Dennison had a very different way of working from us, and had a very different focus in mind for the film. He wanted to concentrate on some of the local people in the area we were shooting, and their relationship with the ocean.

A non-reef animal, the crocodile, featured heavily and he and I clashed a little.

It was his film, however, and one must always let a director exercise their vision.

It was wonderful working with my nephews, but in my opinion the film suffered somewhat without Ron's expertise.

We did attempt to finish our Fiji film, though. We already had two acts, and all that was needed was a third. Ron and I thought that if we went to Fiji and dived together we would be able to find that last act.

'This will be my last trip,' Ron said to me once while we were preparing. He meant it too, regardless of his future health outcomes.

'Well, we'd better make the most of it,' I replied. I could see Ron struggling. He kept sitting down with his eyes closed, sometimes even going to sleep in the daytime, something he had never done before.

We didn't make the most of it. Ron was too weak, too sick. He did dive a couple of times, even managing to film a little, but early in the week he told me he was finished. He simply couldn't go on. I kept diving, but after each dive I would come back to a darkened room where a thin, old man lay asleep on the bed.

We returned home never finding the end of that film.

Once we were back in Fairlight, Ron had his ups and downs. There were moments of hope and weeks of energy but also setbacks and despair. Once, in a good moment, and after I had brought him his tablet and special drink, he thanked me. I remember it because it was the only moment in our lives that he ever did.

On Father's Day 2012, Ron turned the final corner.

It was very early in the morning. I heard a crash. Ron had got up to relieve himself, but lost all muscular control on the way. When I got to him I thought he was dead, folded as he was between the drawers and a glass partition. He was alive but bleeding and barely conscious.

I cleaned Ron up, put him in new clothes and called Manly Waters Private Hospital to let them know I was bringing him in. They met my car with a wheelchair. I stayed with him for some time but he just lay there, eyes closed. The nurse brought me a cup of tea after which I went home. The following morning at 6 a.m. Ron died.

It was the end of my love, and in many ways the end of my life as I knew it; the loss of the man who was as much a part of me as my arms and legs left a void that engulfed me. Yes, we were co-dependent and damn the modern connotations of that word.

He was the most wonderful man I ever met, the most capable and intriguing and complex, and while he didn't show love in a traditional way, I felt the loss of what he had been giving me so gravely. I was seventy-seven years old and I didn't know what to do with myself.

I knew there were a thousand things to organise; accounts and deeds and bills and paperwork and arrangements and archives and slides and film and drives and contracts, but for the first time in my life, I had no idea where to start. So, I didn't.

The only thing I managed to do in that first week was read the sympathy letters that came in a dozen at a time. I would read them and think: How highly people regarded Ron. How humble and gentle they saw him, how clever and kind.

Oh, you never really knew him at all. But I did. Ron was a very special man, incredibly intelligent, totally aware of his place on the planet. I loved him because of, and despite, who he was. He was my other half. After so many years of Ron and Valerie Taylor, I now had to learn to be on my own. Just Valerie.

CHAPTER FIFTEEN

Tidal pull

I have all but finished this book, but now there's a film being made about my life. I don't know how that happened. I ended up agreeing to it, and here we are. It's 2019 and I'm eighty-three. Ron has been gone seven years and it feels like yesterday in some ways, yet he has missed out on so much more. Age may have slowed me but I have still been diving, writing, painting, creating and it feels like I blinked and now I am here. Looking back to put my life on the page has been a strange experience. So many years, places and people to remember. It is always hard to know what will be interesting to others. And now I am telling stories again for the documentary. While filming I've said a number of times that this will be my last film.

Today, the producers have me at the Lagoon Resort, Fiji, the hotel Ron and I used to stay in when we visited Mike

Neumann and his bull sharks. I'm here because that's where Mike's dive shop is, not because I'm staying at the hotel.

The room where Ron lay in darkness after his last dive is just a short walk from the dive shop; past the open thatched dining area, past the bar in which gin used to flow and soft music used to drift over a large blue pool towards a green river.

The bar is still open and the music still drifts over the pool, but I don't know who drinks the gin there these days.

This resort was built in the 1980s and was once grand: the realised vision of the first owner, a Middle Eastern arms dealer. The hotel was also once, in the 1990s, refurbished to be a majestically gauche bordello for Korean tourists. The prostitutes never arrived, though. The new owner hadn't factored in the Christian conservatism of the locals.

The resort has changed since we used to stay here. The owners of the hotel went bankrupt some years ago and now the place has been taken over by the local government.

I can see a boat on the river: the MV *Predator*. There is a man preparing tanks and regulators, tea and biscuits. This is Ben Saqata, my dive buddy on the trip.

Sadly, Rusi, the most amazing shark feeder, has passed away. Rusi knew every bull shark by name; he also knew their different personalities. Now younger men have taken on the task of feeding. Ben is a local pastor and a marine biologist, but is also a bodybuilder and dive master. He has become my assistant and protector. All the guest divers have a protector to watch their back. Bull sharks can at times be very unpredictable. Ben helps me suit up and step off the boat. He will also watch my back when the bulls are being fed. I have many friends in the diving world and Ben is one of them.

When Ron died I didn't know where much of the paperwork was. There are some things I have no idea about to this day. Business letters arrive and they are a puzzle to me. I wonder what business Ron had with this person or that company.

I was angry and lost after Ron died, and I still feel dismayed sometimes. Even though it happened slowly and predictably, I was unprepared for his death. There is a time in your life when being unprepared can be terrifying. I'm not well practised at being terrified. Now, I am worried about some of the most mundane things, such as bank statements and letters from lawyers.

Things that other people are fearful of – sharks and deep dives, strong currents, storms and wild waves tossing the dinghy around like a cork – roll over me like a breeze. And I feel sad that so many young people today have little idea of the exciting world they live in. Young, suburban folk who can't see the manageable reality of risk, only the images on the iPhones they hold in front of their faces.

I do wish Ron had prepared me for a life without him, or that I had prepared myself, but while we're wishing: oh, how I wish he were here.

I never understood melancholia until Ron died. There's never a moment I don't wish he were here, and there never will be.

Being in Fiji makes me miss him even more. On this trip, Mike Neumann is diving with me, along with his partner,

Natasha. Mike has been single for all of the time I've known him, and I feel pleased he now has a lovely woman as a partner. Natasha is a former criminal defence lawyer from New York. She's young, strong and distractingly beautiful.

Along with Natasha, Mike and the filmmakers, I board the *Predator* and speed towards the open ocean.

Jono is with me. I hold his hand. It's warm. He is working as an underwater cameraman for the filmmakers, but he's here for me. All my three nephews look out for me. I am a very lucky aunty.

I'm sometimes amazed by how weak I have become. Sometimes amazed, sometimes disgusted. Above water I am an old lady. Underwater I am forty years old again. Gravity drags me down; I step through the surface of two-thirds of this planet and enter a liquid world where I can fly in any direction.

There is no gravity under the ocean.

I am ready to dive but I am part of a film crew and we must all enter the water together.

They have to get the cameras ready, get the crew ready. Shooting a film is very different when you're the subject, not part of the crew. I can't say I'm comfortable with it. They're mollycoddling me. It's not something I'm used to, not something I'm comfortable with.

Ben holds my tank and leads me to the edge of the boat. I could once climb a ladder wearing twin steel tanks. Now I need a strong hand to lift the weight of an aluminium tank from my back when I walk across a moving deck.

Once I'm in the water it all disappears; the years are behind me. The water is warm and blue and the visibility is great. There's no current, no swell. The conditions are almost perfect.

Ben leads me down; down a sloped coral wall and down to where the sharks are waiting. They know there is a feeding about to happen and are ready for action. Unchanged in many millions of years, sharks are the perfect predators. They move with speed towards the tuna heads being dropped above us, competing for the food. I can hear their teeth grinding as they eat. Some of the females are pregnant. There are dozens of sharks and thousands of fish, every size, many species. It's a wonderful scene of ordered chaos.

This dive is perfect. I'm thrilled. I try to remember a better shark dive and I can't. What an amazing experience. It seems each dive I do with the Beqa sharks is more exciting than the last.

The sharks are so close their tails hit me sometimes. One knocks my mask and it floods but is still on my face. I clear my mask without a thought. A day earlier I bumped into the corner of my bed, a moment of insignificance that caused an injury that won't heal for weeks.

I love being down here and I wish I could stay. Maybe I could. If this were my last dive, would that be so bad? If I never came back up again, just staying down with these sharks, would that be so bad?

The sharks swim around me, sharks who have been named, some by Rusi and Manasa, some by Mike, many by Natasha, who runs a program called 'My Fiji Shark'. The program allows people to 'buy' a shark and therefore contribute to shark research programs and local fisheries initiatives.

I bought a shark for my nephew Jono's pre-teen son Luke some time ago. Luke thinks he actually owns one of these beautiful sharks. I wonder if Luke's shark is here. His name is Batman.

A thought occurs to me: Luke will soon be old enough to get his open-water diving certification. I could bring Luke here and teach him what 'his' shark is really like, how wild and wonderful, how useful his shark has been in rebuilding this reef. I could bring him back here, and Jono and I could film it. That could be the end of *The Sharks that Saved a Reef*. That could be the last film.

Ben motions to me that it's time to go up for our decompression stop. As I hang on the anchor chain, I wonder if I can ever do this dive again? Another film, another trip, another dive? While I think, a lovely sicklefin lemon shark moves below my feet, and reef sharks swim around me.

Of course I can. Of course. All I need to do is step through the surface of the ocean and enter that other place where I feel free, where I can fly without wings.

I have had the best life of anyone I know, love, adventure and wonderful friends.

Mother of all life

Our marine world is a precious gift – a gift from nature that sustains all life on this planet yet we treat it harshly. We pollute its waters and harvest its life without thought for the future or a care for the destruction we leave in our wake.

It is said that you can't miss what you don't know. This is true. If you have never seen them, you can't miss schools of fish that take twenty minutes to pass, or twenty silver tip sharks along a reef edge if they are no longer there. What I have just written used to be how it was.

The disappearance of these sights happened quickly. In fifteen years they were no longer a common sight, in thirty they, like so much marine life we took for granted, were gone.

The underwater world is still a unique and wonderful place. It offers the visitor adventure and excitement but if we continue to despoil this precious gift, marine life as we know it will cease to exist. A farmer reaps what he sows; a fisherman just reaps. Marine animals are free for the taking but unless we change our ways one day there will be nothing left to take.

I have known our marine wilderness in its full glory untouched by man's destructive ways. With my husband Ron I have slipped into virgin waters on far-flung reefs where a kaleidoscope of colour and life dazzles the senses. I have reached out and touched the new, the undiscovered. I have had the best life of anyone I know.

Sadly, if the human race does not control its ever-expanding defilement of our oceans and the life they support, my great-nephew Luke and a million other children like him will never know even a little of what his great-aunt took for granted so long ago.

It pains me to think this, but experience is a great teacher. We humans hold the future of our planet in our greedy, careless hands and that means our own futures.

All governments should be doing more to protect this planet yet in the name of progress they allow continuous clearing of forests, more mining of arable land, more pollutants to flow down the rivers into the sea. They bleat about more jobs, they call the destruction of forest for woodchips 'progress', the harvesting of fish breeding aggregations in the ocean 'necessary'. One day not very far away there will be no more breeding aggregations.

We need marine sanctuaries, where humans don't take and destroy. We need our reefs to be protected and the impact of mining, run-off and pollution taken seriously and short-term economic gain needs to be balanced against long-term damage to the environment, especially to our oceans. This is what the planet needs; it's what we need to survive. Sadly, without a huge change in the way we live I don't think it is going to happen.

I grew up in a world without plastic. We didn't miss it. As I said, you can't miss what you have never seen. My mother used three string bags for shopping. They worked perfectly. I saw my first plastic bag when I was sixteen. I thought it was marvellous. I think the whole world thought it was marvellous. Now, sixty-eight years later, I see plastic everywhere above and below the water. A plastic bag can last hundreds of years; a plastic bin maybe a thousand. Plastic is a death sentence for many marine animals and birds yet our rulers ignore these facts. One day it will be too late. The ocean will be a sea of lifeless plastic and poisonous waste. In some areas it already is.

There has always been global warming and global cooling. The planet always survived. Nature adapted and life went on but now nature has to deal with overpopulation and a billion tons of plastic.

I have had my day. I have lived through the very best times the Earth has ever known. I am a most fortunate person. I have seen enormous changes; sadly, only a few for the better. Young women often ask me, how can they experience a life like mine? I tell them you simply just go for it. Most parents expect great things from their children. My parents expected me and my two brothers to find our own way and we all have.

The world is still a wonderful place; it offers a wealth of adventures both large and small, for each person's idea of adventure is relevant to the limit of their ability and imagination. So I say to all: dream big, chase the life you dream of. We are only here for a moment, we have one great chance and it's entirely up to us whether we go for it, or sit back and take what comes.

Most of all, I hope sharing my story reminds everyone that we are part of a natural world and we need to care for it and protect it before it is lost forever. If our mother the ocean dies then so will we. I don't have time to stop the decline but younger people reading this book can. They have been given the gift of life, they alone hold the future of this world in their hands. I wish them a wonderful exciting life, good luck and every success.

Valerie May Taylor AM,
An original member of the Women Divers Hall of Fame,
Knight of the Order of the Golden Ark

ACKNOWLEDGEMENTS

I wish I could thank all the many wonderful people who have helped me on my travels but it would take a book by itself to name them all. However, I have done my best.

I thank my parents, Edna and Allan Heighes, for giving me the gift of life and the passion to grab it and run.

Ron, my husband and my love for over fifty years.

Vanessa Radnidge from Hachette, without whom there would be no book. And to all at Hachette, including Karen Ward, Jenny Topham, Christa Moffitt, Claire de Medici, Fiona Hazard, Louise Sherwin-Stark, Daniel Pilkington and the rest of the team; Selwa and Brian Anthony. To Ben Mckelvey, thank you!

A special thanks to Lars-Eric Lindblad and his little red ship for giving Ron and myself the opportunity of meeting amazing people and travelling to strange and exotic lands. Also to Sven Olaf Lindblad and his son Jeremy for keeping me travelling on the *National Geographic Orion*, a ship I had the honour of christening.

To adventurer Mike McDowell, a partner on so many adventures. Sir Peter Scott for teaching me about water fowl and how to draw underwater. All my dive buddies, especially Hayley Bailie, Jayne Jenkins and Douglas Seifert, who share my love of underwater photography. James Bailie, Hayley's husband, for taking care of the four boys so Hayley and I can do yet another dive trip. Colin, Jayne's darling husband, who is always there to fix things I break and allows me to steal his wife for dive trips. Dear Joe Harvey, who helps me with the computer. Dick and Pip Smith, wonderful friends, a million thanks for taking Ron and me into the sky over Australia. Rodney Fox, our partner on many great white shark filming trips, and his son, Andrew, who has always been my friend.

Marilyn Georgeff and her fabulous husband, Patrice Richards, for taking me sailing on their yacht. Lyn Tutt, the best dinner guest ever, and her partner, Russ White, who is an angel without wings. Bettina Dalton and Sally Atkins, who have set the story of my life in motion. My nephews Mark, Gregory and Jono Heighes, who love and take care of their aunty. Also Monique, my niece, who gives me calm advice when I am drowning in confusion. My younger brother Greg who I have loved all his life.

John Harding, our fine companion on a hundred adventures, for his mateship and help. Jean-Michele Cousteau for his friendship, many visits and taking me to dive with dolphins. James Abernethy, who introduced us to great hammerheads and Emma the sweet tiger shark. Mike Neumann, long-time friend who loves the marine world and has saved many wonderful bull sharks from the finners' longlines. Also the Fijian warriors who with Mike run the best shark dive in the world.

Howard and Michelle Hall for being my friends and helping me after a blue shark bit my leg. Chris Atkins, star of *The Blue Lagoon* movie and much more. Chris is still my friend today. My English friends Carinthia West, and Gael and Francesco Boglione, who open their homes to me when I visit Great Britain. Sir Basil Charles, a delightful friend who opens his heart to me and makes me laugh. Will Rummens, the seaman who handled our tinny during the Belgian scientific expedition to the Great Barrier Reef in 1967. Will sends me an email to make me laugh every day. Bret Gilliam, another friend who keeps me updated on funny stories and photographs. Michael Awe, a friend for many years and Todd Tai, a lovely man of a hundred talents.

Peter Gimbel, Stan Waterman, Jim Lipscomb, Peter Lake, Tom Chapin; all companions on a great journey, and Peter Matthiessen, who wrote a book from my diary, *Blue Meridian*, about the greatest adventure. To Jim Packer, who found the original *Blue Water, White Death* footage and had it remastered. Peter Benchley for writing *Jaws* and his gracious wife, Wendy, who is my friend. Madeline McGraw, my flatmate for many months. William Cooper, a talented artist and friend whose paintings grace my walls.

Thanks to Kyle Seymour, Dinah Halstead, Sarah Bursle, Kevin Contras, Mark Sheriff, Christiana Carvalho.

B. S. Ong, who took us to strange places. Jane Hawkins, Richard and Judy Flax, Dr John Randall, Richard Vevers.

My first boyfriend Johnny Warren; we are still friends.

To author Mark Twain for giving a little girl who could not walk the story of *Huckleberry Finn* that gave her hope.

My life has been full of beautiful, helpful people. Far more than I can name here. They all know who they are and I thank them from my heart. I have had the best life of anyone. I am a most fortunate person.

Ben Mckelvey is a freelance writer and editor from Sydney who has filed for *Good Weekend, GQ, Voyeur, Rolling Stone, The Bulletin, Cosmo, Cleo* and the *Age* and *West Australian* newspapers. Ben's previous gigs have included editing *Sports & Style* and *Juice* magazines, and working at the *Sydney Morning Herald* as a Senior Feature Writer. He has been embedded with the ADF in East Timor and Iraq, and has worked independently in Iran and Afghanistan. He is the author of *The Commando,* that shares the life of Cameron Baird, VC, MG and has previously worked with Deng Adut and Mark Hunt on their bestselling books *Songs of a War Boy* and *Born to Fight.*